Midnight Sun to Southern Cross
Those who go and those who stay

Midnight Sun to Southern Cross: Those who go and those who stay

© Ruth Bonetti 2017

Published by:

WORDS & *Music*

Words and Music
PO Box 422
The Gap Qld. 4061 Australia
Phone (+61) 07 3300 2286
Mobile (+61) 0411 782 404
http://www.ruthbonetti.com

National Library of Australia Cataloguing-in-Publication entry (paperback)

Creator:	Bonetti, Ruth, author.
Title:	Midnight Sun to Southern Cross : Those who go and those who stay / Ruth Bonetti.
ISBN:	9780987544247 (paperback)
Subjects:	Finns-Australia-Fiction.
	Families-Fiction.
	Finland-Politics and government-Fiction.
	Finland-History-Invasions-Fiction.
Dewey Number:	A823.4

Photo credits: Eric Back; Ruth Bonetti; Brunswick Valley Historical Society.

All rights reserved. No part of this publication may be reproduced, stored in a retrieval system or transmitted in any form by any means without the prior permission of the copyright owner. Enquiries should be made to the publisher.

This book is copyright. Apart from any fair dealing for the purposes of private study, research, criticism or review as permitted under the Copyright Act, no part of this book may be reproduced by any process without the written permission of the publisher.

Midnight Sun to Southern Cross
Those who go and those who stay

Ruth Bonetti

There are those who stay at home and those who go away and it has always been so. Everyone can choose for himself, but he must choose while there is still time and never change his mind.

Tove Jansson, *Moominvalley in November*

For Karin, Gretchen and Pia who enabled and supported my research.
For Rolf; I hope you enjoy your happy Ascension.

I will utter hidden things, things from of old—
> things we have heard and known,
> things our ancestors have told us.
We will not hide them from their descendants;
> we will tell the next generation
> the praiseworthy deeds of the Lord,
> his power, and the wonders he has done.
>> Psalm 78:2–4

Then we your people, the sheep of your pasture,
> will praise you forever;
> from generation to generation
> we will proclaim your praise.
>> Psalm 79:13 (NIV)

Author's Note

This book relies on archival letters and documents to sift truths from myths. In recounting this story, I have interwoven research with imagination. Information gaps were filled with suppositions based on verified facts.

Conversations and points of view are often imaginary but also illumined by quotations from letters. The genres of magical realism and creative non-fiction have widened horizons for me to better understand my ancestors and heritage.

Beyond this, I have attempted to do justice to the people and the stories, and consulted with Finnish family to ensure veracity as far as possible.

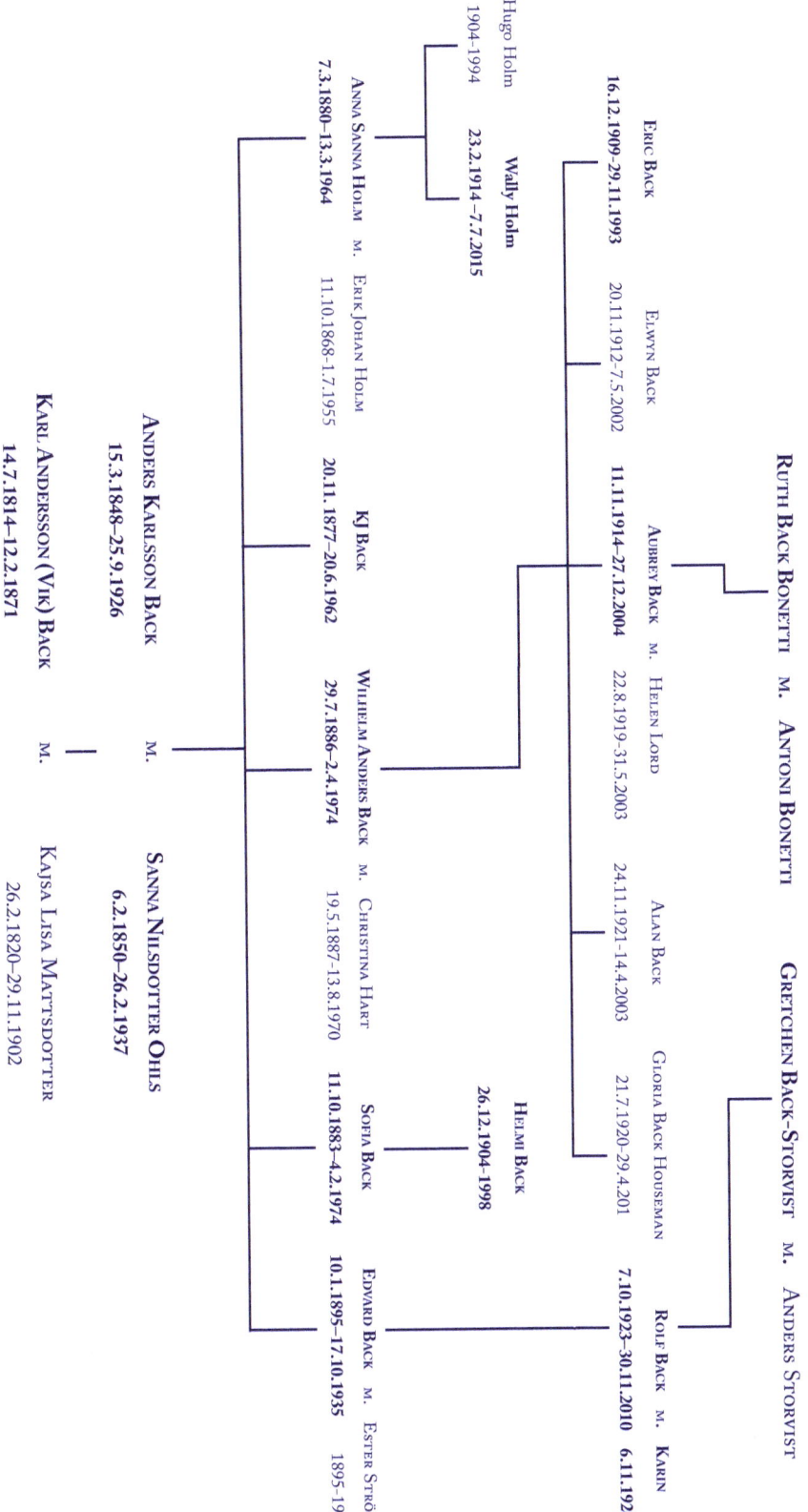

Contents

Author's Note	ix
Preface	xvii
Förord	xviii
Prologue: To the Easterly Point	1
The Outback, where I began	3
Driving South	6
Byron Bay	11
Granddad's Saga	13
Escape from Repression	16
Finding Finnish Heritage	18
Voyages to the South Land	20
The Big School	22
The 'Big House'	26
Brothers Reunited	31
Christina	33
Meeting Sanna	36
The Mooball House	40
Wilhelm Spreads His Wings	45
North of the Border	50

Getting an Education	53
University of Queensland	57
Sister Anna Sanna Sails South	60
Assassins and Decoys	63
Last day at Damskata, Finland	68
The New Emigrants	72
The Grand World Tour of 1924	78
Time Warp in Munsala Farmhouse	84
Latter Day Noah	87
Finland Summer	90
Christina in Europe, 1924	93
Idyllic Summer, 1924	96
Downward Plunge	101
Horse-trading through the Depression	104
Karl Johan Struggles	107
Unresolved Conflict	110
Drought and Birth	114
Bankrupt	118
KJ Saves the World	122
The Brisbane Base	126
Western Provinces	131
Ruth's Parents	135
Last Days	139
Dark Valleys and Green Hills	146
Entering the Promised Land	150

Full Circle to Finland	152
Ruth Explores 2008	155
Finding Finland	158
The Archipelago	161
Sofia is Strong	164
Helmi	168
Back to Munsala	171
Edvard and Civil War	175
A World Apart	179
So Near to the Promised Land	184
David and Goliath: Finland Vs. Russia	189
The Continuation War	194
Hero Rolf	198
Rolf's Birthday—and Death	202
To Russia With Caution	205
Back to Helsinki and Jakobstad	211
Leaving Home	214
Finding Sibelius	217
Hanko Port	219
Bringing Them Home	222
Homing Bird	226
Books quoted or consulted	235
Acknowledgements	239

Preface

My grandmother was the daughter of 'a living man's widow'. She told me stories about those who chose to venture out for a better life in faraway lands. Her own father was one of them, leaving his wife, too ill to travel, and two children behind. He never returned from Australia.

This history of lives disrupted by famine and wars at the beginning of the twentieth century touches my heart. Ruth Bonetti tells about her relatives, emigrants from my own home village in Finland. She bridges both time and continents with the puzzle she has pieced together from family records, letters, old newspaper clippings and her own travels across the world. Through the colourful painting of history that she so vividly creates in this book, I glimpse into my own great grandfather's struggles in the land down under. I might have shared such experiences but fate chose otherwise.

History tends to repeat itself. Wars are still disrupting peoples' lives, only the names of the people and places keep changing. Ruth Bonetti's first book (Burn My Letters) and now this second book, gives insight into how the destiny we choose for ourselves will affect those around us, and how trauma can be carried across generations. Can we understand ourselves without understanding where we originate from? This quest has driven Ruth to dig into her family history. We readers become co-travellers to both those who stay and those who go.

Annika Wiklund-Engblom, PhD
Third generation of those who stayed and always wondered.

Förord

Min mormor var dotter till "en levande mans änka". Många var de historier hon berättade om emigranter som valde att pröva sin lycka och skapa ett bättre liv i främmande länder. Hennes egen far var en av dem som åkte och lämnade kvar sin fru och två barn. Han förblev i Australien resten av sitt liv. Den här historien om liv som rivs upp av hungersnöd och krig i början av 1800-talet berör mig starkt. Ruth Bonetti berättar om sina släktingar, emigranter från min egen hemby i Finland. Hon överbryggar både tid och kontinenter med det pussel hon sammanställt genom sitt sökande i familjearkiv, brev, gamla tidningsurklipp och hennes egna resor runt världen. I den här boken skapar hon en färggrann målning av historien, genom vilken jag får en inblick i min egen gammelmorfars kamp i landet långt under. Det kunde ha varit mitt eget öde, om min gammelmormor hade haft hälsa och kraft att göra den långa resan.

Historien tenderar att upprepa sig. Krig fortsätter att riva upp människors liv; endast namnen på människorna och platserna byts ut. Ruth Bonettis första bok (Burn My Letters), och nu den andra boken, ger insikt i hur våra val i livet påverkar våra nära och kära och hur trauman ärvs genom generationsled. Kan vi förstå oss själva utan att förstå varifrån vi härstammar? Denna fråga har lett Ruth Bonetti att gräva i sin familjehistoria. Vi läsare ges chansen att bli medresenärer till dem som gav sig av men också till dem som stannade kvar.

Annika Wiklund-Engblom, PhD

Prologue: To the Easterly Point

May you in your youth be as welcome as the sun when he rises his golden crest out of the Pacific Ocean and bestows his morning's smile upon the eastern coast.

K. J. Back, *The Concentrated Wisdoms of Australia*

What would my life have been if Wilhelm Anders Back, my grandfather, had stayed in Finland? If he had joined his brother and nephew to expel the Russian overlords, been conscripted into their army? If he had married a blue-eyed, blonde Finnish Swede and fathered his dynasty there I would weave between three languages like my northern relatives do.

But on 26 November 1902, Wilhelm Anders Back ('WA') and his father Anders Karlsson Back embarked on that 15,000 kilometre voyage south to safe haven near the pounding breakers of the Pacific Ocean.

The oppressive regime forbad lads to emigrate after their sixteenth birthday. The older Back son, Karl Johan, had slithered through their net even when they tracked him to Suez. Anders knew Russian spies snooped around Hanko port, hoping he might lead them to KJ, the black sheep. Anders trumpeted, 'We are heading for America' as they boarded a ship for Hull in England, from where they made their way to Australia.

In the Great South Land, enterprising settlers might make a fortune, or they might lose all. Some ventures would be dashed, like waves breaking on rocks. Others would take wings. WA had an eagle eye for opportunities and the talons—or gnawed fingernails—to seize them. In tough times he would horse-trade dairy farms, houses, a Barrier Reef island, factories, Italian art.

Granddad journeyed long distances from his hub in the lush New South Wales hinterland to forge his pastoral empire in the arid outback. Where his sons worked the land and raised children, but escaped to the coast to replenish their spirits. The sea is in our blood. Salty seas, unlike the flat brackish waters of the homeland, Finland.

In my DNA is imprinted the urge to travel across this vast continent and the world. Like a migrating bird, I also wove circles around the globe, to Finland, land of my heritage, and back to Australia.

Near Byron Bay lighthouse, a sign proclaims 'Most easterly point of the Australian mainland.' Leaning on the railing that protects from a drop to foaming sea, I pay tribute to my great-grandfather who read of a large continent, mostly desert. 'It can't all be dry,' Anders Karlsson Back told Karl Johan before he fled Finland in 1899. 'Head for the most easterly point, son. There must be rainfall.' And so my family story radiates from Byron Bay like beams of its historic lighthouse.

Let me take you on a typical childhood journey from the Queensland 'outback' to the green hills of the Northern New South Wales.

The Outback, where I began

Out in the Australian bush I find the pure dove, as well as the bloody tiger cat, the simple and harmless bear, as well as the sneaking dingo, the wide-awake cockatoo, as well as the stupid wallaby, the gifted lyre-bird, as well the unintelligent night owl—all seems odd; but the oddest of all is...there sits the laughing jackass in the weeping willow. Such is the mixture of life in Australia.

K. J. Back, *The Concentrated Wisdoms of Australia*

A floorboard creaks as I tip-toe through my parents' bedroom to the bathroom.

Dad groans. 'Go to sleep, Ruth! We leave at dawn. Is your bag in the car?'

'Mm.' How can I sleep when, above my bed, daddy-long-leg spiders chase each other across the ceiling? One eats the other and leaves its ghost of despairing legs to hang.

Besides, worry worms gnaw at my innards. This journey south to Brisbane troubles me for we will stay there for a whole agonising year in its suburb St Lucia, with daily purgatory at Ironside State School.

In the outback, correspondence 'school' is the only option because the nearest town, Hughenden, is fifty kilometres away. My mother oversees studies in the verandah schoolroom at one end of the U-shaped house. The home Dad built to house his eight children, of which I am sixth—the female runt of their litter. Mum is slim from sprinting between this and, at the other end, a large kitchen where she cooks for a family of ten as well as the stockmen. She has a stick to rotate the washing in a big copper before pushing it through a mangle. Before I start formal lessons she draws pothooks for me to trace and bluebells to colour in. At times governesses arrive, raw from the city. Wide-eyed, I watch them clean their teeth while the tap gushes. We children are meted out a beaker of water and rinse our brush in the residue.

Aged six, I have all week to fathom twelve sums and write neat answers in an exercise book. It is sealed in an envelope after we finish the pages of parsing and compositions. Each week we leave a canvas mailbag at our train siding, a wooden outhouse that stands like a dunny[1] beside the railway line. We throw the bag on the bench and collect another filled with our post. The fun resumes in the back of the utility; we stand and balance, hands-free, over grids, rocks and potholes.

On the way back we deliver some mailbags to Dad's sister Gloria and her family who live at the neighbouring property. Apart from my siblings, three cousins are my only companions. I shiver at the prospect of a big city school, teeming with live teachers and strange children. Now, an unknown teacher in Brisbane corrects and returns my work, showing more concern for the curve of my pothooks than mathematical skills.

Wide-awake, I look out my three windows. These are my escape hatches to wider worlds. They take me to different time zones; now, then or next. Though often a view through to the future loops me back into the past, long before I was born.

Trillions of lights pinprick the sky—masses more than we'll see in the city. The Southern Cross constellation shines brightest. A shooting star trails across the dome, through the Milky Way. Is it a spaceship packed with green men come to kidnap me? They experiment on people—I heard that on the 'Journey into Space' serial that blares through the fibro partition from my brother's Bakelite wireless. Do they deliver aliens here? Is that why I feel like a misfit in my family, in this land?

Other bush kids muster sheep. Our pony Micky rubs me against barbwire fences. The outback is more fun for boys than for girls. Brothers drive jeeps, trucks and cars as soon as they can see over the steering wheel. They round up stock on motorbikes. When they reach an age eligible for a licence, they drive in to town to the police station for a routine test; there is ample room to park in wide streets and it is too flat for a hill start.

We girls have to hand wash dishes for a dozen people three times a day. We bake cakes and biscuits to take to the shearers at morning and afternoon tea, called 'smoko'. In my free time I prefer to read books about people who live amongst green pastures dotted with bluebells and daffodils. They climb mountains and see the world stretched all around.

But my only 'mountain' is the vantage point provided by the tank stand. One day I'll fly to northern lands where colours change with the seasons. Where snow thaws in spring to wash the lands clean.

Here, everything is brown. After years of drought and grasshopper plagues, Dad offers us a pound if we can find a green blade of grass. He keeps

---

1   Australian colloquialism for an outhouse toilet.

his money. Mum tries to grow roses but our motherless pet lamb eats them. Or the kangaroo joey does. It hops into its home in a hessian bag nailed to a wall; we feed it milk through a bottle and teat.

We build cubbies in the oleander shrubs. Mum warns us that their sap is poisonous. But we prefer to risk that than the sharp thorns on the bougainvillea. We find fossilised shells and dinosaur bones amongst the litter of white chalky sheep and cow remains—for long ago these plains and inland sea were the ancient home of *Muttaburrasauras*.

***

Must sleep. My tummy squirms to think of morning. I push off a sweaty sheet.

A spaceship would speed up our sixteen-hundred kilometre journey. I will be squeezed with squirming siblings into the Holden station wagon. Even in the car, Dad will wear his battered Akubra hat that stinks of sweat, sheep dip and lanoline.

Crows ark–ark their harsh morning chorus. I pull a pillow over my ears.

'Rise and shine!' Mum calls. Already my nose is shiny with sweat. After a hasty breakfast we jam-pack the car and lurch away over potholes. It's my turn for a window seat. Our station *Hazelwood Downs* is lost in a billow of dust.

Through the dirty glass I glare at the prickly acacia, gidgee trees and anthills. Maggots crawl over rotting sheep bogged in dried mud around water holes. Flies buzz into my eyes, nostrils and mouth, pesky as brothers. Perhaps southern hills, green grass and flowers may ease the terrors of a big school.

I poke out my tongue at the flat horizon whose 'Mount' Walker barely lifts above it.

You are not my land.

Driving South

From my earliest childhood I was very eager to leave home. If you had only given your consent I'm sure that I would have left many years earlier.

K. J. Back, *undated letter*

The three-day journey south from Hughenden to Brisbane is an ordeal, a blur of prickly pear cactus, stubby Mitchell grass and spindly gidgee bushes. The first morning south traverses a horror stretch, a short-cut dirt track through dry creek beds littered with dead tyres and hubcaps. Dumped rusty cars warn us that we must take care. A murder of crows pick the eyes out of dead sheep carcasses.

Dad sees a strong eucalypt tree and brakes, our bodies thrown together. It's time for a pit-stop. Girls on the right, boys to the left, we seek some privacy behind bushes. Dad pulls out the suitcases (known as 'ports' in Queensland at the time) to find his hammer and placards. He defaces the gum tree with a big sign: '*All have sinned and come short of the glory of God.*' Mum retrieves the picnic basket and thermos for a lunch of bread with choice of tinned camp pie or Vegemite.

Back in the car, the game of *I Spy* falters into bickering after 'grass, horizon, road, car, sheep' are exhausted.

–Who farted? It was you, no him, no her.

–Wind down the window, quick!

–Too much dust, wind it up.

–Yuk, I just swallowed a fly.

The landscape is broken by listless poppies. Sometimes we run out of petrol. We play hopscotch on the open road for an hour or more while Dad walks to the nearest station homestead with a jerry can, to borrow or buy 'benzene.' Goannas scuttle away from our game of catch, played with a rock.

Through all the hours of glaring squinty sun, our car noses forward to a flat horizon. The only distractions are when emus run along beside us, bewildered by the fence. Or we see brolgas and hope they will dance. Kangaroos are drawn to the best grass like wasps to a honey pot.

Sunset splashes a riot of colour around the dome above, vermillion, gold, blood red, fading to pink, all the more dramatic after a volcano eruption in Asia. Our wilted spirits lift. This signals the end of a day, dinner and a bed somewhere. A town nears. Augathella—or Muckadilla or Barcaldine or Chinchilla—is only a hundred kilometres away.

–Where will we eat, a pub meal or fish and chips?

–I'd rather a café. The Greek one does great milkshakes in those tall tin mugs.

But which one? The *White Swan* is dubbed the *Dirty Duck*. Arguments flare.

Signs display the dwindling distance. Nearly there, who pinched my shoes? We drive into a town whose main street—often the only one—is wide enough for three semitrailers to pass. Towns consist of three or four pubs that bear names like *The Commercial*, *Tattersall's*, the *Union* or *Railway Hotel*. They are timber or brick with galvanised iron roofs. Cast-iron columns support wide awnings and verandahs decorated with iron lace. Plaster cornices and ceramic tiles speak of earlier prosperous times.

Public Bars are segregated along gender and racial lines, so even a child notes it's a male sanctum. They do a brisk trade selling Fourex beer and reek of vomit. Carousing, off-tune singing and fistfights will keep us awake long after the official closing time. Drunks sleep off their inebriation on benches outside.

Women are banished for a genteel shandy in the Ladies' Lounge, if accompanied by a male. A dining room serves cheap meals. We wolf a dinner of T–bone steak, chips, slivers of cucumber and tomato, the ubiquitous tinned beetroot. We puff and lug our cases up several flights of rickety stairs to our bedrooms, bare except for an iron bedstead, rough calico sheets, a lumpy pillow and mattress stuffed with prickly coconut fibre and horsehair. There is an enamel jug and basin but other ablutions require a trek down a draughty corridor to the bathroom whose craw-footed bath and cracked smelly toilet are stained an alarming red from the artesian bore water. Sleep is fitful as I toss in the lumpy bed, exhausted but dreading our arrival.

We stagger down for another day on the road, sustained by porridge, fried eggs, bacon and white bread toast. For tedious hours we cramp and squirm in the car. This time I am in the 'dog box' boot of the station wagon. I give myself a headache trying to read.

We recite the names of the towns along the way, imprinted in our memories from many such journeys. They all look similar, their wooden houses are surrounded by yards of red or brown or black soil, decorated with big clamshells and swans fashioned from old tyres. Goats and 'poddy' lambs strip shrubs to mouth level, but mango, orange and lemon trees are laden with fruit.

'Nearly there!' we chirrup as a second sunset heralds that Roma is near. We will stay in what we consider the ultimate of sophistication—the *Wishing Well Motel*. This offers ground–level self-contained units each with a carport outside. Our room boasts the luxury of a kettle, tea bags, milk and sugar.

'Bitumen from now!' We pile into the car next morning with renewed enthusiasm, after jolting over gravel roads for two days. The prospect of our own beds in Brisbane by nightfall dulls that distant thunder grumbling on my mind's horizon—Big School.

Toowoomba gardens are a mass of colour, like my paint-box, with roses, hydrangeas and gerberas. We weave down the road over the Great Dividing Range, stopping at roadside stalls to buy local produce to squeeze in amongst a tangle of arms and legs. Dad buys over-ripe cheap bananas that fruit flies love as much as he does.

Arrival in the city is signalled by the toll bridge crossing the Brisbane River at Indooroopilly. We argue whose turn it is to blow a whistle with the ticket. Suburban streets blur before our eyes until we pull up outside number 160 Highland Terrace. Which Granddad vacated when he built the Big House at 209 Hawken Drive.

We unpack from the front street because the garage is below a steep driveway. The gate opens onto neat manicured lawn gardens, free from the 'bindii–eye' prickles common in the bush. Tomorrow we can play barefoot games of *Red Rover Come Over* and *What's the Time, Mr Wolf?*

This home is palatial after *Hazelwood Downs* homestead. The carpet, wallpaper and plaster ornamented ceilings are the height of elegance.

We make up our beds, arrange the mosquito nets over them—and sleep.

Next day we drive through dairy farms out to Long Pocket to tell the milkman, Mr. Redhead, that we are in town. Each night he will climb the back stairs calling a cheery 'Good night,' and pour foaming milk still warm from his cows into our jugs.

Mum must stock our new household so we venture *en masse* into Adelaide Street, the centre of Brisbane. Lips purse at her expanded waistline and fingers count the heads. Seven children and one more on the way! To reduce the entourage, Mum checks in my sister and me at the *Kindercraft* childcare centre for the day. It is in the City Hall that dominates the skyline in the days before high-rise buildings will overshadow it. We skip over King George Square's paving and admire the sculpture friezes.

Don't dawdle, children, there's so much to do today.

Resonant sound draws us into the cavernous auditorium. The Queensland Symphony Orchestra is playing a free lunch hour concert. (How could I imagine that ten years later I would be on that stage, playing with that same orchestra?) But Mum pulls us away towards the ornate elevator. We venture into the cage, an attendant slams shut the grille doors, presses a button. It zooms up three flights to the kindergarten, way up in the clock tower. After the peace of the outback we jolt every quarter hour when the gongs reverberate.

New toys, puzzles and books are a novelty but we feel gauche amongst unknown children, an uncertain forewarning of school. We escape back to our home surrounded by trees where kookaburras laugh. They alight on the railing to eat meat from our hands. If we can beat the bats and flying foxes, we pick luscious yellow pawpaw from trees that lean against the sun porch.

The brick and white stucco house perches above a steep hillside down to a wild scrubby gully. This is heaven for my brothers who build billy carts and whoosh down the slope in lathers of dust. My father sees the potential use for a corner of empty land; city butchers charge outrageous prices. Does he merely voice his bright idea to carry a live lamb in a box on his lap during a Trans Australia Airlines flight from Hughenden? Siblings deny memory of it. But that is the kind of thing my father would do. He is an original thinker, often compared with his uncle KJ.

The family speaks little of KJ except to dismiss him as an eccentric black sheep, whereas Granddad is revered by family and peers, and will continue to be even past his death in 1974. We peep through the door into the office, where his secretary clatters voluminous carbon copied letters from the Remington. These are sent across Australia and to Finland.

'Do it now' is his motto and this often means phoning Dad or my uncles at five a.m. to detail how they should fall in with his latest plans.

By sponsoring land ballot applications for family, Finnish emigrants and colleagues, Granddad expands a kingdom of western sheep grazing properties. He develops prime land in New South Wales, Western Queensland and Brisbane.

When he builds this landmark mansion at 209 Hawken Drive in the 1950s, I am embarrassed to be the 'granddaughter of the man with the elevator in his house'.

209 Hawken Drive St Lucia

Elevator at 209 Hawken Drive

The 'Big House' is circled by manicured gardens with a goldfish pond, palm trees and greenhouse. Its tiered three-storeys perch over the river like a Rhine castle, adorned by stucco ledges, irresistible to my daredevil cousins. Do I also brave these, scaredy-cat that I am? If so, terror has blotted any recollections. But then, memories of the Big School are etched in my mind.

But first, I'm given a reprieve.

Byron Bay

In the salt-sea plunged he headlong,
In the deep sank the magician,
Sidewise turned he to the sea-shore
On his back to rock forever,
Thus the boundless sea to travel,
Thus to ride the rolling billows.

Kalevala

We drive south to that lighthouse spire at Byron Bay, where passing humpback whales leap and frisk their cheeky tails.

Our family cram into the 'White House' at New Brighton near the sea. Granddad has towed a garage to the yard, added windows and a lick of white paint. (Much later I will recognise it as the quintessential Scandinavian holiday cottage.)

At nearby Brunswick Heads, we visit relatives in the waterfront red house. Mum's idea of bliss is to row into the Brunswick River with a lemon and a knife to cut oysters off the rocks.

At its surf beach, massive waves terrify, dump and yet invigorate. Brothers catch fish from the foot bridge. My mouth waters as the catch sizzles in the pan. After bush dinners at the Homestead of roast mutton and potato with tinned corn and peas, it's magic to pick sweet corn at farms and guzzle on cobs slathered with hot butter. Mango glides down my throat. We gorge on passionfruit and pawpaw.

We visit Dad's cousins inland, where bananas grow rife, swung by flying fox down the hills. Bellbirds 'ding' in rainforests and the sad calls of currawongs curl. Kingfishers flash their gaudy wings through trees.

I play princess, twirling hollow hoop pine rings on my finger. Wait-a-while vines grab me and nettles sting my bare legs, lantana bushes scrape my skin. Fronds of staghorn and elkhorn plants remind Dad of Finland;

he tells of moose and reindeer.

A highlight of the holidays is afternoon tea at *Ocean Shores*, the dairy farm run by Dad's cousins, the Holm family. Their wooden house perches at the top of a steep hill. The dirt track is slippery and fetid with cow manure. So we bicker who should open the gate because that person must then run up the hill. Our Holden revs, roars up the boggy track, then baulks.

'Everybody out and push.' A dozen legs turn the station wagon into a centipede. Wheels churn mud onto our visiting–best clothes. We squelch up the rise, skid in cowpats. Paspalum grass shimmers with raindrops under cloudbursts, mist and rainbows.

Dad's cousins flock around us, chattering in lilting rhythms. Their squat dumpling mother Anna Sanna beams and gestures for she speaks little English.

Uncle KJ emerges from his cottage nearby, bearing pawpaw, passionfruit and bananas. His back curves with a question mark posture. In the dining room an embroidered cloth is barely visible for sponge cakes, gingerbread and biscuits.

When baying cows hang their pleading heads over the fence, Dad's aunt Anna Sanna ties a pinafore around her girth and pulls on gumboots. She beckons me to follow her to the cow bails and 'dricka melk.' She draws up a low stool for me to 'sitta' next to the cow's flank, washes the teats with water and sprays warm, sweet milk straight in my mouth. As a Finland Swede, she speaks Swedish, yet somehow we connect. I whisper secrets and giggle; she sings *Rida, rida ranka*.

The Holm farm milking shed

As the sun slithers down the hill, we pile back into the Holden. The lighthouse beam sweeps the sky, tracing fingers along the ridges. I look back at the waving relatives.

I wish I could stay here. And ask more questions. Not go to the big school.

Back then, I knew little of Granddad's life or why he spoke with a strange accent. One titbit of information resonated with my own life; he left home at an early age to live far from his parents and returned only for brief visits. Over the coming years I collected more jigsaw pieces of his story.

Granddad's Saga

Even in the last stage of darkness and desperation there is a spark of hope. Our sorrows are mixed with joy.

K. J. Back, *The Concentrated Wisdoms of Australia*

Wilhelm Anders was 12 years old when Karl Johan left their home in 1899 so suddenly it was as if trolls took him. Memories of the big brother who challenged him to think and to go to school faded like snow in spring. He remembered a voice raised in arguments with Pappa; of how KJ set everybody off laughing with his ridicule of the Russians, or of the priest's pompous sermons.

With KJ gone, that constant tinder–flash tension between him and Pappa eased but Mamma's worry hung like a shroud. It stilled the laughter between his sisters, Anna Sanna and Sofia, and little Edvard. Pappa and Mamma huddled in the barn whispering.

By day Mamma kept a strong face, her mouth straight in a line, and muffled her weeping in the pillow. She held Wilhelm close sometimes, for he must emigrate also. Wilhelm brushed her aside. He hated fussing. He was 15 or 16, depending on which version of family lore one believes. Did his father, Anders Karlsson Back, use his position as church warden to change the parish records? Lads over 16 were forbidden to emigrate.

Pappa said, 'Wilhelm, be gentle, she grieves deeply after losing the babies, and then Karl Johan. Now you. Maybe she will never see you again. It is hard for a mother.'

Wilhelm longed to escape from the oppression in his homeland. As a Grand Duchy of Russia since 1809, Finland was allowed its own laws, language and religion. Until Nicholas II became Tsar in 1894. Four years later he appointed Nikolai Bobrikov as Governor General, and the first Era of Oppression began. Russia occupied Finland. Soldiers, officials and inspectors were brutish smelly creatures, unlike the Finns who took weekly saunas and swam in lakes.

Finns were pawns for the Russian invaders. When their hard work produced a good harvest, the invaders brought a cart to shovel away their potatoes. They eyed their strong plough horses and stole them. Peasants were powerless—those who complained were executed. Anders warned his son not to challenge the Russians, 'Do you think you can withstand the might of the Tsar? Do you wish to spend your days in some hellhole in Siberia? How would your mother cope to lose a son that way?'

The Finnish army was abolished in 1901 and Finns forced to fight anywhere in the Russian empire—Siberia, the Baltics, and the East. In 1902 Anders determined to take Wilhelm far away, to find freedom in Australia. All were on edge and worked round the clock to bring in the harvest before his ship would sail.

Mamma, Edvard and the sisters clung and wept. Tears clouded Wilhelm's eyes and he gulped to dislodge a lump in his throat. That last day at Munsala he walked around the village. KJ often asked for seeds from trees, so he put some in his pocket. A few last fruit clung to the cherry tree and the pine trees were losing their needle-like leaves.

They heaved their luggage onto the trap. At Kovjoki train station, Mats Wiklund and Otto Nyholm joined them. Their parents' faces were as long as Mamma's, teary and hugging. Anders and the three boys waved handkerchiefs from windows until the train steamed out of sight around a bend.

Further south the land was more fertile and crops burst out of the ground. In Helsingfors, called Helsinki in Finnish—they admired the grand Classical architecture.

Pappa took Wilhelm to Stockmann Emporium on Aleksandersgaten to buy a new outfit of clothes. This impressive building had an amazing contraption called an 'elevator' to carry them up flights to the clothing section. They walked into a box, lined with walnut wood, with gold stripes and mirrors around the walls. The operator slammed shut the steel doors. Wilhelm clutched Pappa's arm as the floor rocked and jolted and creaked. It lifted higher in a gliding motion so he was glad to sit on the leather bench. Two gas lamps illumined the cage. Once Wilhelm realised it was safe transport he rode up and down many times until Pappa said 'enough, we must return to Hotel Kämp'. This also had an elevator which excited him even more than his new suit.

Next day Pappa had business appointments so Wilhelm rode the elevator until Otto and Mats said no more; they wanted to visit the Saluhalle again. This market in an ornate brick building was not long built. 'Who knows when we will eat such food again?' They gorged on many kinds of fish, caviar, cured reindeer, rye bread and Karelia pastries.

Another steam train carried them to Hanko where they boarded the steamer *SS Arcturus* bound for England. Pappa chewed his fingernails till they bled, worried that Russians might stop them in port. They must guess that the three young lads in his care tried to escape five year's conscription.

Did Wilhelm and his friends escape Anders' surveillance briefly, to dance their last night in their motherland on its granite cliffs? Cold rain splashed through their last view of home as the ship unfastened its moorings and ploughed into the stormy Gulf of Finland. When the bar opened to sell cheap whiskey, beer and wine the boys celebrated their future. People lurched against each other, dancing polkas and waltzes to an accordion, mouth organ and fiddle.

The stone Russarö lighthouse—the '*Eye of Hanko*'—waved farewell to the emigrants. Long after its glow slipped below the horizon this spiritual beacon would linger in their minds to light their way to unknown futures.

Wilhelm breathed easier when they arrived in England. Maybe the Russians would give up.

They did not catch KJ so they will not catch me.

Escape from Repression

One should never force his advices upon others, for an advice that is not sought for is rarely ever followed, and, therefore not appreciated.

K. J. Back, *Concentrated Wisdoms of Australia*

A letter Granddad wrote to a 'Baltic Migrant' in Bonegilla Camp, Albury touched me with his grace, forgiveness and gratitude to his new country.

Brisbane, 10th December 1947

Dear Miss Naksim & Fellow Migrants,

I take this opportunity of writing a few lines of 'Welcome to Australia.' In today's paper, I read your comments of how nice everybody has been to you. I can assure you all that you have made no mistake in coming to Australia—a far better place than ever you dared dream. Nevertheless you have to adapt yourselves to Australian conditions.

Australia is a young country with vast resources and opportunities in every direction. Every one of you eight hundred and fifty will be needed and only time will tell who will be the best off—'The first shall be last and the last shall be the first.' You are fortunate indeed to have the Government care for you to such an extent and give all the migrants a preliminary schooling in this camp, and undoubtedly the quicker you learn the language, the better it will be.

I feel I can talk to you just the same as if I were speaking to you in your own country. I came out here as a boy, in 1903, from the Swedish speaking part of Finland, Munsala, Ostrobothnia, married an Australian girl in 1908, have four sons and a daughter, eleven grandchildren. God has richly blessed me in my adopted home.

The corner of a page is torn. I must guess some words and a name—my first awareness of this crucial history of his land:

I will always remember Governor_

was sent to Finland in 1900 to Russianise_

person most hated by all the Finns_

and as a boy I hated him too the same as everybody_

very pleased when a Finnish student shot_

is all old history to you people, but I_

this incident, so that you will know why I make it my adopted homeland.

If I should go back there for a trip one of the first deeds I would do now is to put a wreath on_

–rikoff's grave, as he was the Providence which pushed me out of Finland. After a few years you may say the same thing too–

'Thank God there were so many persecutions and hardships because those hardships forced us to leave the old country.'

—What persecutions, Granddad? Please tell me.

Finding Finnish Heritage

Circumstances are like a ship without a rudder. It may take the traveller to safety, or it may take him to ruination.

K. J. Back, *The Concentrated Wisdoms of Australia*

A quick internet search soon supplies the Russian governor-general's name as Nikolai Bobrikov. I read of his tough regime of Russification that propelled my grandfather and KJ to emigrate. Thus far I'd known little of the strictures that drove them to flee, now my role of family historian filters into various aspects of my life.

In 1899, General Bobrikov convinced Tsar Nicholas II to sign the February Manifesto. The laws of the Russian Empire overruled the laws of Finland. Religion must change to Russian Orthodox. Any person heard to speak ill of the Tsar would be punished. In 1900 Bobrikov tightened the edicts, insisting the Russian language be used to deal with government officials and in schools. Together with half a million Finns, Wilhelm signed a petition to Nicholas II begging him to revoke the manifesto. But the Tsar did not even look at it. He dismissed them as 'all crooks in the relation to Holy Russia.' The nation hated and feared Bobrikov.

When the Sibelius Violin Concerto is programmed for Brisbane Symphony Orchestra in which I play clarinet, rehearsals are illuminated with poignant and teasing thoughts: 'Sibelius was writing this around the time Granddad left Finland.'

I immerse myself in the distinctive harmonies of his symphonies that he called his confessions of faith. 'Never write an unnecessary note. Every note must live.'

The music's dark Finnish mood gains an edge when I discover that the hated Bobrikov was shot by a young clerk, Eugen Schauman on 16 June, 1904.

Such research paths lie ahead of me. Granddad's letter to the Baltic refugee continued:

> Forgive me if I am preaching to you. I don't want this letter to become a sermon, but to state that you are very fortunate people to be here in Australia—the best country in the world. You have the same opportunities as anyone who is born here. At least that is how I found it! It is wonderful the way the Minister for Immigration (The Hon. Arthur A. Caldwell) has battled through all sorts of difficulties to make this migration a success. Therefore make the best of it now, as you can see you have the support and backing of the Government.

He added that though 'no doubt the Hon. Arthur A. Caldwell will see that you will get a good Christmas dinner, but there might be something that you want to have prepared for this—your first Christmas in Australia' and he encloses a cheque for £50 'to help make your first Christmas in Australia a happy one.'

In a radio interview of the 1960s the interviewer began by saying 'You're looking well, Mr Back' to which he answered:

> And why shouldn't I be? Nothing to care about, everything is cared for me. I have a Lord and saviour to guide and direct. When I look back about my sinful life I just doubt myself but then St Paul said to not look back over the past but just look forward, go forward.
>
> I don't want to be a preacher but I just want to tell people about some of my mistakes in order to save them from making the same mistakes which I have done all through my life. The main thing is to believe in the Lord Jesus Christ and to confess Him. Hasn't he told us that if we keep His commandments 'I and my father will come and take our abode with us'? That's the greatest promise what we can have, to have Christ in you the hope of glory.

Granddad, I wish you had been more explicit about those mistakes. They would show the human side of the businessman who became a powerhouse determined to prove himself in his new land.

I want to know more about your early life, especially about Finland. Google and libraries are limited, and you spoke and wrote little of it all those years.

My Finnish relatives sent me photographs of the early family and a treasure trove of folders of family letters.

Voyages to the South Land

Every sea has its waves and every ocean its breakers. The one who expects to sail where there are no dangers or difficulties will be sadly disappointed.

K. J. Back, *The Concentrated Wisdoms of Australia*

In 2008, Gretchen, daughter of my father's cousin Rolf, emails her plans to visit Australia in February—a tough month for Europeans to brave the Australian heat and humidity. Wilhelm and Anders arrived in Australia in summer but they acclimatised during their sea voyage.

KJ's earlier voyage contrasts to his brother's, as adapted from family journals.

The first morning the ship was out in the English Channel and many of the passengers were sick and on their backs in their cabins or on deck chairs. The Finns did not miss a meal. Wilhelm, Otto and Mats explored their ship, the *Ophir*, with four masts and two funnels. It was built in 1891 and had been refitted as the Royal Yacht to bring British royalty to open Australia's new Federation Parliament the year before.

Anders had afforded passage on the best ship. It would sail to the great Southland in 60 days, if winds prevailed. 'Son, you travel in king's style. Aim for such heights and you will do well in your life.'

Next day was sunny and the water blue, tipped with white foam. A steward brought out the Deck Quoits. On rainy days they played draughts and chess. The ship was equipped with a library containing fine books bound in Morocco leather. But they were written in English. Their cabin had comfortable bunks, space for washing in a basin and a bucket in case they felt queasy.

In hot weather they took off their coats. They spent much time on deck and in the swimming bath. On Sunday mornings they attended church in the First Saloon. As Wilhelm could not understand the long sermon, he searched in his Bible for the meaning of Ophir. King Solomon's Phoenician sailors brought gold from the rich country Ophir and he gave some to Queen of Sheba. God blessed Solomon with great riches.

Pappa says He will bless me also in my new land.

The Finals in the Quoits were played off; the first game had been won by Wilhelm in three throws. The Captain presented the prizes at a concert held in the Second Saloon.

Passengers were a mix of people: German, Dutch, Scandinavians, many Irish and English. Wilhelm sought out those who knew Australia, trying out his English in preparation for a new life there.

Once they arrived in Sydney, Pappa conducted business with brokers and bankers. Then they boarded a coastal steamer that transported cut sugarcane, freight, butter and cream, and headed north to Byron Bay.

Rich volcanic soil from a mountain crater grew abundant plants. They wrinkled noses at sharp eucalyptus smells and their drab colours, not bright green like the birch. Other trees were covered in flowers, purple and yellow and red like flames.

'But, surely we will see spring blossom, and brown and gold leaves in autumn? Strange.'

Wilhelm fingered the seeds from a pine tree back home in his pocket. He'd brought a small part of Finland to plant on his new land. The trees would grow strong, like he would. Soon people would look up to him. He had big plans.

Ruth with sons André, Paul-Antoni and Simeon under trees grown from these seeds.

The Big School

A child's mind is like an Australian garden, in which, on the same soil, can be produced an almost unlimited variety of plants.

K. J. Back, *The Concentrated Wisdoms of Australia*

Our holiday near Byron Bay draws to an end after the family Christmas dinner with relatives at the redbrick riverside house at Brunswick Heads. Uncle KJ wears his Sunday best, though I barely notice him. I am too concerned with my own rumbling tummy. Being small fry, I am demoted to a coffee table overflow. My nostrils flare as plates laden with turkey, ham and vegetables pass along the tables—then halt. Granddad pronounces the blessing. Over the rattle of cutlery I chirp several times before they hear, 'Where's mine?' Mum scrabbles another plateful together.

We drive back to Brisbane where I am photographed holding a koala at a wildlife sanctuary. It shows fair hair scraped back off a wide brow into a bow; for once my sea-coloured eyes do not squint into the sun's glare.

It's time to face the ordeal of a city primary school. My brothers tease me with harrowing stories about discipline and 'The Cane'. This formidable instrument of discipline is wielded by the fearsome headmaster, Mr Murray, otherwise known as Mister Mo, or just Mo. I am warned to stay clear of children who chant in the playground 'Uncle Mo with the forty-foot toe' in case I 'get the cuts.' Girls might escape the cane but not wooden rulers on hands.

Mr Murray is a freak, over two metres tall, and most of it spindly legs like a praying mantis. We have seen him driving his brown Vauxhall around the suburb, compressed in it with his knees higher than the steering wheel.

That first morning I awake with my stomach a mess of fear. I don my uniform of white blouse and grey cotton pinafore and sandals. We pack my brown cardboard port with a handkerchief, an apple for little lunch, and a Vegemite sandwich wrapped in greaseproof paper for big lunch. Flanked by brothers to protect me from barking dogs, I venture the kilometre walk along Highland Terrace to the cavernous red brick school.

Our route passes a shop near the school that does a fine trade of bulls' eye and Jaffa lollies and decadent cream buns. I watch a lad wolf these down and note that their colour matches his pale face. Mum would never allow us such 'tooth rot.'

We all assemble on the large front parade area in lines radiating from the flagpole. The deputy principal shouts, 'Parade, attention!' and we snap to command for the National Anthem. We place hands on hearts and look to the flagpole as *God Save the Queen* blares forth. I am allocated into a class of forty children who chatter and giggle and poke out tongues. We march into class to wheezes of *Colonel Bogey* piped through a loud speaker. Straight after roll call, we chant spelling and times tables by rote, then comes the ordeal of arithmetic. Teachers are strict and students meek.

We sit on backless forms, eight children to a desk. Most writing is done on slates with thin slate pencils. The headmaster will inspect our Copy Books of copperplate written with push pen dipped in the ink hole in the desk, and pressing blotting paper over it. I enjoy colouring blue sea around maps of Australia. A highlight of the Grade 2 week is Friday afternoons when we mess our fingers with pastel crayons. 'Today we will draw a day at the beach.' At Brunswick Heads we had a sandcastle building competition; with this fresh in my mind I reach for the crayons.

Sandcastles at Brunswick Heads

The creators of the twenty 'best' masterpieces are chosen to display them to the class next door. Right in the front row sits Elizabeth Palmer. She pulls a face at my painting and says a loud 'yuk!' and I wilt. For decades I will draw black and white, charcoal, conté, and pencil—but avoid colour.

Each year group has its own set of 'reader' books and I soon demolish those stories so make good use of the library—an unknown asset in the country. Back home, over the years I devour and reread our many books: Biggles, Anne of Green Gables, L.M. Alcott; the *Billabong* series over and over. By age ten I will tackle the classics and venture to Dostoyevsky.

Once a week the 'Proddy' sheep—Protestants—are separated from 'Cattle ticks'—Catholics—and fielded off to Religious Instruction. In single file we march across Swann Road to the red brick Presbyterian Church. We fidget through a sermon and sing *'Jesus Wants Me for a Sunbeam'* stirred on by swelling tones of the organ.

In those days I don't notice that a plaque on the organ proclaims it as 'The gift of Mr. and Mrs. W. A. Back'. Or that Whitehouse Brothers built it at a cost of £2,365. It was dedicated at the morning service on 13 June 1954 after which the Brisbane City Organist, Archie Day, gave a recital. As in Mullumbimby, Granddad was an elder of the church, which was built in 1952.

Later my university music student colleagues who practise on the organ will tell that it has two manuals, seven speaking stops and tubular pneumatic action. Cousins will be married here: why did my parents not worship here and encourage us to attend?

Just before little lunch, class monitors are sent to fetch the crate of glass milk bottles. The contents are warm from the sun rather than the cow. During little lunch and big lunch strange, jeering children terrify me. Like dogs and horses they sense my fear. Rather than brave the hopscotch or Jungle Jim climbing frame and swings, I find sanctuary in the toilet block. Or I wander around the vast asphalt oval, throwing listless swings of my yoyo. I wear that vacant fixed smile of the loner that says, 'I'm fine, quite happy by myself, thank you.'

Marauding Mister Mo prowls through the playgrounds, his eyes vigilant behind magnified thick-lensed glasses. It's whispered that one day he pounced on a small lad for dropping litter; the child escaped through his stick legs.

During class, arithmetic is torment. The staccato orders of 'answer down' and 'hands on heads' paralyse my brain. I keep scribbling after the volley fire second command. Stilt dinosaur legs bear down on me. Mr Murray's manacle hand pounces. Freakish long arms lift me aloft by my collar. I flinch from his yellowed parchment skin and sour hot breath and tuba-bellowed rebuke.

My mind has been a blank on arithmetic since.

I will hear later that John Murray's sadistic behaviour and use of the cane derive from his experiences in prisoner-of-war camps on the Burmese railway. Newly returned from World War II, he is Headmaster from 1946 until 1964.

By that time, when I leave for high school, there are 1114 students, a fearsome cohort.

After a torrid day at Ironside State School, I seek a haven in a red brocade armchair in the 'Big House'. Granddad jiggles me on his pneumatic lap and croons *Rida, rida ranka* about a horse called Blanka. He soothes my shattered esteem by calling me his 'bestest little girl'—later, I realise, so are all his granddaughters. But the words pour balm into my troubled little soul.

The 'Big House'

Your home is the image of your mind.

K. J. Back, *The Concentrated Wisdoms of Australia*

As a child, the house at 209 Hawken Drive St Lucia seemed enormous but when I tour inside as an adult it has shrunk. Granddad built this house in the early 1950s and he lived there until 1963.

For two decades, the 'Big House' was the home of Quentin and Michael Bryce. Quentin's roles as Governor of Queensland and then Governor–General of Australia took them to live in resplendent official government residences. She, like me, had grown up in the outback, a little further south at Ilfracombe. Before they sold the St Lucia house, Michael invited me to come with my husband and sons for a tour. After years of driving past, craning my neck to note any changes, I am grateful that two subsequent owners host me for visits inside.

Viewed as an adult, the house has shrunk from my memories. I remember the garden as being bigger, but then it didn't have a hedge. Granddad owned the whole section. He said, 'You must always own the property next door to you.'

They and the next owners preserved the Art Deco style architecture. Jane Bartlett, a later owner, told me, 'There's something special about this house. It's one I'm entirely comfortable in.' People leave behind a sense of their spirit in a place, especially if they create it.

But meetings with both these subsequent owners showed they knew nothing of the man who built this house. It's time to go back and tell his story.

The St Lucia development began when in 1922 Granddad was part of a syndicate of graziers, accountants and businessmen who developed land in the Brisbane back blocks of St Lucia. They acquired 148 acres of the best land in the district on terms from the National Bank. Land sales were slow even before the Depression hit. When people defaulted on their rates payments, WA Back's huge investment was jeopardised. In 1926 the £55,000 Mayne bequest saved him from ruin; it bought much of his 140–acre Coronation

Estate developments of St Lucia and Taringa to build the University of Queensland—the university that I would later attend.

When in Brisbane, Granddad first lived in the house at 160 Highland Terrace, while planning and building his mansion at 209 Hawken Drive. He said 'We'll throw a shilling into the cement mix for good luck.' Building materials were at a premium after World War II; as soldiers were demobilised, so the demand for low cost housing rose. Restrictions on size were tight. Granddad argued that this mansion would house two families; their second son Elywn and his family joined him and Grandma.

Granddad's son Eric wrote of the opposition and controversy over such a big house:

> Dad assured the authorities he had the material; he was bringing it from New South Wales. Dad took a lot of stopping when he decided what he wanted. It was as solid as the Rock of Gibraltar, but I think that an architect should have been consulted. At least he may have noticed the stairs and lift were too small to take the furniture up to the top floor. They had to get a crane to lift it on the outside.

A cousin remembers that WA called for architects to submit designs. Perhaps they found plans in America when they visited in 1950 with letters of introduction to Boston wool firms.

An illustrated feature article written in Finnish about 'Australia's Richest Finn' shows photographs of my grandparents posed against the iconic house.

Pencil pines and hydrangeas flank the white painted front gate; walk with me up the path beside a lawn garden. Or we park in the driveway near a white stucco garage wall where Mr. Ives painted an alpine scene of white-capped mountains rising out of flowered meadows that I longed to visit, having read the 'Heidi' books many times. A fence is punctuated by brick pillars of a convenient height for grandsons to perch and call 'Penny a look' to gawking by passers. The front drive is classic 1950s style with a grass border surrounding a central bed. A striped awning shades the entrance from the fierce Queensland sun.

Now I reach for a photograph: at the open door stands Granddad in rolled up sleeved shirt, braces holding his trousers up over a stout belly, Grandma in pearls beside him. My father wears shorts. Three children cluster around him; another—myself—sits on a step away from the group observing them.

A sign proclaims the name is *Munsala*—his home village in Finland. Which he spoke little about.

W. A. Back owned a real estate agency; he knew how to tout the best angles of his land in an advertising brochure that attempted to sell the Hawken Drive house in the 1960s:

> The house is situated only five miles from the heart of the city in a pre-eminent locality, on three allotments (66 perches) of land with the frontage of 142'6". Set in beautifully kept terraced lawns and gardens, the building ensures maximum privacy while commanding fascinating glimpses and full panoramic views of some of Brisbane's finest city, river and mountain scenery. Construction is in reinforced concrete and brick on three floor levels with a total of fourteen rooms. There is also a spacious roof garden area and excellent accommodation for three cars. All floors are fully AIR-CONDITIONED ...serviced by an AUTOMATIC ELEVATOR and linked with a highly efficient INTERCOMMUNICATION SYSTEM.

Very modern, Granddad. Your vision was ahead of your era. There were many telephone lines; you ran a busy operation. The green curved glass bricks would be difficult to replace. It was pivotal to the design, built around the air-conditioner. A plate in the basement notes it was built in 1952, a '*Carrier Weather Maker*' reverse cycle. It still works.

Through my child's eyes, the furnishings were the pinnacle of elegance; rich red wall-to-wall carpeting, Chinoiserie wallpaper, venetian blinds and heavy curtains. A genesis of my later attempts at wax and clay sculpture were the two marble statues in the lounge room. One showed a girl threading a needle, another pulling a prickle from her foot. The sliding glass door curved around the lounge must have created some decorating challenges. (I have always preferred the curved line to the straight, perhaps in reaction to the governess who set me to making straight lines when I asked her to teach me to draw.)

The kitchen, which opened onto a balcony, was equipped with built-in cupboards and late-model refrigerator and electric stove. The breakfast nook seat was upholstered in dark green leather. We loved to slide along that padded bench while Grandma buttered slices of Dutch loaf.

They entertained guests in the formal dining room. Often, Granddad invited people at short notice, so his enterprising wife stretched the food around extra mouths.

In 1950s Brisbane a house with an elevator connecting all four levels was a piece de resistance. An accordion–grille partition slid open to step into the cage. Grandma worried about the cost of operating a lift at sixpence a time and, as she grew more forgetful of shutting the door, it often became stuck on one level. The staircase was rather too narrow for quick sprints by a portly grandfather.

Upstairs were four wall-to-wall carpeted bedrooms. Three opened onto private balconies. The master bedroom featured elegant custom-built maple suite of twin beds, dressing table and built in wardrobes—progressive for the era, as were the small washbasins in the bedrooms. There was plumbing everywhere.

A tiled, mirrored and appointed bathroom with toilet 'completes an arrangement to provide the ultimate in comfort and convenience for up to eight persons'.

Granddad didn't describe the three bathroom mirrors, placed at right angles so we saw multiple profiles of ourselves. They were a highlight of our visits.

As a youngster, cousin John fell asleep in the bath and didn't hear efforts to rouse him. As the door was locked from the inside, Granddad had to break down the fixed ventilation louvres in the door and crawl through. They were replaced with a piece of timber, but all other doors had slats so the air conditioning could circulate.

Cousins tell that a distressed Granddad telephoned them in the 1960s.

'Please come quickly, there's a woman in the bath and she won't get out.' A vagrant had knocked on the door and the ever hospitable Grandma offered her food and drink. In her dementia, she agreed when the woman announced 'I would like a bath.' Police evicted this uninvited guest from the bathroom.

The top eyrie was an open promenade deck with views of the river and hills in the distance.

> The automatic lift provides effortless access to all floors and to the roof garden area…delightful views looking over the nearby shopping centre towards the City and across one of the attractive reaches of the Brisbane River.

A photograph shows Granddad posed on the upper deck, surveying his kingdom against a backdrop of houses along river.

Taking the lift down to the basement we slid the grille doors to textured glass bricks. There was a security safe and carpentry workshop with lathe; Granddad worked with wood since his youth in Finland. A bullet hole still commemorates the gun building escapade of cousins John and Bob.

Used to outback yards where lawns were rare, I loved the unique sunken garden with decorative fountain, floodlit pool and glass-louvered fernery.

With so many offspring and grandchildren, we were occasional visitors. One photograph shows my brother Stephen standing against the fernery louvres with his bright red wheelbarrow, a present for his third birthday. Soon after, Mum would be in hospital for the birth of Rodney, the youngest child. They came home weeks later because the baby picked up a germ in the ward. (I imagine fluttering chubby fingers reaching for some strange small object. How does a germ look?)

On this occasion a retired missionary looked after us. She scooped out ice cream with a big spoon, rather than counting the heads and making dividing marks on the block before cutting slices. She prepared meals and sandwiches and read me stories before bedtime prayers.

But life would not always be so charmed.

Brothers Reunited

Who shall hear the cuckoo calling,
And the birds all sweetly singing,
If I seek a foreign country?

Kalevala

Wilhelm, his father and friends arrived at Bangalow station on 17 January 1903. Alighting from the train, Anders Back waved an arm at the green hills nearby and pronounced 'So this is the promised land. May the good Lord grant to my descendants some of this land.'

That prayer was fulfilled sixty-five years later when members of the Holm family were led to buy that same Barby farm.

I turn to Granddad's letters to find out how he progressed with learning English. On 20 May 1959 he wrote:

> When I first came out to Australia at Coorabell Creek I was bossing 20 hands for KJ. I practically lived with those Hindus for 12 months and the Indian smell was very upsetting to me and in a friendly way I asked one of them how is it that they can live in such awful smell. He just shook his head and said, our smell is not as bad as your smell is to our countrymen. The same thing can be said about the aboriginals, their own smell is not disagreeable to them, but it is to us whites, and yet the aboriginal people say that we white people have an awful bad smell to them. I think this should be our first starting point without casting any judgment.

I imagine his interactions.

'What's your name?' peoples asked.

'Wilhelm.'

'Vilhelm? You mean W–W–William? Like, Bill? We'll call you Billy, OK? Billy Back.'

It suited him to become 'Billy' and not need to get the right w–w–w. He learned to shape his lips forward, as when Swedes say 'sju' and to say 'welcome' instead of '*välkommen*' but still confused 'willage' for 'village' which drew sniggers.

It was easier for Otto Nyholm and Mats Wiklund. Their names did not cause laughing. Karl Johan was called Jacky or KJ for short.

> –What do I call you, Granddad, now you're in Australia? I can't continue telling your story as Wilhelm, can I?

> *–Especially once we get to World Wars when aliens were regarded with suspicion. We could have been sent to an internment camp. My business was W. A. Back.*

> –Grandma called you Will, but WA is easy. Sorry to interrupt.

An early photograph shows three men on a hilltop, possibly Chincogan, looking out at valleys razed bare. I imagine thoughts that ran through Granddad's mind:

Here is so much space to grow, after Finland's patchwork quilt of fields, every inch put to use, people living close in each other's shadows. Cows were crammed into dark barns but here they graze free. All this land, and who owns it? If it can be developed—as I will do—there are fortunes to be made. People can build big houses for their families, on their own land. The scope is as endless as that horizon miles away, as high as the great dome of blue sky. Once I tame that wilderness, this Promised Land will grow healthy food; bananas sprout like weeds, oranges drip with juice, to build strong offspring. It will be backbreaking work, but I am young and have my life ahead. My land will expand as far as the horizon, my family will reach wider still, numerous as the stars of the Milky Way.

Newspapers provide me with the main events in WA's settling. On 30 July, 1908, the *Mullumbimby Times* noted that the Back brothers were building a large sawmill at Devil's Lookout near Goonengerry. W. A. Back was offered £16 per acre for his Burringbar farm of 296 acres; he was naturalised on 18 February, 1909, and the next year, in 1910, he owned a thousand acres of prime land along the railway line and 1280 acres at Mullumbimby. He turned his attention to finding a wife.

Christina

When I saw her I felt like one who is in the company of angels.

K. J. Back, *The Concentrated Wisdoms of Australia*

W. A. Back's story involved many figures; acres of land, head of sheep, wool clip bales, pounds sterling. But let us look behind the activity to the man and his motivations. And meet the love of his life, Christina Hart, who will bear their five children.

***

The Hart family worked long days to put food on the table, milking cows, separating the cream, churning butter and growing vegetables. The sisters were expert at dressmaking and mending. As Christina adjusted hand–me–down clothes, she dreamed of buying ornate new dresses.

Music lifted their spirits; they sang around the piano, songs like 'Annie Laurie' and 'I'll take you home again Kathleen'. Their parents insisted they attend school between farm chores. Christina walked with her brother John to a little wooden schoolhouse at Wombah. When the family grew, they tripled or quadrupled sisters on the pony. At their next farm, Mororo School was close enough to walk. The Hart children could read, write and calculate sums.

Christina's parents grieved for the two daughters who died before she was born; Elsie May at nine months and Fanny Elizabeth was just ten months old. Both were buried at Maclean. As the oldest surviving daughter, born in 1887, Christina patted her mother's shoulder and brewed cups of tea.

In 1905 the family loaded their possessions onto a dray and headed north to a rented farm at Billinudgel. They drove livestock overland. Christina's father John Hart worked hard to become a respected dairy farmer. He bought a hundred and eighteen acres at Upper Wilson's Creek in 1908. It was thirteen kilometres west of Mullumbimby. The basalt soil proved fertile but the family was frugal. In pioneering communities money was scarce, the work long and arduous.

The Harts rented land on the other side of Wilson's Creek to grow bananas. They hauled wooden boxes of bananas, 25 kilograms when full, that Stan Robinson's horse team freighted to Mullumbimby railway station.

Christina and her three sisters were excited to move to a populated area and its afternoon teas, musical evenings and dances in the local halls. When a neighbour's daughter Inez Whittall drove a horse and sulky in the first Mullumbimby show in 1907, Christina's brother Jack watched her closely—his future wife.

WA owned land at Goonengerry. The locals talked about his enterprise and diligence, making his way in this part of the world—alone except for an unreliable brother who only worked when he put his mind to it.

This persistent young man ignored the fact that another suitor escorted Christina to local picnics and concerts. WA borrowed a Model T Ford and drove to Upper Wilson's Creek. Lace curtains parted and villagers' eyes widened; in the district the usual means of transport were walking, horseback or sulky.

'Would you care for a jaunt in an automobile?' he asked, opening the door with a flourish.

'Dare I? They say it frightens horses and is dangerous on poor tracks.'

'I shall honk the horn to give them warning.'

He helped Christina up onto the footboard, settled her dress within and cranked the engine. Next week he asked John Hart for her hand and blessing.

What a turnaround, to meet and marry Will! So she called him, being of British heritage. Christina realised that what this young man set his heart upon, he won. How could Christina resist this young man who grasped prospects and created opportunities with such ingenuity. With him, she could escape dreary years of cribbing a subsistence on a selection.

Christina preferred household duties indoors to farm chores. She had never felt comfortable to face the pigs and their fifty head of mixed dairy stock.

Will understood and promised, 'We will employ share-farmers to do the milking on our farm.' Already he showed a knack for assessing and auctioneering stock and property.

WA's high spirits were dashed when his corn crop failed. 'How can I support a wife and family on this poor soil?' he fretted, chewing his fingernails. He mortgaged it to the bank and built a home on a farm at Mooball.

There in 1908, Christina married Wilhelm, the young man from Finland—a place she barely knew existed six months earlier.

> –Grandma, in 1974 Granddad wrote about your wedding in a letter just before my own marriage. He was lonely after you died. That left a chasm in his life.

>   —*Who is this?*
>
>   —Your granddaughter, Ruth, Aubrey's daughter. Just before my own wedding, Granddad wrote that he gave you a piano on your wedding day:
>
> > It was certainly a great surprise to Christina and the Hart family and even KJ. Christina was very much taken with the Lipp piano and she received it with the greatest admiration and wanted to know if she could get somebody to teach her. So after the visitors had gone we rang a piano teacher from Mullumbimby and she was most delighted to become Christina's teacher.

WA had a photographer take pictures to send to his family back in Finland. In one of these they posed at the lace–clothed table. A maid poured the silver teapot for Christina, whose hair was coiffed in a beehive, lace white blouse held with a brooch. Their eldest son Eric, dressed in a sailor suit, rode on a hobbyhorse. Chubby baby Elwyn wore a lace bonnet and frilled dress. Posed in his wicker chair in a latticed verandah nook, lush with pot plants, 'Billy' Back sent a message of contented prosperity. I imagine Grandma says:

> —*I wore my georgette gown and jewellery. They must not think me a mere country girl from a poor family.*

WA's son Eric took on the role of family chronicler from age 14 by writing a daily journal of the family's overseas tour, which is complemented by his photographs. Eric gives a more complete overview of his father's busy career and of life on the land in his witty and astute diary and unpublished memoir of 1991:

> I was born at a maternity hospital near the railway in Murwillumbah on 16th December 1909. A couple of years later the three of us went on a delayed honeymoon and I think we went as far as Adelaide. There was a lot of scrub on the farm which had to be cleared, and my father supplied all the poles for the telephone line from Lismore to Casino. Elwyn was also born in Murwillumbah on 20th November 1912, and it was about this time that Dad acquired his first motorcar.

As WA said, 'go forward.'

Meeting Sanna

But a mother may gain with her tears
What the father has lost through his oaths.

K. J. Back, *The Concentrated Wisdoms of Australia*

My Finnish cousin Gretchen sent me family photos from 1890 and 1900. I see my great-grandmother Sanna as straight faced—but so are they all, posing for posterity waiting for the daguerreotypist's flash to explode behind a blanket. In the second picture she holds her young son, Edvard, who looks about three years old; his white bib lightens the black clothing. Her hands hold his legs and his hands curl near hers. She has an intelligent face, but contained; her eyes speak of resignation, while a tight mouth tells of her suffering.

In a photo taken in the 1920s, her broad forehead is unlined, in spite of age. Anders stands tall and broad beside her. She has the sad eyes of a woman who has lost sons. As I have—but only temporarily.

I stumble through the knots of my worries. It's close to Christmas and weeks since I heard from my sons who travel around Europe on overdrawn credit cards. Are they ill? Do they eat enough?

My stomach is replete with barramundi, salad, and a glass of excellent white. Does my son share a bowl of goulash soup or spaghetti with his partner—as we did on our backpacking travels? Our main sustenance was a big bag of muesli, until mould got to it.

The temperature is zero in Europe. If only I'd mailed another pair of socks. Has our ancient feather-down sleeping bag disintegrated? Maybe they can't afford a youth hostel—or find one that's open. In our days of struggling around Europe on an unrealistic budget over the festive season, we learned the words *geschloßen* and *chiuoso*, since most Youth Hostels, once located by plodding up some hill, were closed.

Through fitful nights my imagination roams down dark alleyways of poverty in strange lands, where empty bellies ache all the harder in cool temperatures. As I doze the distance between us narrows. In restless dreams, stinging vines and strangler fig trees knot their roots over rainforest paths, tripping unwary walkers.

'I wish he'd ring reverse charges—though we said that's for emergencies. Or Skype.'

A little dumpling woman has fallen into step beside me. She keeps pace in spite of a limp. Her hair is pulled back from a no-nonsense parting into a bun. She snorts:

> *—Bah! You cannot even begin to know the depths of worry, for you hear news of your sons many times.*

—Sorry, I don't think I know—

> *—You don't know the pain of separation from a son. You play at your fears and blow them into gusts of wind, but they are nothing.*

I pull my shirt tighter across shivering shoulders; the rainforest has given way to tundra of spruce trees, pines and alder. A sprinkling of snow spatters over moss and lichen. Fingers of frost circle my neck and ears.

> *—What do you know of nightmares? Of seeing a son captured and shot as a deserter? Or to hope that he is alive—but he fights in Siberia? Where he pulls hay from the animals' manger to stuff into his boots against the cold?*

I'm chastened. My sons live convivial lives, sampling all the beers their budgets allow in pubs across Europe. Yet my fears are real enough to draw me from my bed to pace out my worries.

—Maybe he's sick? He might be feverish and has no shelter, no—

> *—Wilhelm suffers from bronchitis. I wrote some folk remedies. But do lungwort and fenugreek and wild cherry bark grow there?*

—Wilhelm? Was your son? (I turn to scan her face for resemblances.)

> *—Or try eucalypt. I understand that grows aplenty and is medicinal.*

—My grandfather was Wilhelm; he was called WA.

> *—I know. He left too young.*

—So you're—

> *—Sanna. And you are Ruth, his son-dotter. You inscribed the family tree.*

At least you can express your love to your sons, even now when they are adult. I lost two sons to the other end of the world, and one I never saw again in this life.

–That's tough. I'd be wretched, Grandma Sanna. Or—what do I call you? Should I rewrite you as Sanna Carolina? Update all the births and deaths since? (Groaning)

–Just call me Sanna. Karl Johan could barely say a farewell.

I think of our rush to the airport, the last strong hugs.

–They send you picture postcards, yes? Karl Johan could not even send a postcard for our mail was watched. Ochranen spies. My own husband did not dare say much of his escape to me—his wife and mother of his son—for fear of ears listening.

Half a year passed before we heard word that Karl Johan survived the journey, had escaped those who chased him even across the oceans and earth. He ordered us to burn his letters, but many I hid, or cut out information. Anders bought good land for each son. But… (Sanna's voice fades.)

Edvard planned to leave but died just before he could go. His branch of the family remain in Finland. Pushing my hands deep into my pockets, I huddle against the cold, glad I knitted earmuffs for both boys. They were light to post.

–Bonds between mother and son are close. My son Simeon was independent, even as a toddler. 'I can work it out,' he'd say. Will he call on us if he needs help?

–He could telephone if he needs. If only I could hear my son's voice! Jakob Näs was the first to have a telephone in our village. WA telephoned, and told us about his pretty wife and children and success, his fancy automobile. But Karl Johan I never saw again.

–He arrived safely in Australia and loved his new land. It helped when Wilhelm joined him, and later a sister, Anna Sanna?

–Anna Sanna left home as a grown woman of forty years, with her husband and five children. But KJ went alone and without support. They were opposite temperaments. Will tried to keep him on a stable path, to reason with him, but KJ would not listen. He wrote often in the

> *early years, pleas for money, or to urge us to sell our farms and join him.*

Sanna leads me down the mossy path behind the cemetery, skirting the edge of a hayfield, to the orchard behind her red wooden house.

> –See, these are the cherry trees he planted before he left, still bearing fruit. In that field he grew his maize. When KJ emigrated, it was sold and the money sent across to Australia to buy his first forest land near—how do you say it?—Goodenerry—

–Goonengerry. It is lush and green. KJ made a good life in Australia.

> –During long nights I lay awake, pleading with the good Lord and angels to protect my sons. A mother always feels for her child, even when he is grown to manhood.

I sigh. So it doesn't get any easier? When my children were small, we could cuddle on the couch as I read them stories.

> –We told sagas like Kalevala around the fire; and on summer nights when children could not sleep. Did you sing them lullabies?

–Of course. Granddad, *min farfar*, sang one to me as a child.

> –Let me guess. It was Rida rida ranka, ja?

I sing. She winces at my pronunciation.

> –Please, sing it for me, teach me the correct words.

I cuddle up to her, under the cherry tree. She sings:

> *Rida, rida ranka, hästen heter Blanka.*
> *Vart skall hästen rida? Till en liten piga.*
> *Vad skall pigan heta? Jungfru Margareta.*

My dream fades. I hold a photograph of a woman with sad eyes.

Did I write many letters home to my own parents when I was living in Europe? After phone calls after Mum reported that I answered with 'Ja' and spoke with an accent. When one lives in a foreign land, that language seeps into the very timbre of our voices.

The Mooball House

And it was here their joys were bred
And it was here their tears were shed
Those who for us our burdens bore
So many years before.

Johan Ludvig Runeberg, *Our Land*

Photographs show Granddad relaxed in his swimming costume in the river or in a boat. They document his travels all over the west of Queensland, the north of New South Wales, to Europe. We see him as a family man, with his wife and children, and in Finland with his parents, brother and sister.

What motivated WA Back to become a reputed millionaire? Did he need to prove himself to the folk back home? A genuine priority for him was to see his family secure in the this new land. Through crippling droughts Granddad wrote optimistic letters urging his sons, 'Have faith; rain will surely come soon. God will bless us.'

Research in the Mullumbimby area brings me closer to Granddad. But I feel overwhelmed. How can I outline all his diverse ventures? His flair for seeing opportunities others missed? He could think laterally, and would try anything. An old-timer told me Granddad said, 'If you tell me there's gold there, I'll find a way to get it up.'

I draw on houses for their ability to express the essence of their owners, whose personalities seem to permeate the wood and plaster. Once shy, I become brazen enough to knock on doors and introduce myself. No stranger is safe in their own house if my grandfather built it.

'My grandfather built this house, would you like to know more about him?'

Most invite me in and I prowl through the rooms, camera snapping. Some become good friends, like Ruth Fox, who now owns the red brick house at Brunswick Heads. Granddad bought it in 1917. She invites me to stay and together we enjoy breakfasts looking out at the peace of the river. Together we explore the Goonengerry area, looking for the site of KJ's sawmill. Her son, Ian Fox, has given me maps and his photographs of the aboriginal artefacts he has found in the area.

These lead us along the potholed Mill Road to visit a cottage said to have been KJ's. It looks out towards the Byron Bay lighthouse and is close to Devil's Lookout. The present owner produces title deeds signed by W.A. Back. A local historian Nicholson Hollingworth puts me in touch with more old–timers. Through his connections I visit Granddad's first house at Mooball. My oldest living relative, Wally Holm, gave me directions.

'You can't miss it,' he said. 'Between Mooball and Burringbar, look for the big pine trees that grow all around. He brought those seeds out from Finland in his pocket, planted them at his new land as a memory of home.'

I drive up to a white timbered home with latticed verandas perched on a green hill. This is the house you describe in your letter, Granddad, that you finished building just before you married Grandma. After you realised the Goonengerry land was infertile.

> –*That worried me after Christina had agreed to marry me—*

> –Is it true you gave her two engagement rings?

> –*The first was poor quality. My wife must have the bestest.*

> –Today I drove on Mill Road, looking for signs of a sawmill.

> –*The Goonengerry land was more suited than Devil's Lookout for KJ's sawmill.*

> –And Mooball was on a railway line. It was more fertile soil?

> –*Once I cleared the land. Do not glare; all settlers did so, to make a livelihood.*

> –Photographs dated 1910 show your first home, called *Rosedale*, with bananas growing like enormous weeds all around. One shows cows grazing after rain, and is inscribed '*Eight feet deep of water.*' That's your writing, Granddad? The hill, naked except for stumps, would appal today's environmentalists. We can't remove trees on our land.

Rosedale after rain

–*I had a wife and children to support. How else could we grow crops, graze cows, grow fruit trees?*

–You wrote *'Three year old orange tree'* on the photograph. And you posed in your natty coat against lighter striped trousers and white Panama hat, holding peeled fruit. You looked trim still—

–*I soon put on weight. Christina was a good cook.*

–Granddad, I felt close to you today when I visited your home, stood on the steps under the hanging sign *Rosedale* and looked out to the view of rolling green hills. I sat a while where the photographs were taken; the veranda festooned with banana leaves, ripe bunches hanging above your head.

A maid pours tea for WA, Christina, Eric and baby Elwyn at *Rosedale*

–*We loved that verandah, we could sit and look at the view, right to the horizon.*

–And there in the corner you held your tea party for a photograph. Uncle Eric wrote about driving his tricycle around a circuit of the three verandas and kitchen. Walking through the lofty corridor to the kitchen, I imagined

Grandma cooking your dinner on the wood stove, looking out the window as you burned the tree stumps.

–In your living room, by the ornate fireplace under high plastered ceilings, I imagined Granddad scribbling postcards, sighing, 'If only Mamma could see our boys!'

Grandma interupts: *I worried that little Eric might tread on a snake.*

Granddad had no time for letters, preferring the speed of postcards, always driving to the next appointment with land agents or clients. Such industry left Grandma with fretful babies wriggling with prickly heat rash. Years later, Eric writes of his father's whirlwind life:

> For many years he owned a number of farms, worked by share farmers. He also bought bigger properties like Jasper Hall out from Rosebank. Dad subdivided the properties into three or four farms with dairy and house. Dad sold the [Mooball] farm before the first war broke out.

The same family still owns this when I visit. They make cheese in the outhouse. I relish eating Brie made from the descendants of Granddad's cows, and buy a bag of their manure for my vegetable garden at home. I pick grapes, wondering if my grandparents planted them. Granddad described his early life:

> When the AMP society in Lismore got to know me as a good valuer of land they approached me to become their district valuator. And so I sold properties all over the North Coast. It was continuous work, night and day. Sometimes I would get a telephone call from Casino or Murwillumbah and even Grafton at ten and eleven o'clock at night and I would have to be ready to go out early in the morning in my little Ford car–

I interrupt, pointing to Eric's memoirs:

–Uncle Eric described that, Granddad:

> His T model Ford had a high straight windscreen with two big leather straps to the front to support it, and I think the two brass lights used carbide. The roads were narrow and rough, the car noisy, and every horse drawn vehicle we met looked like an accident as the horse plunged and reared in panic.

–He writes well, doesn't he? Granddad, did you ever sleep? You'd rise and shine before dawn; did my parents and uncles groan when you phoned so early? I can't do justice to your varied ventures in this book. Life dealt you aces, and you played the cards well. Though you had an easier start, compared to KJ—excuse my saying. Your brother could have played lay down misere.

–*Life was never easy! I worked hard for my success.*

–Your life was a kaleidoscope of projects and properties; your fingers mixed so many pies. If I try to document all that, this book will blow out to the size of *War and Peace*. You put the Northern Rivers area on the map. Susan Tsicalas of the Brunswick Valley Historical Society described you as the richest person in Mullumbimby and possibly the whole of the Northern Rivers. She said you were a leading figure in the growth and direction of Mullumbimby, and an influential figure in the region:

> He is probably up there with the status of the Chairman of Norco, Chairman of the BGF and Chairman of CSR–the three most prestigious positions governing the economic fortunes and way-of-life of about 100,000 people. And speculatively, he seems to have been a behind-the-scenes political mover and shaker, perhaps bankrolling Liberal candidates for State and Federal elections along with local councillors.

Granddad, do you agree with that? I can barely hear you—you're so faint.

–*It's hard, talking English, back in my first decade here. I'm tired. Write your book about KJ. You don't need my help.*

Fine. It's been a packed day, driving along muddy dirt roads, talking with people, taking photographs. I head back to my bed in Ruth's house by the Brunswick river. My mind buzzes with all the sights and nuggets of information to integrate. I am exhausted yet cannot sleep. Is it over-stimulus or am I too wrapped up in your story? Leave me be for now, Granddad, and you also, KJ. Please go away for now and let me sleep.

Wilhelm Spreads His Wings

Imagine, see how the bird swoops
You too have your wings
And your mighty space to fly.

Runeberg, *Third Book of Poems*

After Granddad sold his own Mooball farm, others asked him to sell their properties. He moved to Mullumbimby; there the opening of his office attracted the elite in their best finery for photographs splashed in the newspaper.

WA is seated in the white car, fourth from the right.

This successful Stock and Property Agent claimed he sold most of the farms in the district at one time or another. He placed advertisements but word of mouth built his reputation as an honest and frank person who would not sell poor land. Buyers flocked to him. WA bought Morrison Park, about a quarter of the municipality of Mullumbimby, and subdivided allotments off the frontage to the town.

After a cousin sends me plans of his extensive development of Mullumbimby, I drive along Morrison Road to *Park Farm*. It looks out onto grassy lawns that roll down to the river. Photographs show the boys in canoes and WA and Christina standing on a pontoon. Nearby is another home, called *Munsala*, as was his later St Lucia house. This is white stucco with three archways.

KJ wrote home on 26 June 1919:

> Wilhelm has nine properties at the moment. His daily job is and has been for a long time now to buy and sell land for others. When he hears of a good farm selling cheap he buys it for himself and if he gets a good price for his own land he sells that. He has more work than he can do and it is not uncommon for him to earn a hundred or two hundred pounds a day and very seldom does he earn less than fifty pounds a day. He has the best house in town and a motorcar. He has 25,000 sheep and several hundred cows.

While WA was on the road, Christina valued family support from her sister Ada, brother John and his wife Inez. Will offered the widowed Ada a home with them all her life. As they often entertained important visitors, Christina sewed frocks and trimmed hats to present a suitable image. In visits to Sydney, Melbourne and Adelaide, and later London, Zurich, Paris and Helsinki, she bought stylish clothes to reflect an up-and-coming man's standards.

But that takes us ahead in the story of WA and Christina. My father Aubrey was born in Mullumbimby on 11th November 1914, Old Halloween in the Gregorian calendar, and shadowed by the brooding clouds of World War 1.

Eric wrote:

> Dad decided towards the end of the war that instead of renting a house he should build a new one. No doubt he had this in mind for a long time because he had accumulated a large amount of red cedar timber, boards and other sizes all seasoned. It would be worth a lot today. My parents called the

new home 'Cedarholm.' All the doors and cupboards were made of cedar and between the lounge-dining room, as a divider, were two cedar columns, one each side, from floor to ceiling. We moved into 'Cedarholm' at the end of 1918.

There were lead lights in windows and a tiled front verandah. All the furniture came from Beard Watson, the best place in Sydney. Gloria was born in the front bedroom on 21st July, 1920 and Alan on 24th November 1921.

A crucial clue to WA Back's success is the partnerships he forged. He could exercise creative flair and control in many ventures, but outsource the day-to-day running to manager-partners. Eric wrote that 'My father had the ability to choose good honest hard-working partners and he did know good land when he saw it.'

From 1920 for the next 56 years, Vincent Nelson came to work for WA in the office 'and he stuck with him through good and bad times until Dad died in 1974 and then he finalised his estate. Like the others, he was a very honest person.'

WA expanded into Western Queensland, by applying for Land Ballots in partnership with his friends. The first success was when Walter Ellem drew a block of good downs country called *Mellew* in the west of the state near Barcaldine. Walter brought the news and a load of logs on his bullock team up the hill. Christina was confined after Elwyn's birth, but she threw on her wrap and ran outside to share the excitement. A jubilant Walter threw his hat in the air, forgetting his bullocks. Eric told that they toppled the dray and 'finished up in a mess in town.'

That was the first of many ballots. Thus WA helped friends and family to become established on their land and shared many long–standing partnerships. Eric wrote:

> Sometimes there would be 12 blocks up for ballot, then more the following month. Dad had backed about twelve applicants for the twelve blocks of Saltern Creek–144 chances. We must get at least one! But 600 odd marbles went into the box each time, and none of ours ever came out. Then Hugo Holm, my cousin, drew a block at Mount Cornish towards the end of 1929. Dad bought some more ewes near Tamworth and Hugo and I took them to Barcaldine by train, then a drover took them to the Promised Land. Hugo called the new place Stockholm. It could be cut off by floods for weeks at a time, so I suppose he felt like Robinson Crusoe.

With inventive spirit typical of Finns, Hugo built a bridge across Cornish Creek, to the surprise of people in the district.

My parents (L and R), Hugo and Tilda Holm holding Jill, grandmother Tilly Miller.

A desert property called *Rocklea*, between Jericho and Barcaldine, proved to be a poor place:

Dad had no experience of western land, but he learnt from that experience... They shifted the sheep from *Rocklea* to *Mellew*, the Ellem block, and as the boundaries had to be fenced, they only had use of part of the country. Walter said they put 3000 sheep into one small paddock, marked the lambs, and in twelve months they had 6000 sheep there. It was a very good season.

That was the start of the WA Back–Walter Ellem partnership, which lasted until he died.

Another partnership formed with A.J. Cameron who had drawn a block which he called Cremona. Cameron drew *Lillarea*, a large selection about 20 miles from Stockholm. The years following the First World War were good as pent up demand for goods saw prices rise and likewise property values.

And then the Great Depression hit.

North of the Border

Man's life is only short and the impression one makes upon humanity is often like the footprints of the caravan, which remains on the surface of the desert sand until the first puff of wind comes and then is swept away to be seen no more.

K. J. Back, *The Concentrated Wisdoms of Australia*

In his memoir, Eric wonders what took WA from the green hills near Byron Bay for arid western Queensland properties.

> My opinion is the area where he operated in New South Wales was quite small. To grow bigger would have been difficult, whereas the vastness of Queensland in a good season astonishes visitors.

Aha, Uncle Eric, here's the answer: Granddad wrote in a letter:

> While we were living at Mooball up until 1913 I became very interested in growing sheep and wool. I thought we would start with sheep on the 320-acre farm between Mooball and Burringbar. When I went to Sydney and consulted with Pitt Son & Badgery, a very old man (I think his name was Badgery) condemned the idea of trying to grow wool on the North Coast of New South Wales. He gave me a lot of information and good reading, clippings from newspapers, setting out all the failures that people had gone through on the North Coast to grow wool. I am pleased that I accepted his advices.
>
> Always I listened to good sound wisdom before buying land. A sales manager came in with a bundle of properties for sale all over New South Wales and Victoria. I became so interested in it that I went to my old friend Mr Badgery; when

I picked out something that might suit my requirements he gave such a hearty laugh. Nothing seemed good enough for a young man like me starting off in life.

Next he took me into another room—the Queensland room—and unrolled a big map on the wall and with a pointing stick he picked out Blackall, Barcaldine, Longreach, Winton, Hughenden, Muttaburra, Aramac, and he said this is the place for a young man to go. All this was interesting for me but I had my place at Mooball and I proceeded to get a dairy herd established there after a hundred and fifty acres was felled and grassed. But neither of us learned to milk—

—Granddad, I'm surprised you didn't. Surely you had cows on the farm in Finland?

—A family ran the dairy while I devoted my time to my business.

A main factor was that being on the road every day in the wet Northern Rivers district affected WA's health.

I suppose I was careless too. Every February and March I was laid up with bronchitis, I was completely down to it. This made me feel so tired that I could hardly walk, and Christina often used to say to me 'shake yourself up, you will be all right.'

Doctor Kellas told me: 'You will never get rid of this unless you go out west.' By then we were settled in Mullumbimby, a nice home and office; business life appealed to me very much. I said what about Longreach or Winton? After looking on the map Dr Kellas felt sure that the climate would be most suitable for me and I could count on being free from catarrh and hay fever there.

After I pulled myself together and sold the farm at Mooball in late 1913, I took the train to Barcaldine and Longreach, and as soon as I got off the train and walked up the street all ailments of hay fever had left me. The dry climate suited my lungs and ever since, when I had any bad attacks of bronchitis I went out west and it was the best cure.

Eric and his brothers managed their father's enterprises 'out west' including *Fairview* which became an albatross around their necks.

> On paper it looked fine with a good homestead and other buildings right in the middle, a flowing bore and drains taking water to the paddocks. 1926 was a real drought with stock numbers falling to 9000 sheep. The bore pressure was falling and eventually it stopped flowing. A thirty-foot Southern Cross mill had to be bought and a 14-inch diameter pump installed. Even so, it was always a battle for water, especially in summer.

> We would kill [a sheep] late in the day, have fresh meat for one day, and salt meat with a variety of sauces and pickles until it was finished. Butter was a doubtful quantity if you got it home to a drip safe. Vegetables were just the basics, potatoes, pumpkins, onions and sometimes hardened peas that never got soft. It was claimed that if you cooked a galah [bird] with the peas when the peas were soft you could eat the galah.

The newspaper *Mullumbimby Star* in 1931 commended WA's sons Eric and Elwyn whose wool clip topped the market for the state:

> They are the right type of young Australian settler that the country requires to develop the land and with the zest and enthusiasm they are putting into their work, provide an example that many others might follow. With the optimism characteristic of youth, they discount their present discomforts and the setback by drought, and look forward to 'next year' to lift the clouds.

Options were more slim for daughters. My mother saw that education would give us passports to wider horizons and supported our studies in Brisbane.

Getting an Education

*The one with brains and will to toil
May carve his way through life's turmoil.*

K. J. Back, *The Concentrated Wisdoms of Australia*

After my tour, I drive along Hawken Drive mulling over three years' schooling at Ironside State School interspersed by stints back at the sheep station outside Hughenden. From Grade 7 onward, I remained in Brisbane for secondary school and university.

In that red brick house I played with my first city friend. Here I was photographed with a transistor radio to my ear, my hair combed down—Beatles–style—an improvement on the short toothbrush fringe of the serious–eyed portrait some years earlier.

Above our house is the stop where we waited for the Number 11 bus into the city. Or, more likely, where I rushed up the steep terraces from our home on Highland Terrace, along the gravel short cut. Mornings were a scramble; as my mother was mostly absent out west with my father. The sensible solution to live together with older brothers and sisters in the St Lucia house worked—after a fashion. We 'batched'—the shorthand for a bachelor existence.

If I had been a school boarder I would have escaped the pressure of washing and ironing my uniforms (at high school we wore an unflattering lettuce–green colour), making sandwich lunches, and catching the bus by eight a.m. I would have shrunk from a dormitory of strange girls, but adapted after an initial shock like plunging into a freezing lake after a sauna.

Instead, frequent stress headaches brought me to the school sick bay. Like a watermelon, I developed a strong independent outer frame that held inside a mush of insecurity and tension from getting myself to school on time, unaided.

From the bus we caught glimpses of the river sparkling in the morning sun. At night, I would wander down to the pontoon, seeking solace under the smile of the stars. In my naivety, it didn't occur to me that danger could lurk in the shadows.

Opposite Ironside State School I see the red brick Presbyterian Church. I wished we attended this church during our teenage years. Instead our absentee parents sent us to the unassuming Joyful News Mission, in the inner suburb of Fortitude Valley.

The Mission was formed at the turn of the century to help the poor of the area, but the Sunday Services were later attended by all levels of society. Bedraggled children were picked up for Sunday School from the Spring Hill area – slums then, but now areas full of expensive renovations by the upwardly mobile. Being a fundamental church, many things were frowned upon – dancing, makeup, and even women's 'trousers'. In this environment, normal questions which are common in the teenage years were discouraged. When seeking to know 'why', my Sunday School teacher would tap her Bible brick and say, 'It's all in the Book, dear.'

We spent the day in church and various meetings, until at dusk we walked a few blocks to the hub of iniquity where we stood in a circle to 'witness' to drunks and prostitutes. My mystified probings about the latter met with replies about fornication and wanton ways. Answers that only raised more questions. Clutching our Bible bricks we each in turn stepped forward to read a verse of Scripture or 'give our testimony'.

My rebellion was sparked by the prospect of a science excursion to the beach. How could I bend over to prise limpets and sea anemones off rocks while wearing a skirt? When my peers asked why I would not attend the Year 12 formal, I had no answer. What 'witness' was it to be rigid, sober and joyless, and to miss a rite of passage? Mum heard my distressed pleas and relented. With lips as tight as her stitches, she sewed a demure pink gown. A swain was enlisted to escort me through an agony of slipping on the dance floor and awkward ambling through unknown territory. Would I attend future formals? No. But I had made a step towards emancipation.

In the 50s and into the Swinging 60s, women and girls still wore stockings, attached with suspenders, taking care that the back seams were straight. Even on the hottest days, gloves and hats were *de rigueur*, part of our uniforms for school, church, and for Saturday morning jaunts to town.

After shopping at McWhirters we enjoyed a crushed pineapple juice from the little shop opposite the Canberra Hotel. Or lunch in wooden booths at the Shingle Inn, with its aroma of freshly baked goods. A High Tea offered three-layer cake stands of ribbon sandwiches filled with cucumber and cream cheese, elegant small cakes and scones with clotted cream and jam.

Or we salivated at the waffles with ice-cream and vacillated over the choice of butterscotch or chocolate sauce.

Each day I travelled to school, first on the bus to the city centre then by tram over the Grey Street bridge to South Brisbane. My school, Somerville House, is centred around a historic building, *Cumbooquepa*, built of stone with red brick trim, with a stylish blend of arches and verandahs. It is topped by a jaunty polygonal tower and flanked by palm trees. These historic buildings were occupied during the Second World War by the United States Army's East-Asian Command under General Macarthur, when students were evacuated to Stanthorpe, a town over a hundred kilometres west.

The mathematics teacher chirruped about logarithms and square roots. She had no idea of the fog that blanketed my brain because I was too shy to ask for any explanation that might lift my poor results.

In my first year of high school I was voted class captain and, in the last year, prefect. So why did I assume that my peers considered me a loser? Each lunch break the in-crowd congregated in a large circle, each sitting on their 'ports' on the oval, chattering like budgerigars. To join them was as unthinkable as a cold war crossing from East to West Berlin. I lurked with other losers, or in the bathroom. In the turreted library I devoured engrossing books. Two teachers took me under their wings; one slipped to me the sort of books that evangelical Christians burned, like *Catcher in the Rye*. I surprised others as well as myself by topping the year group—once.

Seated at my desk I read poetry and play characters with relish. But when I was given a lead part in the school play, I froze. Eagle eyes pierced me! I was relegated to the back of the Greek chorus.

In later decades I evolved from that shy 'bush' child who hid in the toilet block rather than face fearsome peers. I became an adult who welcomes any platform to reach out with words and music. When I now coach people to boost their confidence in presentations, I can say 'The person you are now is not who you will be in a decade or two or five. If I can conquer such shyness and fears, even welcome public performance, so can you.' The outback child would run a mile at the prospect of speaking in public. Now she enjoys and invites such opportunities.

How did that change? Experience, maturity. Speaking foreign languages.

School classrooms were perched on a hill overlooking the city. Summer storms painted the sky lurid colours worthy of El Greco. Prefects at the school gates enforced a strict rule: all top buttons must be secured. They pounced on any sliver of bare neck. A packet of pins counteracted the missing button excuse. Knees were another no-show zone. The headmistress paraded past kneeling students, ruler at the ready. Any skirt that did not touch the ground must be lengthened by the next day. When rebels dyed their hair with peroxide *Magic Silver White*, she supervised multiple shampoo and scrub treatments, to little avail.

At the end of a school day, I walked down the hill towards the tram line, past the Old South Brisbane Town Hall. Its red brick tower, topped with Australia's first electrically–driven clock, was installed in 1904. During my schooldays it housed the Queensland Conservatorium of Music where I learned clarinet from David Shephard, principal clarinettist of the Queensland Symphony Orchestra. For theory lessons, I climbed circular stairs up to the tower studio where, baffled, I sat mute as Alan Lane wrote ant–track marks on manuscript paper.

My painful mental fog matched his chain–smoking haze. Shy, I was too tongue–tied to ask for clarification. Like a tortoise, I scurried back into my shell at the smallest flicker of impatience from a teacher. Yet I thrived on undivided attention for an hour each week from these teachers.

University of Queensland

The life is but one continual school, which opens at the cradle and closes at the grave.

K. J. Back, *The Concentrated Wisdoms of Australia*

My schooling continued in Brisbane through five years at Somerville House high school, and then four years at the University of Queensland.

Visits to Hughenden dwindled and they were more often by aeroplane. One experience from my teens is scalded into my mind. My sister and I were packed to return from the country property to Brisbane. Then Dad remembered: 'Mutton! You must take some meat with you.' He chased down a sheep, slaughtered and hung it. Chopped and still warm, it was wrapped in newspaper and plastic bags and stowed in our 'ports'. This delayed our departure so we jolted all the harder over rocks and potholes in the fifty kilometre drive to town. We caught the flight by a whisker. The scheduled touch down at Townsville airport dragged on. Buckled in, we fanned ourselves against January heat. Flustered stewards trotted up and down the aisle. The intercom announcement crackled: 'Ladies and gentlemen, apologies for the delay. Does anyone have any perishables on board?' Our hands fluttered up as we slunk deeper into our seats. Our suitcases were offloaded for burial near the tarmac, and then the plane took off.

After finishing school I enrolled at the University of Queensland for a Bachelor of Music course. My pen hovered over the options on the application form. My school results were higher for English, History and Art. Why did I not continue with these instead of music, where I had weaknesses? Partly because I surprised myself by winning a competition, when I felt the power of God playing with and through me.

The Highland Terrace house was a half-hour's walk from university—or run, for no one taught me time management. But it became a melting pot of conflicting stresses. Often I escaped to sit in a tree or on a pontoon on the river, crying out to the stars for help. But I recoiled from visits to 'the bush' where the stars sparkled the brightest. There, I felt alien, a cuckoo in the nest. Barely past Christmas, I caught a bus to Townsville and flew south to arrive on a university friend's doorstep for a mattress on the floor. She hosted 70s style parties. We danced to repetitions of a 'psychedelic' recording called *Pink Rabbit*.

The house at 160 Highland Terrace was sold. The flotsam of decades of living was packed off to charities. None of us had the time, energy or inclination to sort it out. I moved into a residential college where meals appeared three times a day with no effort of shopping, cooking or washing dishes. There I skulked in my basement room, still too shy to join giggling discussions about boyfriends and clothes. I ached with loneliness just as much amongst hundreds of other women. I looked out my window at the lights of Brisbane and prayed for love.

My mother did her best but was torn between eight children and a husband struggling with his own life. She provided a large family with food, shelter and education. But she was spread thin.

Education would provide a pathway for her three daughters. The practical outcome was that I lived in Brisbane, sixteen hundred kilometres southeast of the family property.

Somehow I completed my degree. If I kept myself busy, insecurity was less likely to encroach on my thoughts. I hurtled into challenges, prone to overdrive and burnout to prove myself. During holidays I put myself onto a train to travel the 900 kilometres to Sydney, to throw myself into a fresh environment.

At national music camp in Geelong I met a handsome violinist, drawn as much to his singing tone as to his dark eyes. He signalled his interest by gazing open-mouthed at me during rehearsals. We courted during the Australian Youth Orchestra season at Adelaide, where the program included Stravinsky's Petrushka. At a lunch break, Antoni treated me to an unaccustomed cocktail. Before launching into the high clarinet solo in The Bear and the Peasant, I winked at him. He lost his place in the music.

In the days before Skype and emails, our long distance romance was enriched by treasured letters between occasional visits. I waited weeks for Antoni's first missive, which consisted of a cross word puzzle centred around my name. Who could resist that? Distance gave deeper perspectives during a year apart, then I moved to Sydney on completion of my B.Mus degree.

A year later we married and took off for further studies, teaching and playing in London, then five years in Sweden, France and Germany. We learned Swedish on the job, from scratch, and German with an intensive month's *Anfänger* course. Fear of making a fool of myself faded, knowing that most times I opened my mouth, mistakes came out. I got on with living—and speaking.

Many who witnessed my embarrassments became friends for life.

'Your music is fine,' a friend said, 'but why not introduce the pieces with some words?'

'Because we'd make mistakes!' By then our Swedish was fluent but ungrammatical.

'People forgive that, they warm to you.'

We spoke to our audiences and yes, people appreciated that we made an effort. In my future years came opportunities to present workshops, papers, seminars, and adjudications. After publishing my first book I finessed my speaking skills to embark on promotional campaigns.

Like KJ, I embraced challenges to communicate in a new language. Since faint childhood memories, I identified with KJ who was misunderstood and overlooked by his family. Much of mine was a thousand miles away.

After our seven-year extended honeymoon in Europe, the nesting instinct brought us home to Australia. Antoni accepted a position as Concertmaster of the Queensland Theatre Orchestra. We flew on the last plane that would accept a heavily pregnant woman, after final conferences and courses. Our last fling was a gourmet tour of Provence, sleeping in our little scout tent, so small that my man's feet stuck out the end, so that we could eat snails and Bouillabaisse.

Soon after, my once empty arms were filled with babies, hugging our three sons. I poured into them the love and care I had lacked in my own upbringing. Years later, when my sons stood on their own feet, I had time to discover roots and flesh out the family story so they would know their heritage. Which included the pain of a family divided by wide oceans.

Sister Anna Sanna Sails South

I swam beyond my country,
Left the country so familiar,
And have come to doors I know not...
All the trees around me pain me.

Kalevala

Anders and Sanna Back could not be persuaded to emigrate but sister Anna Sanna reunited with the brothers in January 1921. Much of the following is paraphrased from Karl Johan's letters.

KJ: For twenty years letters crisscrossed back and forth with plans for my family to immigrate to Australia. We waited so long for them to pack up their possessions and move but they felt it all too hard. In 1913 Pappa lost money when the Nykarleby bank failed. Wilhelm wrote many advices in letters and telegrams. Plans faltered then stalled when Civil War intervened. In 1920 I was close to booking a ticket to Finland to bring them out. I planned to travel via America.

> There will be dark winter when I come to Finland. It is now twenty years since I last saw snow, and that will be something to have a real winter again. If I could hear it's so cold and frozen that the house will creak then perhaps I will appreciate the Australian summer.

Anna Sanna argued that the money spent for my ticket would cover the cost of passage for the whole family, including costs to tip stewards. Our parents baulked. Edvard must remain in Finland to look after them as they aged. Besides, men had a duty to rebuild Finland after so many died in the Civil War. He felt frustrated because Pappa bought land for him at Wilsons Creek in 1903. I wrote him in 1920:

> It is a pity that you did not travel here sooner as you could have looked after this land yourself, a saving of about £4 per day. It is the same here as in Finland; it never pays to have a farm if one has to depend on others for labour. Hired hands can bring ruination to an absent owner.

In 1920 Anna Sanna sent word that passages were booked to Australia for herself, husband Erik Johan Nyholm and family. How I longed to hear the details of her life since we parted!

***

We could imagine that Munsala was agog when in 1899 Erik Johan Nyholm returned from work in the redwood forests of California. He saved money to buy a farm in Finland. Many emigrants wasted theirs on gambling. One night Erik Johan won money playing card games. Walking back to his lodging, he heard footsteps gaining on him from behind. He ran to bolt himself in his room. 'There was no sense losing my life for a game of cards,' he said. Though he watched games and could not resist displaying his speed to shuffle the cards, he never played again.

Erik Johan bought a farm at nearby Damskata. His mother, Susanna, widowed years earlier, worried: 'The Russians may conscript you to fight.'

'The Russians won't take me,' Erik Johan said. 'I am flat–footed so couldn't march all day.' Others told of conscription in Russia, tramping from sunrise to sunset with barely a halt, over rye fields that stretched to the horizon. And, true, on 21 January 1900, Erik Johan received an official letter stating he 'is not called for war and for this reason is always free from this.'

Next day Erik Johan was on Anders Back's doorstep to ask permission to court his eldest daughter. Anders approved, for the families were close. He had brought Otto, the younger Nyholm son to Australia with Wilhelm in 1902. He returned to Finland.

Anna Sanna's sister, Sofia, sized up Erik Johan as he walked up the lane to the house.

'Anna San, he's thirty–one years—too old for you,' she hissed.

'Twelve years difference is not much,' Anna Sanna said. 'Better a mature man who has proved himself hard–working, reliable and who cares for his family, than a young lad who seeks only good times.' His worldly–wise ways and ingenuity made younger lads like Sofia's fiancé callow by comparison.

Sofia tossed her head: 'My fiancé has prospects.'

Erik Johan, a shrewd judge of men and horses, shared misgivings about Sofia's suitor, known as a philanderer.

In American logging camps Erik Johan had worked with those whose hands blistered from the great saws—and yet other types of men who avoided hard work.

'Those saws are heavy and men die if they stumble in their path.' So he found safer employment, sharpening the saws. 'Work slowed if those blades dulled.' He was also in demand with smaller blades; his skill as a barber meant he trimmed a hundred or more heads each Sunday.

Animals trusted Erik Johan; his skills as a horseman were known all around the neighbourhood. Governor Stanford of California respected him and made him head of his stable, the finest in the state.

Back in Finland Erik Johan bought the best possible draft horses, a mare and a gelding. He boasted of their strength—so partisans noted him for a dangerous mission against the Russians.

The banns were read in church. In midsummer of 1900, the couple stood before God for His blessing on a loving union which would endure fifty-five years. In her best dress, with a wreath of June flowers in her hair Anna Sanna followed Wilhelm Munsin the fiddler up to the altar where the priest read the marriage vows. As they walked back down the hill villagers threw blossoms. Mamma and Pappa set up in the orchard trestle tables decorated with birch branches. Jugs of *saft* washed down the wedding porridge. In her happiness Anna Sanna barely noticed Sofia's furrowed brow.

They began married life living with Anna Sanna's parents, Edvard and Sofia while Erik Johan built their own red timbered house at nearby Damskata. After working long days ploughing, haymaking and butchering, Erik Johan worked another shift to craft its innovative iron roof. In September 1904, as Anna Sanna nursed her firstborn, Hugo, Sofia's own belly was swollen with the seed of her fickle fiancé.

'What example does this set for others that the churchwarden's daughter bears an illegitimate child?' Anders roared. Sofia tossed her head. Of all of the family, she was his match.

But no one made a fool of Sofia without consequence. For all that the banns had been read she sent her fickle fiancé packing.

Assassins and Decoys

Land, which a thousand lakelets hast,
Where song and honour dwell!
Shore upon which our life was cast,
Land of our future and our past!

Johan Ludvig Runeberg, *Vårt Land*

We may never unearth the truth from myths, due to the secrecy by which the Finns sought to avoid the Russian authorities. Some stories may have been intended to mislead the authorities. An amazing story of Erik Johan Holm bravely taking an assassin by horse-drawn sled across the Monäs Pass ice to Sweden has been passed down through the family. The shortest route from Finland to Sweden was from that village south of Munsala, from where so many escaped by boat to Sweden, it was called a 'Monäs passport'. In recent frozen winters, cars and trucks have driven across an ice highway at such a place.

Erik Johan's story was retold by his daughters in the ripe accents they had learned from their parents. But their eldest brother Hugo—who was 20 years old when they left Finland—also said 'They don't know the half of it; they couldn't cope if they did.'

Perhaps it happened earlier during the Civil War, but Hugo's daughter thought he remembered it from childhood. In this case the assassin might have been Lennart Hohenthal who on 6 February 1905 killed Eliel Soisalon-Soininen, a prominent Procurator (Chancellor of Justice). But Hugo was born in September 1904, too young to have first-hand memories.

Gretel Kummel tells me it was Erik Johan's brother Viktor who drove the Procurator to safety but there were many conflicting stories about the actual escape. She sends me a book *Udden in Munsala* written by Viktor's son, Runar Nyholm, her father. Viktor worked in America and returned to live at Damskata, 700 metres from the cape called Udden. Since 1885, when District Judge Berndt Hällsten and his wife Betty arrived, they had regular contact with the Nyholm and Back families. Hällsten sold 400,000 square metres of land to Anders Back and Johan Eriksson Nyholm for 5,000 Marks. Betty hosted the neighbourhood children for cake and juice on birthdays and name days.

Runar's book confirmed that the couple were active against the Russian regime, along with other prominent figures like Jakob Näs, member of the parliament, who lived in Monäs.

> The district judge and his wife were warm patriotic people and engaged in the passive resistance movement. Because of that they were also involved in the spreading of 'Fria Ord' ('Free Word'), a propaganda newspaper. For that purpose the isolated Udden was particularly suitable. In 1902 during the pilot strike Mr. and Mrs. Hällsten were active. Also in 1915-1917 when boys travelled via Sweden to the 27th Jägar battalion in Germany, Udden was used as a halting-place where the boys could stay while waiting for a suitable transport to Sweden.
>
> Other refugees who were sought after by the Russian authorities found temporary asylum at Udden. In the home of my childhood there was a lot of talk about such an incident 75 years ago because my father was to play an important role at the departure of the refugee from Udden.
>
> My parents' home was situated less than a kilometre from Udden and so it happened on a winter's day in 1906 that the district judge Hällsten called for my father. He had not been gone very long before he returned and said he had to drive a fugitive gentleman. Everybody knew that Father owned a mare that was quick to run and generally was called 'The black mare'. The gentleman said his name was Hohenthal. He was hidden in the sleigh and they took off over the ice to Andra sjön (The Other Lake) and further on through the town of Nykarleby to the Kovjoki station.
>
> The town was dangerous to pass through because gendarmes were on guard so it was no safe journey for the two in the sleigh. Hohenthal asked his driver if he thought someone might catch up to them. To this came the answer from the driver's seat: 'Only bullets can catch us'. Unmolested, they passed also through the town and at the station there were

no gendarmes. Hohenthal could enter the train unrecognized for transportation to Sweden. For sure the driver was relieved when he returned home.

I heard my father and mother tell about this incident several times in my childhood and they lived, of course, in strong assurance that it had been Lennart Hohenthal whom father had had in his sleigh.

Partisans had rescued Hohenthal out of a Kakola prison window by rope ladder. Dr. Torvald Hohenthal told Runar that his uncle hid on a farm for two weeks before being smuggled to Sweden. Another story that may have been created as a decoy for the Russians came from fisherman Isak Flygar in Monäs who said he took him by boat over the archipelago. At sea the man fired some pistol shots at seabirds and said he had shot a procurator with his gun. He added, 'But don't be afraid, I won't do you any harm'. Flygar was convinced it was Hohenthal he had had in his boat. He was one of four decoys who covered the escape route of the real assassin.

Was Erik Johan's story confused with Viktor's? Hugo said the Damskata home was a safe–house for activists and Runar's book backs this. Living close to Udden, it is possible that all the Nyholm brothers were involved with the resistance. But the many conflicting stories are shadowy.

Another snippet lingers in family lore; that Erik Johan declared, 'There will be reprisals. We must be on the next ship for Australia.' In fact, the family sailed from Finland on 11 October 1920, well after the Civil War finished. It took time to sell the farm, pack and organise a large family.

Perhaps two similar stories are melded? Who knows the truth? A wife least of all, in case she might divulge information under torture. We can only imagine what might have happened. Let us place it in the latter timeframe of the Civil War.

During the First World War, Russians overran Finland to quarter soldiers. They plundered produce while Finn bellies rumbled. Erik Johan, a butcher, heard Russian officials tell a farmer, 'You have two cows. Give us one for our troops.' Offspring tell that Erik Johan guarded Russian prisoners on sentry duty in the snow, his boots stuffed with straw.

Russia's 1917 revolution soon spread to Finland. Farmers smuggled guns in wagons of hay, ready to strike. As Finns grasped the chance to expel hated Russian overlords, White partisans fought against Red sympathisers in the Civil War.

Brothers slaughtered brothers and friends. Dad's uncle Edvard fought at

Tampere where fierce battles decimated the Reds and killed many Whites. Further north in Ostrobothnia, fighting was less severe. Nevertheless, everyone lived in fear.

As so many men were buried in cold makeshift graves, how could an able person not be drawn into conflict or activism?

At Västerö near Vaasa, the ship *Equity* neared land to unload weapons from Germany for Civil War partisans. In October 1917, activists waited in a small church high on the cliffs. At the signal, 'It's time,' they formed a human chain to unload the ship. Was Erik Johan one of those? Damskata hamlet, close to Udden and the sea, was just across the sound from the village of Monäs, that escape route to Sweden.

Hugo's sketchy memory is of late-night knocking at the door. That two burly white partisans whose fur coats dripped snow elbowed in and gestured Erik Johan into the scullery. They huddled together, whispering, then sidled out into the night. Erik Johan gave Anna Sanna a quick hug, then saddled the horses to the sleigh.

Did Erik Johan then whip his horses to Monäs, across the ice to Sweden and all the way back again? Family describe white foam and sweat streaming off them. The gulf stream could melt the ice and it was too dark to see cracks in the early spring thaw. Was the route to Kovjoki railway station more feasible?

Imagine Anna Sanna waiting, sleepless, by the window until hooves rattled into the barn and her husband returned.

'After delivering them to the underground partisans I rested the horses while I thanked God for his protection,' he whispered. 'We waited just long enough for their frothing to subside and walked home.'

'You're mad, Erik Johan! You could have gone right through the ice, or been captured. I could be a widow with five children now.' How might he have responded?

'And still might be, unless we escape. Emigrate.'

'Then we must all go to Australia, keep the family together.'

'Karl Johan and Wilhelm will help us settle and find good land.'

It was easy for him to say. He already had experience of emigration, eleven years in America. In Finland, the family was well off. Erik Johan had built a house that towered above others in the district, with the first iron roof. To begin afresh and face hardship in Australia—at their ages—they must leave behind their frail parents.

'Look to the future,' Erik Johan reminded Anna Sanna. 'Anders and Sanna still have Sofia and Edvard. We must tend to our own children.'

True, a mother must think first of her offspring, Hugo, Martha, Ted,

Anne and Wally. Yet Pappa's slow pace showed his days were closing into twilight. Anna Sanna would not hear the bell toll for her father.

Farewell at Damskata home, before the Nyholm (holm) family emigrated to Australia. L-R: Martha, Sanna Nyholm, Sanna Back, Anna Sanna (Back) Nyholm with Ann, Anders Back, a neighbour, Eric Johan with two Arabian horses, Ted and Walter on hobby horses, Sofia Back, Hugo.

Last day at Damskata, Finland

Be religious, but not a fanatic, patriot but not a patrimaniac. Let the whole of humanity be your nationality, and the whole world your native land.

K.J. Back, *The Royal Toast*

Migrating families treasure photographs of themselves with their loved ones—that last view frozen in time. Hands reveal so much, I realise, as I copy a photograph in paint. It shows their last day, 11 October 1920, before Anna Sanna and her husband take their five children to freedom in Australia.

Four generations gather outside the red wood house at Damskata. Anna Sanna stands between her seated parents, as if already poised to fly, a hand resting on each. Anders sits upright, his hands stolidly on his knees. This is a man who sees the future for his daughter that cannot be here. Migration is the best course.

Erik Johan's hands fondle the beloved Arabian horses that flank him. How can I leave these trusty friends, I hear him sigh.

The children, resplendent in their best clothes, look solemn. They will miss Pelli the dog, who lies at their feet.

The family is charged by the tumult of emotions that ricochet between their parents and grandparents. Walter and Ted ride the hobbyhorses carved by their uncle Edvard. Beside her grandmother, Martha holds tight a doll's pram—why must she leave it behind? She promises to write many letters. 'Every week, *Mormor*, you will hear our news.'

What could a caring grandmother do or say? Sanna's hands lie resigned in her lap. Her thoughts speak through that gesture seen in all her photographs; she peers up under lowered brows, her head sunk onto her chest. I imagine her turmoil:

> *—Yet another child lost to me. Of course they are not safe here. They beg Anders and me to follow them to Australia. But our strength wanes. I*

shall not see my grandchildren grow. Little Walter cries that he cannot pack Pelli as we do the hobbyhorse. Hugo stands by the fence beside his aunt Sofia. (What a pity that Helmi sulks in the attic.) Hugo is resourceful, so he will thrive. As a boy in confirmation class he stole money from the poor man statue. He enticed a spider into the slot so its legs would push out the money.

Tumultuous thoughts beset Anna Sanna's mind, as her hand warms Mamma's shoulder:

—What am I doing, a woman turned forty, to sail over the world? Karl Johan wrote how seas taller than houses thrashed his ship. Yet our family must not be divided. Far from his kin, Karl Johan is rudderless, tossed by any wave that takes him.

Pappa prays for travelling safety and gives his blessing amid snuffles and sobs. Faces are wet from weeping. A procession of relatives, horses and cart heads to the station at Kovjoki. Erik Johan wipes the tears from his eyes in his horses' manes.

A plaintive hoot announces the train's arrival. Last hugs are hasty as they fling children and bags aboard. As the train steams around the bend, Anna Sanna tries to retain the sight of her family and of birch trees bare in white fields. But tears cloud her vision.

At Hanko the family boards the *Ariadne* for a tense voyage to London, preceded by a minesweeper. They wait three months in London while the *Benalla* is refitted—the ship is rife with rats. Anna Sanna blames little Anne's chicken pox on them. During dark hours it is a comfort to share her concerns with another woman, and in their own tongue. Ida, her cousin from Munsala, travels with them. With her are husband, Mats Wilhelm Backlund, and their children, Bengt and Astrid.[2]

God hears Anna Sanna's daily prayers and the family arrives safely in Sydney. They board the *Wollongbar* for Byron Bay, and arrive on the third day of January 1921—a new year and a new life. KJ and WA wave handkerchiefs in greeting on the jetty. They have enlisted a fleet of automobiles and sulkies to carry the ten voyagers and their luggage to WA's white timbered house *Cedarholm* in Mullumbimby.

The children run under the canopy of its gated trellis to climb a large Moreton Bay fig. Verandahs surround the home, open spaces where Anna Sanna sinks onto a *chaise longue*, fanning her flushed skin. Exhaustion

---

2   As ensuing letters are forthright, names have been changed.

overwhelms her, from the years of childbirth, famine and fear. During the sea journey she could barely close her eyes while on deck. Always she must count the children's heads in case one fell overboard in their climbing and games of tag.

Now her eyelids flutter shut against sun so brilliant she moves to a bay window. Its lead light design shows dolphins and other sea creatures. Outside her children chatter with WA's family, adding to their smattering of Swedish language.

In between bustling over her wood stove, Christina comes often to check the comfort of her sister-in-law. Her concern is so kindly that Anna Sanna bestirs herself to admire the orchids, fruit and vegetables in the garden. Sign language and giggles aid the tour of a hothouse. Anna Sanna wonders why this is needed in a steamy climate.

Christina cooks a feast for the family's first meal together around a cedar table. It's a hubbub of laughter, tears and stories of twenty years' separation and trials. Russian brutality, famine and civil war could not be entrusted to letters. WA and KJ translate for Christina and the boys. Aubrey, a serious lad of six years, has eyes round as a full moon. 'But if you built a boat, you could all escape,' he repeats.

KJ shows them all the thirty-nine cedar wood doors. 'I milled this fine timber in my sawmill. See how the grain shines through the polish.'

High ceilings are corniced in elaborate plaster designs. WA has built this beautiful house at great cost. KJ points out plasterboard left by the builders scribbled with words he translates as: 'Pay or else—angel of death!'

KJ also has debts and concerns. Rather than right them with hard work he sits for hours on the verandah scribbling long letters home. His sister's arrival lets loose a torrent of words. He has kept in touch with friends back home. Now, fired by tales of revolution and civil war, he urges them and family to migrate and live together in freedom.

'If only we could be together here, all the farmers from Kyrkbacken,' he says. 'I hope that our parents have the benefit of living their last years free in Australia where there is an eternal summer and we can pick fruit every day of the year.'

KJ wants to teach Anna Sanna English—just as in their childhood he helped her read Swedish.

'*Nej,*' she sighs. 'I am too old for that. You and Wilhelm came here younger.'

'English words are often like Swedish. Many words—*Många ord.*'

'*Nej. Jag är för gammal.*' She points to wrinkles on her hands.

KJ insists: 'Man is *samma* – same; *bok* is book. Forty years is not too old.'

'You boys are clever, you learn easily. I am glad to have Ida Backlund with us, even though it is crowded in our cabin with Erik Johan, myself and our five children also. Her man, Mats Wilhelm—'

'Mats Wille we call him,' KJ laughs. 'He's a lazy, weak-hearted speculator.'

'He can be vexing, true, but it eases my homesickness to talk to another woman. Ida's daughter Astrid is learning English fast.'

'You can—*du kan*—*tala engelska*. It makes your life easier.'

'I make a good life here, and raise strong, healthy children. They will be my *engelska* voice. I will milk cows each day morning and night, sew and cook. That's enough.'

'Erik Johan is a fine man. I have written home, saying that you have the best man in all the district, that you will soon begin to make a good living because he uses his hands and turns himself to many jobs. He will make a fine settler. He is far more resourceful than Mats, who so lacks enterprise. How I wish Edvard had not encouraged him to come. He will drain your resources and your energy.'

'Hush, he comes!'

KJ shakes Mats Wilhelm Backlund's hand. 'Mats, so you arrived at last! After twenty years. I thank you again for giving me your passport—that saved me.'

'I told the authorities I lost my papers and showed a confirmation record to get a new passport so I could travel to Alaska.'

'You did not stay there?'

'It's a great country, but we agreed to stay together, so here we are. I know you are grateful and will help me.'

'I have a farm that you could buy, next door to my own property. I intended it for my family but they wait so long. I picture it as yours. I can help you settle.'

But Mats Wille is not so easily settled. Two families crowd a small cottage, but Ida gives Anna Sanna company so there is no rush to find a farm.

The New Emigrants

Foreign food I do not relish,
In the best of strangers' houses

Kalevala

The two newly arrived Finnish families must now adjust to life as settlers in a strange country, a sweltering climate and wild terrain. Anna Sanna struggles to speak with her sister–in–law. She leans on Ida's support yet the inertia of her friend's husband and son drains her. Both families cram into a small cottage near Mullumbimby for eight months.

The following is condensed from KJ's letters between January 1921 and 1922:

> To those of you at home, always on my mind, I thank you for the socks and the blanket that you sent me with Anna Sanna. It is nice to have a memory from my home country and my dear mother. It is a long time since I had a fine pair of socks on my feet.
>
> Anna Sanna brought Edvard's letter. I am happy to see that you are all well and nothing has happened to you during the great disturbances that Europe and the whole world has gone through concerning Germany's doom. There were many things I would have liked to write to you during the war but I feared you would be punished for my sins, so I thought it best to say little.
>
> I hope you all move here now before it is too late since Finland still has many difficulties to go through before the present peace can become a final one.
>
> Since Pappa was here land prices have risen from £5 to about £50. The war did not influence land prices here but we

didn't have boats to take our goods to the big world markets. When the whole of Europe was in famine we had food in such abundance that it rotted alongside the railway lines. Following labour shortages, prices have risen noticeably and it costs more to live here than it did before, but when one has one's own garden one never has to suffer distress. We have hundreds of fruit you have never even heard of.

Incomes have increased so much that one can earn more here than when everything was cheaper. Australia will certainly have a beautiful future ahead of it.

Last time Pappa was here I didn't even have a cabin to live in. Now I have four farms of my own and you could live in any of them. Wilhelm has trouble with his land spread far apart; it would be as if you had your land in Munsala, Nykarleby, Denmark, Sweden, Gibraltar and Palestine.

It would be so much easier for you to live here than in Finland; the long winters make work on the farm such slavery. I cannot see why it would be necessary to wait for summer to travel because then it is winter on the other side. The Red Sea is on your side of the Equator and they have summer at the same time as you. It is the largest sweating sauna you will pass through in all your life and I assure you, you will do better without having experienced that.

If someone asks you how old you are you could say you are 35 years old. If they don't believe you, you could say you have suffered through many hardships and many more are yet to come.

You don't have to worry about Erik Johan and the family; they will get on very well. Erik Johan said yesterday 'Anna Sanna had never looked so good in her whole life. When I first saw her I thought she looked so unhealthy I could have cried for her.' He asks me to tell you that as long as he lives he will care for his children. He is a good father. They are doing well and have learned how to do their daily chores.

I can imagine that you often wonder what Anna Sanna and

Erik Johan do over here. It's best to write a list of what they don't have to do:

They don't have to drive their seed to the mill. They don't have to mind the cows. They don't have to go far to find grazing grounds for the cows. They don't have to bring in the horses in winter. They don't pay anything to the priest or the organist. No meetings where they have to recite the Bible to show they know it. They don't pay anything to the barn to store crops. They don't pay any poor people's tax. They have no spies. They don't have snow and ice to freeze their ears and noses off. They don't have any national service. They have no gypsies or Finns that beg or steal from them, no one that gossips and no neighbours that come over to shout at them.

We would be very happy if it wasn't for our cousin, Mats Wilhelm. He has had many good prospects since he came here and has cost us much and made us very annoyed. I could write a whole book of sad memories concerning my experiences about Mats, in our childhood and youth and now here. I suspect that he has never done a hard day's work in all of his life.

Wilhelm suggested Mats take a banana plantation of 28 acres; he could manage it on his own. They could get as good an income as on a place with 40 cows. Wilhelm said he could build them a cottage to Ida's wishes and they could pay it off in time. It was only three kilometres from Burringbar railway, a half-hour from Mullumbimby. It was a very good place but Mats found it unsuitable. He has seen in his mind a place where he can swim and go fishing. He thought of his adventures in the wild in Alaska where he could trap animals and fish more than he could eat.

I had just the right place, a forest with a high mountain, a little bit looking like Alaska. It was a paradise for the hunter and fisher. A place with big birds like in Finland that he could shoot when he wants to, private from the neighbours although they are not far away. The fish were jumping in the water, the kangaroos were hopping from every bush; birds in all colours of the rainbow were singing from morning to eve and flying from tree to tree. It was in truth a paradise for the hunter and fisher. This was only eight miles from Mullumbimby and the price was £20 per acre, a third of what you'd pay for others. They were all pleased and could see that they might buy it.

My place was the best in the area, and freehold while others surrounding me rent from the government. My neighbours are not self-sufficient, unlike me. I am not a farmer; I am a landowner and independent.

It has mountain on three sides, from the back and the upside you can catch the water that comes down from the mountain, you don't have to irrigate. For animals and fruit growing it was ideal. Money was not the important thing but rather that I should help a countryman. He was a friend from my childhood, we grew up together; his wife was a classmate. I began to see this land as his, this old friend. Mats and I travelled to Wilson's Creek to see this place that I now called his. He decided it was too far away.

A neighbour since Pappa's days in Australia, Frank James, died with the Spanish flu. He left a nice place five miles from Mullumbimby, by the riverside and nearby the church. It was a hundred acres, and good grass. Wilhelm had got the price down to £3300 with five percent interest.

'Yes,' Mats said, 'I will buy it.'

They had everything ready to sign in Wilhelm's office but where was Mats Wille? No one knew. After waiting the whole day, Mats said it wouldn't suit as he was not a good carpenter. He should buy where there's a good house already.

At Coopers Creek Mats and Wilhelm came to see my place with a very high mountain on both sides, about a mile from my cottage, well protected on every side. The soil is rich and there are two big rivers and a waterfall several hundred feet up. You could run everything by waterpower, a milk machine, cream separators and electricity.

Everything on it is new and well built. A fisher could not desire anything more. It is five kilometres from the school, ten kilometres from town, sixteen from the railway station. Mats

Wille was delighted with this house and immediately wanted to buy it. The price was £30 per acre.

Wilhelm hoped to buy it himself so you and Ester, Mamma, Sofia and Helmi could live on it, because we haven't given up the hope of you coming here. Ida would have all that a Finnish emigrant would need in Australia; four beautiful furnished rooms with corridor and veranda, everything was new, very tidy. And nearby you could count ten cottages and see gardens, fig trees, palms, flowers, and birds. From the kitchen window you could see several hundred metres up in the air my big mountain cliff that one of our soldiers has named Gibraltar because of its likeness to that. From the top of the hill there were two creeks that sent waterfalls down the cliff into the river on both sides of the house. On the mountain tops there were very big trees, so high you can see them on the horizon with the big ones on the top.

This place was 78 acres of good pasture, big enough to feed 35 cows and the right size for Mats. Everyone felt very happy. Mr Lessing, a journalist from Finland, expressed our own feelings when with tears in his eyes he said his heartfelt joy to be involved with this affair. 'Never before have I seen an Ostrobothnian farmer setting down in Australia in such a wonderful way; never before has a man from Finland got such a good beginning in such a short time.'

We presented Mats to the new neighbours and they were friendly and wished them luck and success. We introduced them to the people in the shop in the nearest town. Knowing that in the near future they would not be able to travel much we took them 130 kilometres to Lismore and there we had a kvälsvard housewarming and drank the Harja Kannun toast in beer with a good soup. We showed them the Richmond River, the historical place where Dad and Wilhelm arrived nearly twenty years ago. We drove home through Bangalow to Mullumbimby and arrived at ten o'clock at night.

We had taken him to the bank that would lend money to Mats and Wilhelm was prepared to be guarantor. When everything was ready, horse, cows, hens and ducks, Mats didn't come to sign the contract. His moral spinal column broke and he didn't dare to write his name on the agreement.

Another place belonged to Mr Ellem, who lives in central Queensland. Mats was delighted with Ellem's farm and asked Wilhelm to help him buy it for as low a price as possible. He wanted to get Mr Ellem to come to Mullumbimby to have the better opportunity to demonstrate to him. Mr Ellem lives only a little over 1600 kilometres from here, but because of that you can't travel all the way with steamboat; railway travelling costs for him to come here are more than what it cost Mats to travel from Finland to Australia. The whole trip to come 1600 kilometres cost him over £150 and Mr Ellem's time is of high worth but Mats can't understand that. Mr Ellem was busy and couldn't come immediately; we had to send a telegram every day to keep Mats satisfied. He made many visits to Ellem's farm and it was indeed a very good place, 135 acres, the best you could get. It was just one kilometre to the school, three to the church, less than two to my cottage and 13 kilometres to town and the railway. From his door you could see the steamboats on the ocean 16 kilometres away.

I told Mats that it had always been my desire to get this for my brother. This made him more determined and he said with a loud sigh, 'How I should like to have that place.' But when Mr Ellem came Mats lost interest in the whole affair.

Ida is a good farmer's wife, as if she was a man. If her husband and her first-born were even half as good they would do well. They could have a bright future in Australia.

I have now written about five of the different farms that they tried to get for Mats and I have five more to write but I will do that next time. I don't believe that Mats will buy any farm until he finds one where the cows have legs of porcelain.

The Grand World Tour of 1924

Travelled homeward to his country,
O'er the blue sea's watery surface.

Kalevala

After Anna Sanna and her family migrated, letters escalated urging Edvard and his wife Ester to join them. But KJ's description of his trials to settle the Backlund family may have stirred up ill feeling at home. After eight months, Mats and his family moved to New Zealand. At the end of 1921 the Holm family settled at Main Arm near Mullumbimby.

A photograph shows them posed outside their house, cropped trees on the hillside. Their sixth child sat on her mother's knee. Between April 1927 and 1964, the family lived at Ocean Shores near Billinudgel in the wooden house surrounded by verandahs, that I remember visiting as a child. Until they were led to the same 'Promised Land' of Anders Back's prayer in 1903.

A brief letter from Edvard in 1921 replied:

> I am sorry about the problems with Mats Wille but I had written a letter about him coming earlier; you had had the opportunity to write against it but that you didn't do, so because of that the fault is yours too. Brother KJ, Mamma and Pappa will not be strong enough to go to Australia. For myself to travel, it's difficult for me to go and difficult to stay.

Perhaps in response to this, KJ replied:

> I can only say that all this is just a ghost and a little bit of meanness on your part. I had nothing to gain in you coming here and I wanted you to come only for your own sake and for your own good. Wilhelm's letters were always welcome during the long time when you couldn't mention my name

without horrible and disgusting words. In one of your letters to Wilhelm you write that it is understood I have persisted in calling you a coward. I have never claimed you to be anything of such because no one knows what the future will bear. Life is changing and it is easy to lose a lifetime of collections when you can never be certain of what you have collected.

They agreed to differ: 'Edvard, I must respect your fine feelings for our parents, and that you will stay with them. What they have done for us as parents we can never repay.'

But the folder contains fewer letters from KJ after this. Or were his later letters burned?

WA decided to travel to Finland to encourage and persuade his parents to emigrate. He sold his beautiful *Cedarholm* and set off with his wife, a nurse and five children on a year–long Grand Tour. What an entourage it must have been!

My Uncle Eric chronicled their voyage in his daily journal. My cousins lent me this exercise book to transcribe. After years stored in the fierce dry heat of western Queensland, the fragile book crumbled easily so it was a relief to preserve it.

Eric was a true historian and took photos with his Box Brownie camera to complement his journal. In this and his memoir, he describes life in Finland through the eyes of a 14–year–old Australian lad:

> By 1923 my parents were planning a trip to Finland so that Dad's family could meet us all. At that time to travel so far, and with a young family, was unheard of. Certainly, there were emigrants leaving Europe to settle in a new country, but they usually left nothing behind and they came on an assisted one-way ticket. Tourism had not been invented then. It was a do it yourself business, and the only way to travel out of Australia, in any direction, was by ship. To go to England in those days usually took about six weeks, and I think P & O Orient had about one ship per month going in both directions.
>
> Before we left Cedarholm was sold to Dr. Gibson, and then Mum and Dad decided they should take a nurse along to help with the family. There were five of us; I was 14 and the eldest, but Gloria was three and Alan two. They put a small advertisement in the Sydney Morning Herald, and the first responses filled the letterbox in Mullumbimby, but the next

day the post office phoned and said we had better come and collect the mail. They had a mailbag full. There were over 600 replies to the advertisement and they all had to be opened, read and drafted into some order. And the winner? How was she chosen? Nurse Neilson sent a telegram saying she was coming to be interviewed, and she jumped on the first boat or train and came to Mullumbimby. Afterwards I can't remember any complaints about her, so I guess she was satisfactory.

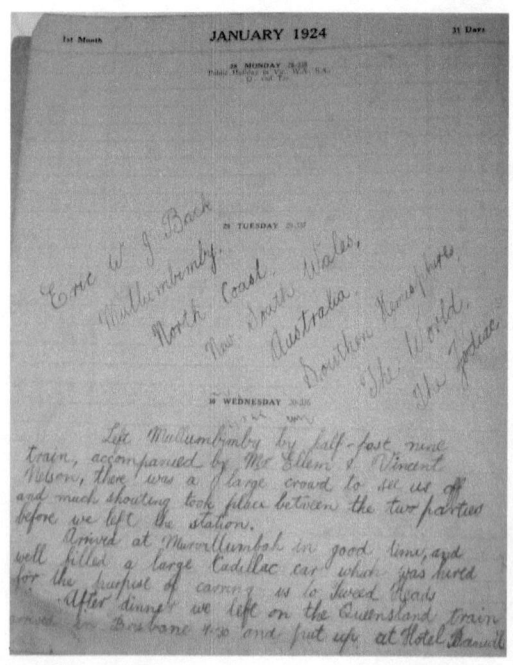

The World Tour started from Mullumbimby railway station cheered by a large gathering of people. On 2nd February 1924 they sailed from Brisbane in the orient liner *Osterley* of over 12,000 tons to Sydney where they stayed on board for a fortnight. The ship then called at Melbourne, Adelaide, Freemantle, Colombo, Suez Canal and Naples. At Toulon in the south of France they disembarked and went by train from Nice to Turin in Italy. Granddad's postcard from Ventimiglia already rued this travelling circus, 'It's so boring to travel with so many to look after, especially with so many children, and fifteen bags. We should have come straight from England so we wouldn't have everything with us.' Shopping expeditions in Paris, Zurich and Helsinki added more.

At the Fiat factory, Dad ordered a large six cylinder car but as it would not be ready for 20 days we took a leisurely tour of northern Italy; Venice, Florence, Genoa and Milan. We had ample time to see thousands of paintings.

In Turin, Dad applied for a driver's licence. He could not talk to the Testing Officer, but he got the car going and weaved through traffic and people around a big square, after which the

> Officer jumped out, wrote out the license and told him to go!
>
> Dad decided it would be safer to get a bit more tuition before starting across Europe, so he picked up a young fellow (via Fiat)–the chauffeur had been driver for Lloyd George doing the peace talks in 1919 at Lugarno–to go with us for some days. As we could not speak to him Dad got a guide who knew most places and languages. So we ended up like a modern tour coach with the driver responsible for the working of the car, and a guide who could get you into a mediaeval town and bring you out on the right road on the other side. He also found hotels, as we had nothing booked ahead. Of course there were mistakes, like when little boys went behind the car to do a wee, and the driver thought the petrol tank was leaking! Sometimes petrol buying was primitive. It was in a very large glass bottles with the plug in the top. Then our driver would sniff them all and make a choice.
>
> You will ask, 'Where did we put all the people?' Well usually the driver, Dad and Elwyn sat in the front seat, then there were two 'Dicky' seats that folded against the front seat and the guide was behind the driver. I had the other one. Mum and Nurse were in the back seat and the little ones were spread around. The car was an open tourer; it had a folding canvas roof and was pretty cold when heading into the Alps. Luggage was strapped on running boards and at back. Mum and Nurse learned to pack a couple of bags on top with smelly clothes to discourage customs officers.

He writes how the family drove north, passing through bombarded battlefields and bomb craters of whole villages in France and Germany. Eric's journal notes that 'Father and the boys climbed on an upended German tank.' I imagine Elwyn thought it all a lark, but Aubrey looks downcast in the photographs.

At Stettin on the Baltic their driver and guide returned to Italy and Nurse to England. The car and family went on to the S.S. *Ariadne* to Helsinki, where:

> Dad took us in the car to a hotel and we said, 'It is up to you to speak to the natives now,' but after a while the receptionist said, 'Sir, if you speak English we may get along better.'

Dad managed the car quite well, and after leaving Helsinki we stayed the night at Tammerfors. The Finnish roads then were not designed for motorcars. On flat country they twisted and turned around small farms, and any granite small hills they went straight over, so it was slow travelling. We got to Munsala about 10 p.m. when the sun was setting, home to a warm welcome, even if we could not speak to our Finnish family. We arrived 29th of May 1924.

Eric's memoir reflects on this time:

At the Munsala home that time was Granddad Back, a little man with a lot of snow white hair, who when walking seemed to shuffle along. He would have been about 76 at the time. Grandma Back was not very big, but energetic and a good talker. When the house was built they had put two large granite slabs down, one on top of the other, as steps into the house. Grandma fell and broke her hip when those slabs had ice on them one winter many years before. She walked with a limp but it did not seem to slow her down. Then there was Aunt Sofia and her daughter Helmi and Dad's younger brother Edvard, his wife Ester and their boy Rolf, a little fellow learning to walk. Edvard had a farm of his own some distance away but he would come over to help with the farm work, such as planting potatoes and haymaking.

We three boys found some nice wide boards on the beams near the ceiling in what used to be Dad's old carpentering room. We asked if we could have them to make a boat. At first Granddad hesitated, then he agreed. Elwyn was the main builder and marine architect for the boat and I am pleased to say it turned out well, because long afterwards we learned Granddad had put those boards away to make his coffin when he died! We had a lot of happy days with the boat. (In fact it came to an unhappy end. In those bootlegging days a lot of smuggling went on across the Baltic. One poor unfortunate appropriated the boat to meet a rendezvous at sea. But the timber had shrunk, the boat leaked and the fellow drowned.)

Uncle Edvard took it down on his cart to 'Udden' and we were introduced to 'Herrin Surlinksa' (it sounded like this). She was the most important lady in the district, I think her husband used to be a governor.

—That must have been Betty Hällsten. Did you hear tales of passive or active resistance?

But Eric does not answer, so I go back to my research…

Christina Day celebration: Betty Hällsten sits centre with Christina behind, 4th from left.

Time Warp in Munsala Farmhouse

Bread never runs out when the Lord blesses.

Old Finnish saying

The two-storey house at Munsala looked big from outside on earlier visits. In 2008 I can explore inside. Wandering through, I wonder how WA and Christina, with their five children, could all cram into it?

I imagine the Fiat brakes outside the red-timbered farmhouse. By lantern-light the children, exhausted from a twelve hour drive, stumble over the rough steps into hugs and voluble Swedish. In the living room, their parents are ensconced on the divan and plied with coffee; the children perch on chairs and accept cheese, a variety of rye and hard bread, marinated herring, gingerbread and warm milk. They long for bed and to escape from the appraisals of all the relatives. Aunt Sofia and her reticent daughter Helmi lead them upstairs, the candlelight throwing grotesque shadows.

I tread over the woven rag rugs, and up the curved narrow staircase. It's a precarious climb in semidarkness over uneven steps. Small windows cast little light.

The attic is a jumble of chairs, carved wooden bed-heads, dressing tables. Saws lie on a bench; on dressers are a coffee grinder, porcelain and rag dolls, a toy kick-sled, photographs and books. Fraying wallpaper forms a backdrop to two prints: one of two children arm in arm, the other of Christ praying at Gethsemane. There is a gramophone and some long playing records.

Mentally, I pick up the straw broom that rests against a wall. I long to prepare these rooms, to make up comfortable beds into which the children can fall; to sort the puzzles and blocks, to repair headless dolls in their prams and cradles that will delight the family when they wake.

I wonder: did Anders and Sanna sleep downstairs and give their upstairs bedroom to WA and Christina? A small room at the side may have been KJ's where he read by lamplight. I look through the heap of books, Bibles and religious tracts, searching for philosophers. KJ quoted Socrates. There are *Tales of Ensign Stål* and *Our Land* by Jakobstad-born Johan Ludvig Runeberg, doubtless a hero of KJ's. A large white-bound book titled *This is Australia*, sent to entice their migration is dated 1948 and inscribed 'To Sofia and Helmi, Christmas greetings from Christina and William.'

Was this pride of space offered to eldest son Eric? Did the other children sleep top-to-tail in these divan beds?

***

Aubrey, aged ten, at Tampere.

The lad Aubrey listens wide-eyed in the shuttered gloom that passes for night in mid-summer. Long into birdcall, sounds filter up: clinks of cups, yawns from Mother. Voices speak Swedish except when Father translates snippets. Since Aunt Anna Sanna came to Mullumbimby, telling of battles and oppression, Aubrey has learned some words that recur; *död* means dead; *krig* is war; *soldat* a soldier; hunger is the same word with a rounded inflection. There is much talk of Tammerfors (Tampere in Finnish) where the family slept last night. It was besieged for weeks in April 1918. Uncle Edvard fought there—in the greatest battle in Finland's history, a turning point in the Civil War. The link is too real between a relative and bullet marks, burned tanks and houses. Six years later people still look thin and hungry.

Aubrey smells and tastes the fear; his brain races with quandaries and solutions; if they were oppressed they should escape! Why didn't they build a boat and sail to safety in Sweden?

Over breakfast, Anders notes his grandson's saucer eyes and tight-held breath. He waves his pipe and the conversation into other topics. 'No more congerichuchin. We must rake the hay.'

But all his life my father Aubrey will be poised, as if on alert to fight or flee from persecution and torture by subsequent oppressors. He will build boats, ready to rescue his family. These overheard conversations are the genesis of his constant obsessions to escape from the red peril, then the yellow peril; any of many various–hued perils. This latter-day Noah determined to bring his family to safety.

Such dread is passed down through the generations.

Latter Day Noah

Life is like a boat on a river. If not paddled upwards it is sure to drift downwards.

K. J. Back, *The Concentrated Wisdoms of Australia*

As an adult, I understand my father's paranoia. Reading Uncle Eric's journal of their days in Finland, I see Dad as the ten–year old huddled under the covers, appalled yet fascinated by the tales of Russian brutality that could not be committed to letters. The history of my people, living in fear of the Russians, has been imprinted in our family DNA for generations, even when they are at a safe distance, living in Australia.

Here is the origin of Aubrey's boat–building sagas, of the unfinished hulks that lay open and bare like skeletal fish bones to disgrace our mother's garden. Such fears compel him into making incessant dire predictions of invasion. With his ears always tuned, and eyes always opened, for imminent disasters, he develops a supposed prescience that creates foreboding miseries.

Some of his boats will crest the seas, only to sink. One wrecks near Lucinda in north Queensland and its retrieval proves an ongoing, expensive headache. Reading Eric's diary of three excited boys about to launch their boat into the sea, it all becomes as clear as the shimmering waters. It's the boat–building Swede in him. And the Finnish fear of invasion.

***

Here in the attic in Munsala, I recall similar forebodings. In the Antipodes, another ten–year old also huddled under blankets, pillow over her head. I tried in vain to block tales of doom. Booming reel–to–reel tape recordings told of Christians tortured in Communist Russia. There was no escaping the stories of fathers who denounced sons and daughters to unspeakable horrors, or children their parents. Even family was not to be trusted. Faith was a dangerous thing. One might be thrown into some tiny, dark cell, tortured—no, it is unthinkable.

In the isolation of the outback, lights shine starkly against blackness. Headlights dance and weave through silhouetted arms of trees. These flashing zigzags along the dirt road signal my parents' safe return home from prayer meetings at the Baptist church in town. There, Dad gleans ever more leaflets and books that ferment the Catholic versus Protestant rivalry and paranoia of that era. Armed with these, he warns that at a signal from the Pope, all Catholics will rise up *en masse* and slaughter us Protestants.

Child Ruth eyes the genial neighbours who invite us to their farmhouse for tennis and fizzy drinks, tea and cake. Surely Eugene of the prodigious Adam's apple, amiable in his white shorts, would not wield a machete on us? Later the enemy changes face and colour: Indonesians will covet our land, they will swoop down on us and we must be prepared, as he is, with barrels of flour and of 'benzene' buried on the property. Nightmares are further fed by books about dinosaurs read by torchlight under the sheet, all the more gripping when fossilised *Muttaburrasaurus* bones are found on the property.

Nights are full of terrible forebodings. Little Ruth knows the meaning of awe, as in *'Thou shalt fear the Lord thy God'* for each night she scans the sky's frightful majesty of God the creator. A massive black dome rides over western Queensland. It is alive with shooting stars, teems with myriad lights patterned into constellations. Through this the Milky Way swoops its highway down to earth. Her wakeful watches have never yet been disturbed by the mysterious *min–min* lights that have spooked many in the outback. But anything is possible in these lavish galaxies and light–year timeframes.

Ancient Finnish mythology calls this *Linnunrata*, the path of the birds. Over this they migrate from the North Pole, below the North Star, to the other end of the world. At the edges of Earth lies *Lintukoto*, 'the home of the birds', a warm region where they shelter during the winter. Birds also brought a person's soul at the moment of birth, and took it away when they died, to search the land of the dead, *Tuonela*. In olden times, people kept a wood carved 'soul–bird' by their bedside to protect their soul from escaping while vulnerable in sleep and being lost in the path of dreams.

Is some genetic memory in me already aware of such concepts?

In my twenties, alive with anticipation, I will board a shiny bird to fly to Europe. Nightmares again fester after a relative gives me a book, *The Late Great Planet Earth*, to read on the journey. With maps showing how Biblical prophecies will be fulfilled, this predicts Russia will swoop down and conquer all of Europe, and the world. Armageddon will be loosed on us. And I am flying into the thick of it!

When my husband Antoni is offered a concertmaster's position with Norrlands Operan in Umeå, Sweden, I am excited at the prospect of living in Scandinavia. But fears lurk in me about this new home. For just across the sea lies Russia, our centuries–long aggressor and enemy. It will again rise up to conquer. Who can argue with the prophets? Who can predict The Rapture, Tribulation or Armageddon? Will the Russians lead the charge?

That becomes ever more relevant in the instability of the world's political chess board.

Finland Summer

We melt away like lumps of ice in the hot sun, for nothing will withstand the pure essence of love.

K. J. Back, *The Concentrated Wisdoms of Australia*

I imagine the children waking to a bustling Munsala farmhouse. Rushing through breakfast so they can continue their carpentering in the barn stacked with a spinning wheel, sleds, utensils and brooms.

On June 5th 1924, Eric wrote:

> This morning we got up early, about 8 o'clock, which is early here, for a day's work on the boat. I spent a good deal of my time in making the nose or bow, and in the afternoon we joined the side of the boat to the bow. We went to bed pretty stiff that night.

Boat–building progress was frustrated by distractions of entertaining and daily chores. They took the cows to pasture and minded them.

> This morning Elwyn went with Grandpa in my place while I went on with the boat …but was very slow work. When Elwyn returned we continued with the boat all the evening, one of the wonders of the far North we think is the Mid-Night sun which is just like a sun in the middle of the night, so far we have not used an artificial light since we came here. (June 11)

A few days later they were packing between the big holes and boards of the boat, mixing paint and tar for the bottom. Did Sanna grit her teeth at the mess?

> As it was raining we could not take the boat out so we laid paper on the floor. We put the tar on first which was like varnish, and afterwards we painted the upper part with red paint.

Two weeks later the boat was ready to sail and moored at Udden. But the next day:

> After we had performed our usual duty of leading the cows to grass, I set to work with Father on a batch of correspondence which had to be attended to before the mail closed; the letter writing occupied half the day.

The hyperactive WA relied on Eric as his own English lagged behind his many plans and projects:

> This morning was the scene of great activities as everybody was busy writing letters under Father's directions, two pots of ink ran dry but one blessing we had plenty of pens, and as there was only half a bottle of ink left we used to dip three pens in at once. As we had missed the mail at Munsala we had an early dinner at 5 p.m. and Elwyn and I set out on bicycles for Nykarleby we had 14 killometers (sic) to cover and an hour to do it in but we got there in time travelling 28 killometers.

A hard day's fencing further delayed the maiden voyage until the 19th June when they rowed towards the sea and landed on shore, opposite an island to which they intended to sail for a picnic:

> As there was a light breeze blowing from the sea we sailed home…This-morning after helping Father clean the car and put benzene in, we set out for Udden where we had our boat moored, and after making the boat sea-worthy we set out for Grassern (Grass island) which is an island covered with grass and Northern Forest trees such as birch and Pine and is also in possession of some summer bungalows.

Snapshots show two boys—for Eric was the photographer—sitting in a chunky oblong boat, anchored close to shore; the sail standing proud. At Picnic Bay, their rug is strewn with hats, apples, a flask and a lunchbox. In true Aussie fashion, a billy swings on sticks over a fire. Elwyn lifts his pannikin in a toast.

Did they play out stories of escape as they launched it from Udden? Visitors told of friends and family who skied through blizzards to safety in Sweden or, in summer, strained at the oars; frenzied rowing stripping the flesh from their hands.

I wonder at the impression this experience made on the lads; such early enterprise set them into 'can–do' mindsets. It is a trait typical of our family right through to present generations that we set out to invent or create that which we lack.

Since reading Eric's journal and family letters I feel more tolerant of my father. A middle child, the third of five, Aubrey was overshadowed by his siblings though he was dux of his school. Eric was privy to his father's business through letter writing and conversations. Elwyn, the second son was blessed with looks, personality and business flair akin to his father's. After living in Sweden, I noticed that my Uncle Elwyn of all the brothers had the most pronounced Swedish accent.

My father made many abortive boat–building attempts—that's the Swede in him. This highpoint of his childhood he tried to recapture all the rest of his life.

He attempted creative ways to move from the bush to the coast; soon after my birth, disheartened from droving sheep all over the state to find pasture, he gained a 99–year lease of Orpheus Island, east of Ingham. He shipped a flock across but the sheep could not survive on the prolific but dangerous spear grass growing there.

If only he had not relinquished the lease and thrown away the opportunity of having a Barrier Reef island! Orpheus is now an expensive resort.

The Swede in me groans. For I also love the sea and, as an adult, choose to work at the renowned seaside town of Noosa for my fix of walks and swims at the beach.

Dad was born and raised in Mullumbimby. When he moved to 'the bush' he wrote a plaintive letter in which he complained of the boredom and isolation. He missed picnics at Byron Bay and the Brunswick Heads surf. 'My two hobbies are gardening, growing fruit and boat building. Both can be better done on the coast.' A true Swede, he was happiest in a boat. Like him, I long to stay forever in this lush area, vibrant with colour, amongst the rolling hills topped by the jutting cone–shaped Mount Chincogan.

But I found opportunities to roam the world; Aubrey was trapped in the outback.

Christina in Europe, 1924

Father's love you leave behind you;
Learn to love thy husband's father…
Fitting language must you utter.

Kalevala

In the upstairs loft, I look out the small windows at the view my grandmother Christina woke up to each morning. I imagine her, homesick, longing to hide under the covers rather than to put on her smile with her modish clothes. Grateful for the coffee pot ceremoniously brought up with the porcelain cow milk jug, white with brown spots. The brew fortified her for the appraisal of more visitors.

***

With little language in common, Christina instead observed people's bodies, faces and manners. They might think her a simple farm girl but she noticed any derogatory gestures and sniggers behind her husband's back. He expected good service in return for his business and hard–earned money. People didn't realise the long days and sleepless nights he laboured to finance this grand tour. WA insisted on keeping up standards and the semblance of wealth, even though this year–long venture strains their resources. It had become a nightmare for him to travel with so many mouths to feed three times each day. Outlandish food upset the children's health.

To afford this venture WA sold *Cedarholm*, the most beautiful house a woman could imagine! Christina pulled a dog–eared photograph from her handbag. Her eyes feasted on the gracious high ceilings moulded in fine plaster and traced with filigree designs. How she loved those airy verandahs lined with geometric tiles, where potted ferns thrived, the red cedar doors, hewn in the sawmill WA had helped KJ build. When the ship *Wollongbar* wrecked near Byron Bay wharf, WA, with his quick eye for opportunity, had bought the saloon timber and installed it in the breakfast room, complete with portholes, exactly as in the ship. When Christina protested 'How can I enjoy my breakfast in such gloom?' Her Will reached for his carpentry tools to bring in the sunshine.

WA learned from Napoleon Hill's *Think and Grow Rich*. But some of WA's many enterprises took him close to bankruptcy. He escaped by selling this beautiful home to Doctor Gibson—the only one who could afford it—but did he underestimate the cost of an overseas trip? He itched to introduce his offspring to his family and also to persuade them to emigrate.

Only the good Lord knew how Christina endured the wrench as she packed their belongings and the children's toys into storage. She was concerned about venturing across the seas to a war-devastated continent. Homeless, she sobbed into her pillow as their path led inexorably to Finland where new relatives would probe and peer at her.

'I will build you a mansion, when we return,' her husband vowed. When he bought statues in Italy, he justified that the expense with the claim 'these are for your magnificent new house.' He would fulfil that promise with the Big House in St Lucia—the talk of 1950s Brisbane.

Her qualms grew as they drew closer to Munsala. How confronting to meet strange people and to not be able to converse with them, to not understand what they said.

Christina bought outfits in the world's leading cities. How could they know the well-groomed woman was a shy country girl who'd been swooped up into WA's big visions? He mixed with leaders of business, even of countries. A letter of introduction from the Prime Minister of Australia opened doors to prominent people. Eric helped him write to organise meetings with mayors of cities and to attend conferences of woolgrowers in England. It was Christina's duty to dress in a manner that complemented his exalted position in society.

Sofia looked askance as Christina assisted in the cramped kitchen, clumsy with strange ingredients and recipes. Sofia made a show of her hard work around the farm—shearing sheep, spinning and making soap, scything hay. Her forbidding manner said, 'What does this fashion model know about hard work?' Women with hair drawn into stern, practical buns tutted over her short bobbed waves that were practical for travelling.

But Christina never sat with folded hands, playing the lady; she was always busy sewing, cleaning and cooking. Her scant words of Swedish could not bridge the gap, but why should Sofia be condescending—especially with her illegitimate daughter!

Christina encouraged WA's projects; gave an occasional word of caution. She was his sounding board, sometimes a brake on his more foolhardy plans. She supported him through thick and thin—and thin was often the case when the family meal had to stretch to include unheralded guests at dinner time. Which would only worsen when they returned to Australia, as WA sponsored a stream of Finns keen to migrate. Painting his adopted country as Utopia, he promised them all a bed and food when they arrived. But he did not shop or cook!

Christina stabilised her husband's whirlwind life. She bore him five healthy children. Perhaps Sanna was envious of this, with her fear that some angel of death hung over her, as she pointed to the deceased children on the family gravestone. When Christina feared such a curse might pass to their own children, Will reminded that they asked God's protection on their marriage and lives. This included the children.

Each long day of this endless summer brought fresh agonies. Christina wearied with the effort of keeping up with her husband and putting on a smile for his family. They didn't mean to exclude her, but photographs were posed with WA seated between his parents, his brother and sister on either side. Behind stood the second-class citizens; the illegitimate daughter and the wife from Australia. Even on her name day 'Christina Day' when she should have been guest of honour, in the ceremonial photograph she was placed to the side or behind. Betty Hällsten sat next to her mother-in-law, resplendent in a lavish hat.

Despite not understanding this culture, Christina fulfilled her duty as a daughter-in-law at WA's right hand, the gracious, well-groomed wife. She paraded bright children for their grandparents to spoil. She would not complain. She could endure this situation for a few months and enable her husband to make his peace with his family, to lay to rest any issues that drove him these past twenty years.

Soon they would escape to England and a ship home. Her duty would be restricted to carefully worded letters. She was schooled in writing; for all that Eric ridiculed her in his journal. When she was hungry for letters from home, she noticed he'd written: 'Mother lasted all day scribbling away (no wonder she doesn't write good).'

I will pour my love, time and energy into my husband and children. In this way, I will win them over in the end.

Idyllic Summer, 1924

Not until we have a family of our own will we fully realise what we owe our parents. Some learn this when it is too late—others never.

K. J. Back, *The Concentrated Wisdoms of Australia*

My visit to Finland in 2008 is enhanced by Eric's insights. Places I have read of in his journal flash past my train or car window. As my cousin Gretchen drives me through Munsala to Udden by the sea, I remember Eric's 1924 journal that described picnics, a motor launch trip to Monå on the sound and a family wedding:

> As Father's cousin was getting married today (15th June) we went to the church to see the sermon, and as they were leaving the church I took a photo of them. The wedding party consisted of two musicians while all the other people filed behind two deep. We went to the wedding breakfast which consisted mainly of porridge and potatoes.

I imagine the faces of the children when served such simple fare for a celebration! The people pictured are lean, unlike WA's rotund figure.

Swimming Finnish style fascinated young Eric who penned on 16 July:

> This morning a picnic was organised and everybody set off at 11 a.m. straight after breakfast for a popular picnic place near Udden with a name as long as Constantinople, but all the same it was very nice, so we had a good swim, but it was a bit cold. Everybody about the country seemed to be in swimming and as bathing togs were (as yet) not introduced into these parts men, women and children were naked. (I am trying to get a good snap with my camera around some of the watering places.)

Photos show WA in his black swimming costume, with a towel around his shoulders. He was used to nudity in the sauna and lakes as a youngster, but he was reluctant to be exposed in front of the locals. His sons, also clothed, stood gauchely on the sand dune above the nude people, uncertain how to respond. In another snap, four young men posed on a rock holding tree branches over their privates in defiant ridicule.

But by 25 July he writes: 'The weather is getting cooler and the swimming season is over, it only lasts for one week (no wonder none of the people here are good swimmers).'

Eric's photographs show his father posing for the camera, pushing the plough, and all the family working to dig, plant potatoes and make hay. Frequent entertaining created a flurry of cooking and preparation for the visitors.

> Father went to Nykarleby and returned with a crowd of visitors after dinner so of course we had to make ourselves look respectable, much against Elwyn's will who thought he

could spend his time more valuably. The people stayed for afternoon tea, supper, and mid-night supper and then thought of going home in the rain.

Snapshots of picnics reveal the grandparents' fatigue, as if this influx of family has taken as much in strain as it gave pleasure. We see a picnic, all the family gathered around the gramophone. Had WA imagined such a scene when he bought it and smuggled it past the customs officials and out of Switzerland under the children's feet?

Sanna looks down as if to escape the camera. Her thoughts reach out to me:
Ah, me, to have a son return from the other end of the world, plump and well clothed. What a pace Wilhelm moves at! Christina seems a fitting wife for him in her beautiful clothes and hats—fancy turnouts, as Eric calls them. She tries hard—too hard—to fit into our ways, which can't be easy. She apologises often that she can't speak our language. Many mothers struggle to accept a daughter-in-law. I am long past such silliness. I released my son to the other side of the world, and am grateful he has the support of a good wife. But I wonder where is the real woman under Christina's smiles and fripperies? I do not smile for the camera just because I am told to do so. People can take me for what I am.

Sofia and Helmi are busy raking the hay, planting potatoes, shearing the sheep. There is endless preparation of meals for so many extra mouths. A stream of visitors comes to meet Wilhelm, to ogle at his automobile and his stylish wife and children in their fancy clothes. They must be given coffee and bullar or a meal. Many produce papers for him to sign as sponsor to migrate. Soon there will be no Finns left in the country, for they follow my son like he is the Pied Piper.

Wilhelm Anders makes some show to assist in the fields but all too soon he is drawn away by his business, to meet some dignitary or write letters. Anders and I shake our heads and wonder if the trappings of money might have become too important. What drives him to make such a lavish display for us, the family who nurtured him and helped him take the big step to emigrate? It has been enough just to have him here with us.

Anders sits with hands folded, his eyes shut. I must accept that he is ready to die; he has seen his son and grandchildren and welcomes death. When we visit Edvard and Ester at Purmo, Wilhelm makes plans to bring them to Australia. 'You will have friends there, for many others plan to migrate.'

Edvard knows his responsibility as the remaining son, so shakes his head.

'You could bring Mamma and Pappa all together,' WA urges.

'We will not travel across the wide oceans to a new land at our age. I have not many days left to me, son.'

'No, Pappa, you are strong as a moose!' WA exclaims but Anders shrugs.

'When the Lord calls me home, I am ready.' He gives the family his blessing. Eric described their final parting on September 1:

> Everyone was up at 6 a.m. this morning busy packing and getting the portmanteaux on the car. Amidst tears we had breakfast and then came the terrible time of bidding goodbye. Everyone was weaping (sic) but at last we got away, and watched Munsala church until it disappeared from view.

Edvard came to Helsinki to see them off for England, via Kiel Canal.

> We disembarked at Hull, Monday 8th, and it was good to belong, to be able to read all the signs and talk to people after being in foreign lands for so long.

Let's compare my own family's three-month campervan tour all across Europe in 1995. After we returned to England our youngest son, then aged five, flummoxed a shop assistant in London by asking, 'Do you speak English?' A photo shows him sitting between two toilet pedestals at the outhouse at Rolf's cottage. Gretchen later told me that shared toilets are common in Munsala, and that a child who jumped between three pedestals fell in.

WA was again creating a cyclone of activity, to attend a wool conference in Bradford, the world wool centre at the time. He lunched with the Lord Mayor. The search started for any of Christina's relations around Whittlesey. Eric reports:

> Dad dug up quite a few. Uncle Richard and Uncle Tom had good rich farms in the Fen Country but they were old men.

The car was delivered to agents to ship to Australia, and they explored London and the Wembley Exhibition. On 16 October 1924, they sailed from Southampton on the *Athenic*, through Panama Canal, via Pitcairn Island and Auckland.

They completed the journey to Sydney and then boarded the *Wollongbar* to Bryon Bay. The family arrived home on Christmas Day and enjoyed dinner with the Hart family. They had no place to go to in Mullumbimby. As *Cedarholm* was sold, they rented a house at the bottom end of Stuart Street, near the Brunswick River, where the boys attended the Mullumbimby Rural School. A branch of the river made a bend right at the school making a swimming hole. They built another boat, a canoe.

Christina grieved the loss of her former home each time she walked past.

Downward Plunge

Debts are an embarrassment to freedom, and freedom is too precious to be pawned for anything that money can buy.

K. J. Back, *The Concentrated Wisdoms of Australia*

How could WA have predicted the uncertain environment to which his family returned after the lavish overseas tour? Fired with ideas, he attempted to implement new ventures for the community and his family. He donated land adjacent to the Mullumbimby railway for a bowling green. Local newspapers reported his plans in 1925 to build a tannery and boot factory on one of his blocks. Hydroelectric power would be used. Whether this proceeded is doubtful. In New Zealand, he noticed the benefits of top dressing soil with fertiliser rich in phosphate and promoted this to the community.

How could he envisage The Depression looming a few years later?

Then his father, Anders Back, died in 1926. WA missed the guidance of his hero, who spurred him forward. It was only sixteen years that they lived together but in that time Anders taught his son all he needed for a successful life. From him WA modelled the faith that became his lodestar, the succour in difficult times.

Mullumbimby October 10, 1926

Precious mother,

I am sorry that I haven't written earlier but the sad news of Pappa's death came like lightning from above. I haven't been myself for a long time and it's hard for me to understand that Pappa isn't around anymore. I was in Sydney a couple of weeks ago on business around the same time that Pappa spent his last hours on earth and I felt very uncomfortable. I didn't know the reason for this but I felt that I had to write to you. On Tuesday September 28 I got three telegrams, two of them told me that one and a half inches of rain had fallen in *Fairview* and Barcaldine, the third one from Christina said the following 'Edvard sends telegram. Father dead. Funeral on Saturday. Send them a telegram. Christina.'

His secretary's clatter of keys halted as WA collected his thoughts. How to express what Pappa taught? His directions echoed even from the other end of the world and they were invariably sound. Like Anders 'Kyrkback', WA became a churchwarden and many looked to him for spiritual leadership. It gave satisfaction to lead others into a faith that could sustain them through the ups and downs of life.

I felt very confused and could hardly believe what I had read. It seemed impossible to continue my business so I travelled home to Mullumbimby on a steamboat headed for Byron Bay.

I visited the Holm's farm and met Karl Johan. We decided to hold a service in my home on Saturday. I read the funeral text from Svenska Psalmboken and Christina and the boys read it in English. After that we sang a few hymns in English. In Pappa's last letter to Anna Sanna, he urged her to read certain parts of a book called 'True Christianity' and Karl Johan read these at the service.

> Both Karl Johan and I have realised that we should have written more to Pappa and thanked him for all the kindness he has shown towards us.

Perhaps Anders' last letter dated 1 November 1921 propelled WA's trip to Finland in 1924. He wrote to Anna Sanna: 'I look through my bad eyes that it is now the beginning towards difficult times. I don't think I will be able to write more letters as I don't feel very well.'

Now that Pappa was not on this earth any more WA felt the great loss of his sounding board. KJ was no patriarch: too unstable. He had lost the will to maintain his crops and fruit trees. He looked and smelled like a tramp.

Sister Anna Sanna was sensible but wrapped up in her own family life. She never learned English, whereas WA's thoughts flew so fast, it was now slower for him to use Swedish. Her children suppressed a giggle at WA's struggles to remember Swedish words. With a secretary it was easier to write letters home in English, which Edvard translated for the family in Finland.

Hearing him sigh, Christina said; 'Pull yourself together, Will, he has had a good life and has gone home.'

Horse-trading through the Depression

Prosperity is no proof of wisdom, but he who can prosper without making a fool of himself is wise.

K. J. Back, *The Royal Toast*

Eric continues his account of the downturn:

Towards the end of the 1920s the economy started to go bad. Commodities came down in price, and my guess is Dad had a lot of farms. Some had been sold but he got them back on his hands, and each one had a mortgage to a bank. He had a very good friend, A.E. Walker on a good farm at Bangalow, and he was in the same boat as Dad. They could not sell their farms, so they went to Sydney together. The Depression hit hard, and there was no past to guide people in this disaster. Every third man was unemployed and there was no dole. The Savings Bank, where most poor people might have a few pounds tucked away, closed its doors. Newspapers carried advertisements like 'have savings book worth £50, will sell for £25.'

Cash was King of those days; those in jobs saw their pay reduced all the time. In Mullumbimby nearly every Saturday night a house caught fire when people were at the pictures. It was called selling out to the insurance company. When people had no money the exchange business thrived, and that is what Mr. Walker and Dad were doing. It was old-fashioned horse-trading.

Many men were given tin dishes and a pick to go into the bush fossicking for gold, others tried to shoot kangaroos and koala bears, and a large number just carried their swags around the country, asking for police rations and handouts from property owners as they passed through. Most were well behaved, but I remember eight bagmen turned up at *Mellew* one day, asking for rations. They had a cattle dog with them, so if you knocked them back you knew they would kill sheep for themselves, use what they could, and the rest will be wasted.

Dad and Mr. Walker met all sorts of people on their trips to Sydney. They traded some farms to Mr. W. S. Friend in exchange for a large block of land between Parramatta and Pennant Hills. But the remarkable thing about the deed was that it was an early Land Grant to one of the discoverers of the way over the Blue Mountains, Wentworth, Lawson or Blaxland. It was a large dairy of many cows producing milk for the Metropolitan Milk Board. There was a share farmer working it; they started milking at midnight, and I suppose midday. I thought, what an awful job! When did they sleep? Dad and Mr. Walker sold in the end, but they missed a golden opportunity. After the war when Sydney grew in all directions, just one small piece of land was sold to the housing commission for over $300,000. At other times WA traded farms that he could not otherwise sell, in return for assets or produce.

Dad had bought marble statues and Venetian glass in Europe. He was walking down George Street in Sydney and came to an Italian Art Gallery. He went in to compare prices. The owner wanted to get out at any price and Dad bought the business for very little.

I imagine the reaction when WA arrived home that night for dinner and said: 'Dear, I bought a shop full of marble statues. Indeed we will sell and make a profit.'

He sent for Vincent and they sold for whatever they could get a thousand marble clocks, dishes and statues. They had cars going around the suburbs selling from house to house. They had to move out of George Street as the rent was too high, but they sold the lot.

At this time we were living at the Park Farm. Dad had bought it from John Morrison to subdivide the frontage into town allotments, but the Depression did not help this idea. It was a good flat farm with a few miles' frontage to the Brunswick River, and right against Mullumbimby. Dad exchanged the Park Farm and a Rosebank farm to Mr. Fraser for Fraser House in Sydney, and he was eventually able to sell Fraser House and end up with £14,000 in the bank! That was big money then.

In the depression there was no profit in anything. Most woolgrowers just sent their wool to the nearest selling centre and hoped for the best. Dad decided the London market had an edge on the Australian sales. Small firms favoured the London sales where they could get their purchases home in a couple of days. Dad then looked into the shipping side of things, and found most wool went in the Conference Line ships. The freight was worked out between shipping lines running regular services and the wool trade. Dad got Clark and Tait, the biggest wool producers in Queensland to join with the Back group, as we were known then, to charter a Tramp ship to take our wool to London. The ships they chartered were not old rust buckets, but modern Norwegian diesels with a fair turn of speed. Then we saved on rail freight as they mostly loaded at Gladstone. Of course the ships had to pick up other loading on the way, and once they loaded copra and weevils got into the wool, so it had to be fumigated in London.

On one occasion Dad asked the ship if he could go along too, and what it would cost. Their answer was 'We will give you a good cabin and take you to London, if you are prepared to pay for your meals.' The last part of this business was the selling broker in London, who happened to be Swartze, Buchanan and Co. Over the years Dad had very close relations with them. There was a constant flow of correspondence both ways, and even in the war years when wool sales ceased, Dad kept up a constant flow of food parcels to the families.

He donated 10,000 sheep to be tinned and shipped to feed the many who endured famine in Europe. In 1948 my father gave 540 sheep to the Salvation Army to distribute a thousand tins of corned mutton in Germany.

Karl Johan Struggles

Every good or bad action that a man does will have its influence upon his happiness in his declining years. Yea, it will stamp its impression on his very deathbed.

K. J. Back, *The Concentrated Wisdoms of Australia*

When Anders died, pent-up hurts bruised KJ's heart. A logjam of justification halted his tongue. All his life, words had been his path to reach out to his family and the world. His efforts to impress the one man who mattered to him no longer mattered. His father's disapproval lingered beyond the grave and made all KJ's words futile.

He wrote in 1921:

> At the end of 1913, I had what I thought a safe income of £1350 a year and although I had quite large debts it was still good. Then the war came and I lost all of my income and had I not been able to sell my forest I might not have been able to keep my land.

Drought shrivelled his crops, his fruit trees. Watering a persimmon, the pain welled up. 'What is the use?' he cried aloud, flinging a bucket of precious tank water at the orange trees. 'Hundreds of trees I planted so their sweet juice would refresh you and Mamma, but you never came to enjoy them.'

The bucket hurtled down the hill.

'Pappa, you stayed icebound while I prepared a mansion for you in the Promised Land, exotic fruits to lavish on you. You could have sat near my waterfall and cooled your feet in Wilson's Creek with breezes blowing through your hair, watched the platypus play while I picked the best of my harvest for you. Heard kookaburras laughing. But you never came. You did not believe I could succeed. Whatever I do, you still brand me a failure. I will no longer broil myself for long hours in the sun.'

A beaten soul cares little for exteriors, for appearances. KJ plunged into a chasm of wounds. In his nightmares, *hamingjas* taunted him; chased him around a barren horizon.

KJ threw aside his pen. No personal letters remain in the family file after 1922. Or perhaps some were so vitriolic they were destroyed.

The next writings available are KJ's treatises to save the world from financial ruin. A letter to the Prime Minister accuses a neighbour of being a spy.

Snippets of letters from the Holm family and Eric gave some inklings of KJ's decline in the following years. He was still productive in 1925, though struggling to pay bills. According to Eric:

> Elwyn and I rode out our bicycles to see Uncle KJ some time ago but as he lives up on the mountains we had a hard job to get there. He has got about twelve men working on his banana plantations, five being Finns. When we were out there Uncle was busy making a road up to one of his plantations, so we watched them blasting stones.

One of those men was Ulf Bexar, an old friend whose passage he'd paid to come from Finland. But this came to grief. KJ's nephew Hugo wrote in November of that year:

'Next month two people will go back to Finland, both have been working for KJ and one of the men, Bexar, is waiting for money though KJ has very little. Solin, the other one has not worked for him for a year.'

Three years later, in 1928: 'Last time I was in town I saw KJ with some parcels of bananas; he has such a low income now that he has no employees.'

I discovered in my research that KJ had become bankrupt, yet the family spoke little of this.

—*A newspaper printed that I was bankrupt? How dare they?* (Wild eyes blaze.)

—It was tough in the Depression, people jumping on the trains to hitch a ride to somewhere they might raise a few bob's work. Children were sent to stay with relatives who could offer them a better home.

—*Even if I did lose all my money, I grew fruit to live on. I didn't need my little brother's condescending rescue.*

—I read a letter Granddad wrote about that to my father—

—*He wrote letters to blacken my reputation and turn others against me.*

–He just said you were ungrateful and blamed others for your problems.

–Just as he made an example of me to his son, Aubrey. He was ashamed of two black sheep in the family.

–Dad also had bright ideas, flashes of genius, but he hadn't the confidence to see them through. I guess Granddad must have been a demanding father?

–Wilhelm dismissed him as he did my gift of writing. Said my books were a waste of money. He constricted me, like a python. Ever since the day he arrived from Finland, when that snake ate the fowls, he dismissed me. Before, I was a successful farmer, my corn crop was the talk of the district in 1902.

–KJ, I appreciate it took courage to self–publish your books.

–I will write a book that will change the world.

But my words hardly alleviate the pain of rejection as he curls huddled like a foetus. Then his thin voice reaches me.

Unresolved Conflict

*But the evil Joukahainen
Nursed a grudge within his bosom,
In his heart the worm of envy,
Envy of this Väinämöinen,
Of this wonderful enchanter.*

Kalevala

Anders Back's sun went down without resolving wrath for his eldest son. How might KJ's future have differed if he found reconciliation, forgiveness and love?

Instead, bitter roots stunted growth in his life's orchard. He dug cankers deeper into its swamp.

I wonder, KJ, what might your fertile intellect have achieved if your heart was warmed by a wife and family?

> *Doubtless Pappa looked down from Heaven and shook his head, muttering 'That useless son, I knew he would come to grief!'*
>
> *Numb with shock when he died, my life lost direction. After all the hatred and anger between us, losing him hit me hard. Never would I expect to miss that tyrant, always quick to find fault in me. While Wilhelm made it his business to stay on his sweet side, Pappa's standards were impossible for me to attain.*
>
> *I grieved most that bad blood still boiled between us and would through eternity. But I could not face a visit to Finland to see him before his death. The Russian web spread to Suez and beyond. So I refused Wilhelm's offer to pay for my trip.*
>
> *My brash brother, fresh from conquering the world, got me a*

bankruptcy clearance but he looked down his nose. Yet I was not always short of funds, I had financial success.

When we sold the sawmill to Joe Hollingworth's estate I guessed Wilhelm was in cohorts with the executor relative. They both stood to share profits— he spread rumours that we had swindled him, expecting all the timber included in the price. I was the one to suffer pursed lips and pointed fingers.

When I lost my land, Will deigned to have me live with him. He fussed that I brought fleas, and left my papaw to ripen on his fancy timber mantelpiece, or ripe bananas that attracted fruit flies. Will always wore a suit, tie, waistcoat and hat, while sniffing at the holes in my boots.

Will's letter to Aubrey fell into my hands. It hurt me dreadfully. My own brother wrote that Satan had 'worked me to a pitch' as if I were demon-possessed, and he the winged angel who swooped down to rescue me.

WA wrote to Aubrey on 24 July 1959:

> I have so many times told you and to the whole family that I had a dread of having to go through any bankruptcy court, as I felt it would not only disgrace myself, but also pass such a slur and degradation on my family, as all that sort of thing cannot be completely washed away, no matter how you strive to get your clearance ... I would not like to go through anything like I did in connection with Uncle KJ's bankruptcy. He was bitter and antagonistic against me all the time—

—Bankrupt. I struggle to form my mouth around that word.

Of course I was bitter. I lost all my land, my five cottages, my crops of corn, my sawmills.

Anna Sanna knew it was not my fault that the Depression hit me along with so many others. She agreed I should be true to my gifts even though printing costs were exorbitant. I walked from Sydney to bring my books home in a wheelbarrow, eight hundred kilometres. Would Wilhelm do that? He drove a plush automobile or slept in a steamship cabin.

Wilhelm slighted me in his constant stream of letters, carbon-copied to all the relatives in both Australia and Finland. He was now the prolific letter writer of the family—much as he could not put a sentence together in English without his secretary or a son to script it. His fancy coloured letterhead showed fat sheep grazing on the type of green grass that Western Queensland graziers prayed for. With 'W. A. Back' in ornate lettering.

I, Karl Johan, the published author, laboured to perfect my English—although my friend the schoolmaster looked through my manuscripts before I published. My treatises in the 1930s summed up my deliberations of several decades, to free mankind from slavery to poverty. Others rushed round, trying to scratch a few pennies together. Many lost all, in the blink of an eye. I wanted to feed their minds so they could use the brains God gave them. Yet was this respected? By some: Prime Minister Chifley consulted me. He asked, 'Do you think we should nationalise the Bank?'

'You'll lose the election if you do,' I told him. And I was right.

Yet, Will was the anointed son, the forger of family fortunes, driving his fancy Fiat into Munsala, the locals' eyes bulging from their sockets.

–KJ, Olavi Koivukangas, a respected historian describes you in his book the first Finnish Australian to write books in English—

–Did Wilhelm bother to open them? He only read his Bible and books about how to grow rich—never the Classics or the philosophers.

–And he describes you as a 'relatively wealthy farmer in Mullumbimby.' But WA overshadowed you?

–He always stood in front of me. When he arrived in Australia, a raw little northerner, I showed him how to survive in this climate. He complained of the heat; I told him the best situation to build a house and catch the sea breezes.

The earth was richer than you could dream of in Finland. A volcano had spewed itself all over the hills and valleys, creating earth so rich that you could grow anything easily. It pulsed with life all year round; never lay fallow as in Finland.

The food was there for eating, even in the Depression years, if one had a mind to making it grow. Bananas ripened on the trees in huge fat bunches. The corn was yellow like the sun that beat on it all year round, and bursting with juice. After the snows melted Finland had a small window of the year for planting, tending and reaping. Then the earth shuddered back into sleep.

***

KJ did not cope with family deaths.

In Finland, carefully preserved folders of letters contain pages that WA wrote after Anders and Edvard passed on. But KJ the author remains silent. No words survive to express his grief when his mother Sanna died in 1937. Were his letters destroyed or had he divorced himself from his pen, struggling to exist?

Drought and Birth

Many men, heedless of the present, allow a bright future to float away to a gloomy past.

K. J. Back, *The Royal Toast*

Granddad's missives to my father chastised him for an idealism too similar to that of my uncle KJ. In Granddad's view, only a realist could succeed and be happy. One such epistle stated that 'the idealist pictures things as he would like them to be, but he can never achieve it, or come any way near his desire.'

I wondered if WA would dismiss my careers of musician and author as fanciful, too. Don't I have a duty to use my gifts, Granddad?

I imagine he says:

> –You have been blessed with nice talents, yes, but God has given you children to raise, to feed and educate.

> –But Granddad, I have been a good mother. Now I have time; someone should write the family story.

That letter my father received just a week before my birth contained much of the dictum according to WA:

> The realist gets pleasure in achieving, and by plodding along he builds up something for better; each success makes him more confident in himself. Most great men whom we admire through history have been blessed with evenly divided minds first as an idealist and then as a realist. And I maintain that you have to have both. The realistic mind is the essential in the finish where the main 'delivery of the goods comes in'. It does not throw anything by the wind and toss everything up on a dice.

His dogmatic dismissal of Aubrey's ideas unleashed anger and despair in my father, which would filter through the lives of my whole family.

'Aub, please read this,' he pencilled at the top of another letter some weeks later, 'Do not be krankey.' But the damage was done. My father battled low self-esteem as well as drought, gained a daughter—another mouth to feed. He paid a thousand pounds' deposit on an aeroplane, money forfeited when he could not afford to pay the balance. His efforts to escape the bush were foiled yet again. His responsibilities trapped him there.

So, Granddad considered creative pursuits, like mine, unworthy compared with business. Beauty in all its forms—music, art, words and dance—draws my spirit, as a revolt against arid landscapes.

Sometimes it felt as if the two hemispheres of my brain were at odds with each other. Reading through Granddad's letters to my father I share his angst:

> I grant you that idealists have made some good discoveries but big mistakes, crime and misery have been brought about by idealists like Hitler and Mussolini, or Peter the Hermit in the Crusades.

'He compares me with Hitler and Mussolini? His own son—he treats me like a child. He is the dictator, not me! He says I will never succeed.'

An idealist cannot succeed. An idealist cannot be happy in life.

Such statements dictate it is dangerous to allow creative ideas free rein. They must be tempered by the rational. Child Ruth will starve her strengths. The sap of creativity dries like parched waterholes. I flinch inside the straitjacket of words that condemn me along with my father.

Aubrey in turn will lash out similar judgments. Adult, pragmatic Ruth realises Dad merely passes on what his father meted to him, and Anders to KJ. Father, forgive us, for we are swept by waves of generational patterns.

But the child in Ruth will shrink into a foetal position wishing for the safety of womb.

***

I am born into drought. When Dad is away droving sheep to distant pastures, my mother's company is all mine and I sleep in her bed—until that strange man rides into my dreamland, sweaty and dusty. He evicts me to the cot.

There are few photographs of my childhood but those show a lopsided child with fair wavy hair squinting into the sun. A nickname 'Cuddles' reveals that I was one who craves affection, but in a family of eight children, to get attention one needs a loud voice—which this ugly duckling lacks. Until I find a voice in music.

The bush culture of hillbilly music is an unlikely breeding ground for a classical musician. The odds are slim. My first experience of music was of a governess teaching her sole repertoire, *Fairy Bells*, on our jangly piano. The piano's tone was crippled by searing heat and the silverfish and mice that nibbled its innards. This flummoxes my concept of intonation for years. But an Australian Broadcasting Commission schools music program changes my life's direction. It demonstrates the wind instruments in turn; this is the flute. Tweet. No. The oboe: too dour. 'Now hear the clarinet.'

'I'll play that,' I decide immediately, loving the rich sounds and colours. With no inkling how to produce them, I have found my means of expression.

While at university, John Curro, conductor of Queensland Youth Orchestra, sees that I need a challenge. The Copland concerto is virtuosic but also allows me to express the instrument's singing tone and lyricism. There are altissimo register and jazzy syncopated rhythms to conquer. And John knows that I will enjoy exploiting its introvert and extrovert qualities.

'Why not?'

'Because the next round performance is two weeks away and I have not learned, let alone played, the Copland.'

'There's nothing to lose. You can fall back on Weber. Just do it.'

How I practise. Never have I worked so. I climb a technical Mount Everest; slay dragons of my weaknesses; my rhythmic vagaries are drilled into precision, altissimo register runs conquered. Day and night I live, work, sleep and finally surmount the Copland Concerto. My performance with the Queensland Symphony Orchestra is already a triumph; there is no apprehension about winning—I did so already. This is my moment, charged with electricity. I shine, ecstatic.

This glorious moment will never be repeated. My feet barely touch the ground as I walk through the City Hall foyer with my parents. Until my father chops my future off at its ankles.

'Why would people pay money to come and hear that?' he asks.

These words cast me into an abyss.

Dad's unthinking remark slams at my solar plexus. The emotional shock stays with me. I have no heart for further competitions. The next year I will make a lukewarm entry for the same competition but a raging temperature justifies my withdrawal.

Music loses its joy, its play, becomes work.

A few nights after my winning concerto performance, I walk from my university residential college to the Highland Terrace home. It is being packed ready for sale; boxes hold a decade's memories consigned to the rubbish. Below the sun porch windows, I hear my parents' voices. They host a prayer meeting, asking God's blessing on missionaries in obscure distant 'fields'. They little know their own daughter cries her heart out in the garden below. There is no blessing for her.

My plans will intensify to put a world's distance between us. Decades later my chiropractor will notice my tight rib cage and shallow breathing; a professional musician and teacher should know how to breathe. Through kinesiology treatment we release that spasm of breath holding that has become a habit since this time. That performance of Copland Concerto is my musical pinnacle; like KJ, I peak early and never match it again.

Bankrupt

It is the debt, and that which was the cause of the debt, that brings on bankruptcy, not the creditor.

K. J. Back, *The Concentrated Wisdoms of Australia*

The first I heard of KJ's bankruptcy was that letter from Granddad to my father, in which he admonished Dad for risking ruin.

The bankruptcy file reveals KJ owed the bank £2443, two shillings and four pence. Wages were unpaid to Ulf Bexar (£100), G. Kastren (£20), Praham Singh (£9) and A. Linden (£95). £100 was claimed by Hollingworth Sawmill Company 'For timber and some Promissory Notes.'

Two sad letters revealed how KJ struggled against inflexible systems, banks and court processes he did not understand. He was depressed, out of his depth and, in spite of his fluency with the English language, felt insecure to express himself in a courtroom. So he picked up his pen, that weapon with which he fought battles. This time it was an attempt to be understood.

The first letter was dated 6 December, 1927 to the Chief Clerk in Bankruptcy in Sydney.

> Dear Sir,
>
> I am in receipt of Creditor's Petition No. A 26939 and I wish to state that I intend to dispute the same on the following grounds.
>
> That the property held as security from me is worth considerably more than the amount owing.
>
> That I can easily find some men who are only too willing to buy it to that price, and on the terms that the Bank has offered for two others, on the condition that the agreement

signed between me and such part with the Bank as a third party, which is exactly the same as the Bank wanted me to do with another party.

At the present time it is practically impossible to sell my land up here to any price for cash, and the only possible chance of selling anything is on terms... the Bank has previously asked me to deal with another man, that man being entirely unknown to me and in my opinion one with very little prospects. I therefore refused to accept the Bank's client. ... One [other] man who was an absolute stranger to me, and who was recommended to me for my guarantee, committed suicide on account of his financial worries, and so the debt was heaped up against me.

Hoping you will register this is the grounds my defence,

Yours faithfully,
KJ Back

A second letter of 16 December 1927 addressed the Judge and This Honourable Court:

Dear Sirs,

As I have no experience in legal matters and feel very nervous in the court I am afraid I may break down and so I am taking the precaution of writing down the main points of what I have to say. First of all I wish to thank this Honourable Court for the leniency that has been extended to me for I can plainly see that the court is trying to give me Justice.

...The reason why I did not defend this case six months ago is that the bank had just then taken possession of the property, which deprived me of all income, and put me in such a fix financially that I could not even have paid my passage to Sydney...

At this particular time everything was at its lowest ebb on the North Coast. It will ruin me for life if the bank puts me Insolvent, and there would be many others who would lose by it also.

Karl Johan urged the bank to sell the farm in question for the full amount of the debt on the nominal deposit, to someone who would maintain and improve the place, 'but I can do the same myself if the bank gives me a chance. In fact I have a man in the house now waiting to start if they only say the word. This man has been waiting there for nearly two years.'

He reminded them that when the National Bank first opened their branch in Mullumbimby he was the first one to start an account with them, and it was on his very recommendations that their branch was started. He found them 25 new customers, and in many instances guaranteed people's accounts in order to give them the fixed overdrafts. 'I did all this for nothing simply with the object of helping the Bank to get a start.'

> At this particular time I owed no money to the Bank and this farm, now in question, had no mortgage on it, but then I got some money from the Bank and did a considerable amount of clearing on the land. I planted 3 acres of sugarcane, which grew splendidly and became the talk of the whole district. I built a house, yards and bales, cream shed and all these improvements cost me about £500. In addition to this I bought a dairy herd and a separator and all other necessaries, which ran me into another £400. Just then when I was ready to start and before I had received one single cream cheque, the Bank put the screw on me and on the whole lot of those whom I had guaranteed and they worried us to such an extent that none of us knew where to turn, in fact some of us were on the point of going off our heads.

KJ submitted a plea in August 1931.

The Hollingworth company had noted 'an overpayment was made in connection with the purchase of an area or quantity of timber at Goonengerry.' KJ wrote in response:

> As regards the Hollingworth account: This was for timber required for the building of a house on the property mortgaged to the National Bank. When the buildings were nearly finished the bank ejected me and stuck to the timber that did not legally belong neither to me nor to the bank. Thus it was not I but the National Bank, the very bank that put me insolvent that is morally if not legally guilty of dishonesty in that respect. The Hollingworth Company realises that too and

they are not now holding me responsible for that any longer.

If I could obtain my clearance now some of my relations would lend me an old horse and a spring-cart and then I would grow some vegetables for the Sydney markets…if I could put in some beans at once I may make twenty pounds in the late Spring and that would keep me for the best part of the year.

The main cause of bankruptcy was the War. I never recovered after that. At the time when I contracted those debts I had a number of beautiful banana plantations and they were all looking well. I was in high hopes of being able to make satisfactory arrangements with all my creditors within a year or two, but the Bunchy Top Disease came into the plantations and I was ordered by the Inspector to destroy them all. Shortly before the Bankruptcy I tried to call a meeting with my creditors but no one came.

A Certificate of Discharge was issued on 8 September 1931.

But the damage was done. KJ, once a successful farmer and landowner, never regained his confidence. He retained his debating skills; the Mullumbimby Star reported on 4 May 1933 his verbal interrogation of a politician A. E. Budd in a community meeting. His battered top hat, worn when he acted in plays in the district, gathered dust and mould.

Decades later KJ sent money to Finland to pay Ulf Bexar his wages.

I begin to see why Granddad worried about idealists. It hadn't been so much KJ's bad business acumen that sent him bankrupt—it had been his desire to help his fellowman. He'd gone guarantor for local farmers to help them get a head start in the area and, when times had gone bad, the bank had used him as a scapegoat.

KJ Saves the World

All mankind must be liberated from Militarism, and from the Moneylenders yoke. The Interest must be abolished. There must be a new system of finance, and there must be peace and unity between all Nations.

K.J. Back, *K.J. Back's Financial System*

As the Second World War tightened its strictures on Europe, WA organised a shipload of provisions to save Finnish people from famine. His office was strewn with sacks of flour and sugar, transferred into kilo–size calico bags. He employed a woman full time and grandchildren were enlisted as a Lilliputian army to pack and stack.

What if the shipments were pilfered, he was asked. 'Thieves have to live too,' WA replied.

KJ applied his pen to save the world from the evils of financial ruin.

The Depression and bankruptcy challenged KJ's mind. He poured innovative and outrageous plans into eight short treatises to 'Solve the Financial Ills of the World.'

He wrote that he had taken out a copyright of a small pamphlet dealing with the financial problems of the time. He interviewed agents in connection with an American copyright 'but they all advised me not to spend any money on it as they do not think it worth the while. I think it would be of some use to the world if I could get anyone to read it, but no one will.'

In 1931 he began *K. J. Back's Financial System* with bold capitals:

> K. J. BACK'S PROCLAMATION TO THE WORLD: Be it hereby known throughout the whole world that the Day of Deliverance is now dawning. In opening this book you are opening up a new epoch in the History of Mankind. For the Old System terminates here. And here the New System commences.

Bad seasons were KJ's lot, but now he wrote: 'There will be no more famine or starvation in any country at any time' and that all the world shall be liberated from the iniquitous burden of the interest rates. With a flourish of his pen he joined countries with railways, connecting links between Scandinavia, Europe and Asia. This would prove a 'veritable gold mine for Finland. Under the New System of Finance a Railway might be built from Åbo, on the coast of Finland, through the Åland Archipelago to Sweden,' linking Russia and Asia to the North Sea. Another would connect Gibraltar to the north of Africa, and a 'railway tunnel between Dover and Calais.'

This undertaking of many millions of pounds, using the most capable engineers, 'would not cost Finland one penny for its construction.' Hydroelectricity from waterfalls would power the stone drills and load the railway trucks with stones.

KJ the visionary turned his attention to taming the oceans of the world. To drain the Adriatic Sea, building a canal around it, large enough to carry away all the water that flows into the Adriatic, from which towns would receive their water by gravitation.

> Thus although Venice loses her gondolier she will still have her harbour, large enough for ocean going steamers. There is a job in the Adriatic for five million men digging the canals and building the dykes. Their wages will soon lift the depression in those countries. Tunnels will be dug through the mountains to lead river waters to distant fields for irrigation. Where there are now drifting sands will soon be beautiful farms and orchards.
>
> So it will go on all over the world. Instead of fighting one another the Nations will be united in one ceaseless battle against the elements. There is expansion for Asia also right out of Australia, and it will all be conquered from the sea some day. The author can see all this, but he will not be able to enjoy it. For although the New System of Finance will put many things within man's reach, man will still remain a mortal, and all those things will only come when the time is due for it.

I cannot give KJ's theories the appraisal they deserve. A lecturer in accounting read his tomes and observed that it was a pity KJ did not have more education as he had an able mind. I gave them to my brother Douglas Back for his comment on the treatises. He wrote:

A Commentary on KJ Back's Financial System

I began reading my Great Uncle's treatise with a degree of scepticism, but it wasn't long before my interest was piqued and my understanding of the intellect of the man grew.

Let me begin as a small boy, near Billinudgel in NSW, at the unpainted hut on the hill where KJ lived. I would peer through the doorway at this old, stooped man with whiskers growing out of his ears, taking in the scene, but ready to run. I don't know if I thought he might put me in his cooking pot, but I don't recall him ever acknowledging me. His smoky hut was stacked waist-deep with old newspapers and books. He lived like a hermit bachelor.

KJ wrote to the newspaper about *My New System of Finance*, like a modern day Christopher Columbus who had just discovered the new world and was enthusiastically presenting it to mankind. His thesis was well thought out, and his vision, presented with conviction, has merit.

To set the scene, the Australian currency had been pegged to a gold standard, which had restricted the creation of finance and put brakes on the development of the economy. Worse still, the money lent out by the Bankers was seen to be their money, because they may, or may not, have had the gold in their vault to back it, and this afforded them the privilege of charging 7% interest on their loans. KJ advised his system 'When it comes will not be a Gold Standard but... a Property Standard.' It would be backed by the Freehold Property and productive capacity of the Australian people. It would transfer the money creation business back to the Commonwealth Government. Because it no longer required a Banker or his gold, the money would be lent out interest free, but with a small fee to the Treasury of the Commonwealth of Australia, for doing the valuation on the property.

This is also the philosophy of the Social Credit movement which had a large following around that era, including a political party and elected representatives. He dreamed of the day when money would be issued as a credit secured by a man's assets, not as a debt to the Bankers, who take the asset as security and issue money which cost them nothing to create, and claim ownership of it. By freeing up the money supply, it would allow the building of great projects. The Trans Australia Railway, had already been built in Australia using his New Financial System, or Social Credit. The First World War was financed in the same way. KJ was a visionary and had huge aspirations for the world. ...

Earlier books were signed K. J. Back, author. Now he had evolved to 'The Liberator of all Mankind, K. J. Back.'

The Brisbane Base

Your wealth may far exceed what now you got,
Your honour may surpass your wildest aim.

K. J. Back, *The Concentrated Wisdom of Australia*

WA was an astute land assessor and, after developing a swathe of Mullumbimby, turned his eyes north, past the Queensland border. When in Brisbane, Granddad stayed at the Canberra hotel in Ann Street, Brisbane. Granddad's business interests had expanded north of the Queensland border, so it became a strain to divide his time between the Northern Rivers district, Brisbane and further west. Once he caught the bus back to his base in Mullumbimby, leaving his car standing unlocked outside the hotel. It was still there when he returned next day.

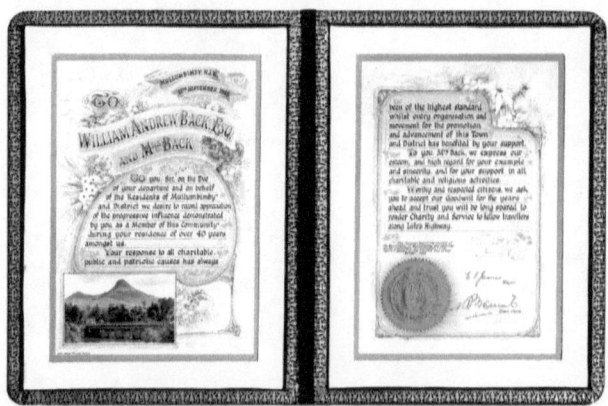

The time had come to move to Brisbane. The Mayor of Mullumbimby gave him a Civic Farewell on 12 September 1949. A magnificent illuminated citation, signed by the Mayor and Town Clerk read:

> We desire to record appreciation of the progressive influence demonstrated by you as a member of this

community... Your response to all charitable, public and patriotic causes has always been of the highest standard whilst every organisation and movement for the promotion and advancement of this town has benefited from your support.

A shrewd move to base himself in Brisbane enabled his outreach to country areas.

Picnic and repairs: Unknown, Christina, Unknown, Gloria, Alan, WA.

Dubbed by some as 'the father of St Lucia', he appears to have headed the syndicate that developed much of the suburb.

Eric wrote about the St Lucia development.

> The purchase price was to be about £24,000. They formed a private company known as Coronation Park Pty and we know it today as St Lucia. The land included the (now) Indooroopilly Golf Club, then along the river to include a lot of the University grounds, but away from the frontage it was mostly undeveloped bush.

Its hills were subdivided into 870 building blocks on a contour town plan system by the best surveyors available to convert dairy land and scrub into a model suburb.

Granddad aimed high. The Governor himself, Sir Matthew Nathan, presided at the opening of the estate. An engineer himself, he praised the layout to reduce the steepness of the grades as one of the civic triumphs of Mr R. A. McInnes, who was to become town planner of Brisbane.

Up to 1926 some blocks were sold but only a few built on. For the next nine years Coronation Park Ltd watched as disaster and near–bankruptcy took over. Many of the blocks passed back to the subdividers or were sold for unpaid rates.

> To most observers this looked like the end of St Lucia… to most that is except Mr Back and his partners. 'From the time I first saw the beautiful hills of St Lucia I knew that one day it would blossom,' Mr Back muses. 'There were times though, that courage, faith–and a bundle of unwanted land–was all that we had.'[3]

The times were against his Brisbane Coronation Park project. Eric wrote that:

> Blocks of land were advertised for £10 deposit and £1 monthly with water and electricity. All might have gone well for Coronation Park if the Depression had not arrived soon after it started. People may have paid a few pounds deposit on a block but then when they got their rates from the Council, they mostly forfeited the land as the best way out. Certainly no one could build in those days.

In *The Telegraph* of 25 January 1962, WA reminisced on those hard times:

> "We wanted to make it a model suburb; and even in the early days each sale contract carried certain development clauses. Trees were to be left intact and only houses costing a minimum of £700 were allowed to be built". St Lucia was just easing out of the economic doldrums when World War II–and the consequent building restrictions–struck another blow to progress. In 1946-47 Coronation Park Ltd wound up voluntarily and the unsold land was divided among the partners.
>
> Mr Back, left with a parcel of about 40 blocks agreed to take over the sale of some of the other land of his associates. "In 1948 there were mobs of Kangaroos all over the place, dirt roads, and no worthwhile shopping facilities" he says.

---

3   The Telegraph, 25 January 1962 p 33 c 3.

> –That gave you many sleepless nights, Granddad? I didn't see any kangaroos a decade later.
>
> –Providence intervened when the Brisbane City Council resumed 200 blocks between 1926 and 1929 for the site of the University. Funds came from a bequest by Dr and Miss Mayne.

The 'Mayne gift' was donated in 1928 but building was delayed as the founding fathers debated the ideal site for the university. A first preference was Victoria Park but that was too expensive. Meanwhile, the land was used for the State-funded St Lucia Farm School, where hundreds of city boys were trained to plough, sow crops and milk cows.

In August 1935 the government announced £300,000 for the erection of buildings and £200,000 for their furnishing and equipment and next year. Premier Forgan Smith was presented with plans and said:

> The suburb is now in the stage of transition from gum boots (the distinguishing mark of men in the dairy yard) to horn-rimmed spectacles (the brand of the student). On the proposed University site the St. Lucia Farm School has been temporarily established.[4]

In the 1940s the army pitched tents on Coronation Drive. This was renamed Hawken Drive in 1950 after the death of Professor Roger Hawken, a prime mover in the development of the university.

Eric continues:

> Then at the other end a large area was sold to Indooroopilly Golf Club. Sometimes Dad said it was 35 acres sold for £3500 but it varied a bit. The company could never get ahead and the bank wanted their money, so finally it was proposed to wind the company up and share the remaining blocks between the partners. …This probably made Dad and Mum decide to shift to Brisbane and Vincent Nelson sold up and came too.

The Courier Mail of 14 December 1949 described WA Back as a Swede who arrived with £200 and now was building 30 rental houses and shops at St Lucia, worth more than £75,000.

---

4 *Courier Mail* of February 26, 1936.

> This 63 year old is 'affable and sprightly for his age'; of his 50 allotments he already has four houses partly completed in St Lucia and is having built an ultra modern home with lift and swimming pool. It notes that building materials are obtained from Sweden, England and the Continent, bricks from Casino. All homes were equipped with hot and cold water, septic systems, and garages. Plans also included community gardens, tennis courts, and shops.
>
> Mr. Back said his office staff would be transferred from Mullumbimby to St. Lucia and accommodated in some of the new houses. He had built 110 houses at Mullumbimby, where he had 'carved out' 30 dairy farms from scrub land. 'Mr. Back sends his wool to London, where it has brought an average of £90 to £100 a bale this year, and twice topped the market.

It was described it as a charming sylvan setting in some of the most picturesque country in Brisbane. After the university was built, St Lucia development expanded.

Eric wrote that his father:

> ...could not resist the temptation to buy land if any good blocks came on the market. He reasoned the place would come to nothing if you sat on a lot of empty land. There was no costing for each job. I would go so far as to say that he never made much money out of his building venture.

Dad had got a fair bit of publicity in the papers for his efforts to create St Lucia given the village shopping centre was his idea. He got Bob Browning to start a small food store first.

I remember our wide eyes when a modern supermarket opened. Rather than stand behind a counter and be served we could push a trolley and choose items from the shelves. Bob always wore a white apron and a smile. Next door was the ANZ bank; both began in a white timber house. WA promised the ANZ bank a lot of accounts, so they opened up part-time.

Decades later my husband and I returned after seven years in Europe. With little banking history, our hopes of buying a house were slim until the bank manager noted: 'Oh, you're William Back's grandchild?' and the loan process was fast-tracked.

Western Provinces

Adversity is like a mighty storm, which breaks off all the deformed and unworthy limbs of the tree of friendship and brotherhood.

K. J. Back, *The Concentrated Wisdoms of Australia*

In New South Wales, both Back brothers' farms were staging posts for emigrant Finns. WA helped them and also his sons and nephews by partnering with them in ballots for land. His pastoral province extended with sheep properties in Western Queensland and provided work for the growing family. Sons Elwyn and Aubrey worked at the sheep station *Stockholm* and Eric managed *Fairview* from 1935. Many were surprised when a drover delivered a mob of a thousand sheep, picked up for a bargain, as the first sign that Granddad was in the area.

WA ran a stock and station business to manage the bookkeeping of forty properties. One partner, Fred Smith, drew a good block on *Afton Downs*, which he named *Wilfred Downs* (Will for Dad and Fred, his name.) Smith and his family were hard working share farmers at Mullumbimby when he drew the block, and worked hard to get a home and other buildings on the selection.

Eric tells of the partnership with A. J. Cameron at *Bundoran Station*:

> The homestead was built on the banks of a big waterhole in Alick's Creek, and the water level was maintained by a bore drain from the bore. It was a wide stretch of water with plenty of birdlife around. Aub and Helen spent the first years of their married life at *Bundoran* and I did envy them, coming as I did from a dry country like *Fairview*. They changed the name of the place to *Lilford*. This is the name of Lord Lilford's fine home and estate very close to where Granddad and Grandma Hart came from in England. When we were in England in 1924, relative of my mother's took us there. He was bailiff or estate manager.

All went well with *Lilford* when the seasons were kind, but there was nothing if it was dry.

> In 1932-33 with all those new places to set up we ran into a drought. No rain in the summer months, and there was no agistment in the sheep country. We boys looked through the cattle country and settled on some empty farms mainly around Wowan in the Dawson Valley. We railed just over 8000 sheep there in different consignments and they were in flocks of 2,000 each at different farms. It was labour intensive, as the sheep had to be shepherded—no fences and plenty of dogs. I used to go early in the morning to the other camps, in turn, and count the sheep out of the yard, to see if any were lost…

> Then our luck changed. There was very heavy rain in the west in the middle of winter, and none on the coast where our sheep were. In the west thousands of sheep died in the wet and intense cold—even kangaroos died. When the grass grew in the spring we were able to bring the sheep home, and we lost very few.

They turned 'a bare bit of dirt with only a few miles of old fences' into a moneymaking business. In September 1936 Mr. Cameron decided to buy WA out.

In 1939 WA became interested in a large property *Aberfoyle*—but the price was beyond him. When war broke out, 'everyone panicked' so his father suggested to Norman Fraser that they buy it as partners, together with *Fairview*.

> The partnership did not last very long. Dad and Fraser were both dominating characters and they had differences on how things should be worked. Fraser saw a couple of station diaries from *Aberfoyle* and floods dominated the picture so when Dad said, 'You take *Aberfoyle* or *Fairview* and I will take the other one,' Norm Fraser settled for *Fairview* and both were happy.

Eric managed *Aberfoyle* 'a rough place of 303 square miles or 194,000 acres' for decades.

> It was a long way from any town; our business was with Hughenden 120 miles away but Muttaburra and Aramac were 110 miles by worse road. We had no direct telephone and had to rely on the bush telegraph to send messages. Most was

covered in scrub, which made it very hard to muster, and the paddocks were big, the largest was 26,000 acres. The Dingo Barrier Fence ran along the eastern boundary so there was always the risk of dogs getting in and this was made easier because 80,000 acres of *Aberfoyle* was subject to flooding and this knocked the fences about. At least we could get good bore water at shallow depths.

The homestead and woolshed were on the western side of Torrens Creek, but all good high ground was on the eastern side so before the wet season set in most of the sheep would be put on the eastern. If the wet season lasted a long time and the blowflies got into the sheep, there was nothing the station could do as there was no equipment at that side. The first summer we owned it about 3000 sheep died of fly. I decided we would avoid this problem in future by shearing half the flock in November.

As well as running the property I had to do monthly accounts for up to a dozen employees on the books and this included stores such as tobacco supplied by us... It was not rationed but it was very scarce. So if men could not get tobacco they would leave and in time I would have no staff. I told the men that sunshine or flood I would guarantee them one tin of Log Cabin tobacco, paper and matches per week and I never fell down on that undertaking although in flood times it came close.

When we started mustering for a first shearing I had sleepless nights worrying about all the sheep that were missing. I would start mustering for shearing six weeks beforehand and pack them into handy paddocks. Mustering calls for six or eight men spread across the paddock, and all had to make a lot of noise to get the sheep running. It also started other animals: kangaroos, emus but hopefully no dingoes. One day an old fellow Sammy Rolfe was riding in sight of the fence when a kangaroo got hooked up in the fence. He dismounted to free it and as an afterthought put his own waistcoat on the roo and headed it in the general direction of the other men. He thought it a great joke until he reached for his tobacco and then realised it was in his waistcoat, bounding through the scrub.

> To muster some of the distant paddocks we had to set up an overnight camp. It was a tough life but an experience I'm pleased to have had; to sit around the campfire at night drinking tea and swapping yarns brought us closer together. Later in bed I would look at the stars and moon through the trees and listen to the horse bells.

But Eric found the job became too big. 'When I was out in a mustering camp and working away from home a lot, who was backing me up on the home front?' When he returned home for a break, Vincent Nelson interviewed girls to work in the office in Mullumbimby, choosing Doris Kohnke. 'Did he realise he was also picking a wife for me?'

> One of early achievements at *Aberfoyle* was the building of a new telephone line to Torrens Creek, a distance of 70 miles. I don't know how we ever achieved it. Manpower was scarce, new phone wire and insulators out, even gidgee posts were hard to find. Today who would set out to build a phone line from say Brisbane to Tweed Heads with an axe, crowbar and shovel?

At the end of 1943, Aunt Gloria and her husband Victor Houseman obtained *Wilfred Downs*, their home until 1960 when they sold it to my father Aubrey. He used some of his share of the proceeds from the sale of *Aberfoyle* to pay for *Wilfred*.

But first we need an update on my parents and other grandparents.

Ruth's Parents

It matters but little what you are to nationality or race, but to be happy in married life, it is essential that one's love should be full-blooded.

K. J. Back, *The Concentrated Wisdoms of Australia*

We are all the result of a combined heritage from two sets of genes. My mother Maud Helen Lord was born in 1919 to strong pioneers, though they would not know the Finnish word *sisu*. Her father and grandfather bore the same name, R.D. Lord, short for Robert Drayton Lord. (Drayton was the village on the Darling Downs where her grandfather was born in 1852.) There is a pattern of passing names on; Mum was called by her second name Helen, to avoid confusion with her mother. And so am I named for my mother but called by my second name.

Mum's father was born in 1884 in Cooktown on the far north tip of Cape York. His father was the Queensland National Bank manager when the gold rush made Cooktown the second largest town in the state. He could add four columns of figures in his head, but an abacus lay ready on the counter, so Chinese gold diggers could reckon the price of their gold.

In steamy tropical heat, the bankers wore white suits and sported long moustaches but they lived hard lives. To set up new banks they rode horses on slushy mountain tracks, camped in the rain and were on constant watch for Chinese bandits or the spears of blacks. This frontier hub was Queensland's most northerly port and each week an escort galloped to the coast carrying leather bags full of gold. In this wild prosperous town the bank advanced money to merchants on the security of shares, mining machinery, land and hotels. Or of tons of rice or opium, that were held in the strong room.

When the gold seams yielded their riches, the floors of the bank, hotels and stores were noisy with hobnail boots. But once the reefs were denuded of their wealth, shares became worthless. The pubs were abandoned, the machinery rusted and the personal guarantors disappeared. Insolvent storekeepers and miners moved on to the next gold rush town, leaving debts behind.

My grandfather was orphaned at 12 years when his father died in 1898. He lived with a family whose son was the same age and who became a friend for life. For eleven years he worked on a large cattle station *Bluff Downs* owned by his uncle Ernest White, at first for his keep, then for a minimum wage. One day White set him to mind a mob of cattle for an hour or two but didn't return until sunset. White was so impressed that he doubled R.D.'s wage and made him head stockman. When his nephew decided to move on, White said: 'With this reference you should get any manager's job you ask for.'

R.D. married Maud Ellen Sabien in Cunnamulla in January 1916. He took his new wife to the remote property he managed called *Gregory Downs*. It was one of the first established in the savannah grasses of the Gulf of Carpentaria called by Captain Lort Stokes 'the Plains of Promise.' Their steamer sailed from Townsville, followed Cape York and headed down into the Gulf of Carpentaria. From Burketown a dray jolted them over more than 300 kilometres of rough tracks to the station. Far from other white people, it was dry, parched land but clean running water flowed in the Gregory River, fringed by cabbage palms, Leichhardt trees and tea trees.

Waanyani Aboriginal men made excellent stockmen. They lived in large indigenous camps with their wives and families who helped as domestics around the house and garden. Old photographs in a family folder show men dressed up in paint and feathers before a corroboree.

My grandmother was responsible for the health of all those on the station, black and white. Medical attention was many days away. Two doctors cared for a vast area of two million square kilometres until, in 1928, Reverend John Flynn formed the Royal Flying Doctor Service. This eased the daily struggles of pioneers in remote areas.

Annual supply orders were shipped in through Burketown and would list two tons of flour, a ton of salt—essential for preserving—Epsom Salts, 'fever mixture' and laudanum for pain relief.

The black women cried as the couple packed to move to their next property, *Lawn Hill*, about 150 kilometres away. 'You come back sometime, Missus.'

'But I'm not going far away, only to *Lawn Hill*,' she said.

There, the creek is carpeted with water lilies and the emerald water spilling through the gorge forms an oasis in the desert. In indigenous mythology, the Rainbow Serpent Boodjamulla carved this gorge from the red and gold rocky cliffs. In a limestone outcrop at Riversleigh near *Lawn Hill* are fossil remains of huge birds, crocodiles, carnivorous kangaroos, marsupial lions, turtles and pythons with girths the size of a dinner plate. They date back 25 million years.

My mother was a toddler when the couple next moved. In October 1920 the Lords bought *Proa* near Nelia. This was sheep country and his experience was with cattle, so R.D. worked as the manager at *Lammermoor* to gain experience with sheep. The owner Mr. H.A. Coldham wrote a reference:

> I may state that I only engaged him [R. D. Lord] for a couple of months originally, but found him to be such a competent cattle manager that I kept him on up to the present.
>
> This year was one of the driest years ever experienced and he proved himself a tremendous success in dealing with drought conditions. He is a splendid judge of stock and I consider him one of the best men I have ever employed. He is honest and absolutely trustworthy and I have pleasure in recommending him to anyone requiring the services of first class station manager.

Proa was less remote but life was no easier. My grandmother fetched water from a bore, fired a woodstove for heating and cooking. A charcoal cooler was the only cooling device to prevent the butter from turning to oil.

In seasons of ups and downs, one drought really broke R.D. The bank refused more loans and so he signed papers to give them the property. That night two inches of rain fell. He rang the bank manager and asked, 'Would you tear up the papers?'

No. R.D. worked to buy his land back again.

Meanwhile, my father, Aubrey Gordon Douglas Back, had moved north from Mullumbimby to Queensland where he met my mother.

According to Eric:

> Aubrey had left home and gone to work at *Stockholm* like the rest of us. Hugo [Holm] had made a good job of turning the old Muttaburra Post Office, plus new material, into a comfortable homestead, so they needed someone to look after it. Hugo acquired the services of an old ship's steward to keep house and cook, and of course everyone had to be on time. Aub was a motorbike fanatic at the time, and when he brought bits of the bike onto the kitchen table at night, it did not help with the cook. He rode his bike from Mullumbimby to *Stockholm* after one holiday, and the bitumen ended at Dalby in those days. The rest of the road was rough and dusty, and Aub had a box on the back with his suit, a few bits of clothing

and biscuits. A liberal supply of dust and a good shaking made for a real mess.

I know little of their meeting, except that my father shore a hundred sheep on the morning of his wedding in January 1941. Grandma sexed the eggs to have a dozen cockerels ready for the reception. On the day before the wedding, she killed, stuffed and cooked them. As my mother went to dress, a telegram arrived. The priest was delayed in Townsville.

Uncle Eric gave his version:

> The Anglican minister who had been asked to marry them must have been an absent-minded type because he set off for Synod, and completely forgot about them. So the Presbyterian man was hastily pressed into service. The marriage had to be postponed a day.

In January heat with no refrigeration, food soon spoiled. Grandma killed the hens and cooked all over again. This was an inauspicious start to a marriage that endured until she died in 2003. In 1945 George Nicol sold *Hazelwood Downs* to Helen. My parents raised their brood there until in 1963 Dad bought *Wilfred Downs*, a convenient ten kilometres from *Hazelwood Downs* from his sister Gloria and her husband.

I was 11 when we moved next door to *Wilfred Downs*, an efficient property with tidy sheds, a cubby house and swing. My aunt left behind bins of clothes and shoes, a delight for dressing up. We hosted a farewell party at which my sisters and I staged the entertainment; a dramatic production titled *King Midas*. One apt line lingers in my memory; I intoned: 'Too much gold.'

Why did we choose that topic? My father read books about lost goldmines, even mounted expeditions. He must have felt pressured to match his father's wealth.

Last Days

When crops are ripe, what we have sown,
We must expect to reap.

K. J. Back, *The Concentrated Wisdoms of Australia*

The Depression took an economic and emotional toll on uncle KJ. A 1945 letter from the Holms to Finland spoke of the family in Australia and KJ's plight.

> We read Uncle Wilhelm's and Uncle KJ's letter to you and we don't know how you can understand all what they have put together. They want you to come over here and I don't know if you would enjoy yourself here but you may do as you please. Uncle KJ has no house but lives in a hotel and writes in the days in Uncle Wilhelm's office. He has some bananas that he sold and got some money for but he borrowed so much for the war loan but he couldn't keep the money and ended up spending it.

He later moved into a cabin behind WA's office in Mullumbimby, and over the following decades KJ owned land; fifty acres at Goonengerry, another place near Yelgun, high on Chinaman's Hill.

–So you had a vantage point.

–*Yes, a bird's eye view for miles around. I could hide if threatened.*

–Ian Fox gave me photographs of old boots, a stove and pots in rough country that might be yours. You were charged in June 1940 for planting bananas in Yelgun without a permit.

He does not answer.

When I drove my father's cousin through Billinudgel she said in an offhand voice, 'This was KJ's swamp. Once he owned all this area but he was elderly and didn't maintain it.'

Her father Erik Johan Holm sought a property with both hill and lowland for Australia's dry years outnumbered those of flood. He bought two hundred acres at Ocean Shores and with hard work, the land realised an excellent return.

WA decided KJ needed a better home and in 1949 built the cottage behind the Holm farmhouse. There he continued to write, much to the consternation of the family. Annie Holm wrote to Finland on 18 June 1950, about a surprise party to celebrate their parents' fifty year wedding anniversary, and then:

> We have been pumping KJ for more information and we have come to the conclusion that he intends writing a book that will include your life history. He is evidently writing to the different newspapers to see if they would print this book. We are hoping that this will never come to pass. He decided against printing in the newspapers as he thought people would probably burn them the following day and all this must go down in history.

KJ the author, ca. 1920.

In 1951: 'KJ has begun again to plant orchids and has stopped writing so it is much better.'

In KJ's will dated 18th January, 1951 shaky handwriting tells that he has 'very important writing nearly ready for publication if life and health permits it.' He bequeaths £100 to his executor, Stan Robinson 'as a token of good will and in gratitude for all his kindness and friendliness in the past.' But apart from this 'I do not bequeath anything to anybody and it is my desire that my estate shall be kept intakt (sic) until it eats itself out in expenses'—of printing costs. And that:

> ... my executors shall do their best to get my writing before the world of publishers, who would shoulder the labour and expenses in connection with same and pay part of the profit to my estate. But if this cannot be done, it is my desire that my said writings shall be

published by my executors and paid for out of my estate.

How can I locate these latest writings, which he tried with his failing strength to preserve? His niece is most likely to know, but she dismisses it as another fancy.

'At the height of his interest in finance he said that he was going to write a book that will change the whole world. We know that the book that changed the world had already been written—the Bible.'

This will may have been lost or disregarded, for an elderly KJ was coerced to sign another.

A niece wrote in her memoir that KJ 'did have some interest in the Scriptures throughout his life, though he did not apply the teachings to his personal life. Therefore we felt at liberty to send the £3000 from his estate to print Scripture and for evangelistic work in third world countries.'

If KJ told the story of the family, it may have been burned or thrown in the swamp with all the other 'rubbish'. Just as his words were censored in Finland, this pattern was replicated in Australia. He remained an outsider.

In October 1952, KJ was hit by a truck as he walked on the road near Yelgun and left at the roadside. He spent eight weeks in hospital with nine broken bones. The driver was not charged because KJ couldn't remember anything.

Even living near the Holms, KJ the bachelor was solitary. He typed a letter to his nephew Eric:

> Billinudgel, 26th December 1957
>
> Your Christmas pressants (sic) and your C. card are due to hand and I wish to thank you for same. I lead a lonely life and it is only very seldom that I see anyone. But I do a great deal of thinking, and what you have sent me serves as a constant reminder of everything that is worth thinking of in the past, present and in the future. I cannot forget the fact that you were always a good boy from the earliest of your childhood, and evidently you are so still.
>
> With best wishes to Mrs. Back (your wife) and to your children and wishing you all a life of prosperity and happiness.
>
> Uncle K. J.
>
> PS. I am sending you herewith some passion fruit that has grown in my garden.

✱✱✱

I imagine these later years as KJ might tell the story.

> *Carloads crammed with children, who is it this time? One of Will's offspring; they breed like rabbits, taking the Bible literally when it said to come into the Promised Land and multiply.*
>
> *Our steep hill is boggy from rain and slithery with cow manure but that does not deter them. They have travelled a thousand miles on worse roads. It's Aubrey and his eight children, I hope they won't peer in my windows and point and giggle. I crave peace and will shoo the bunny children away. I have little energy to talk. Pestering little peoples make me tired. But one asks for copies of my books.*
>
> *My nieces have baked cakes all morning. Anna Sanna welcomes them for all that she cannot understand when they talk at once and too fast. They admire the garden. Aubrey's wife Helen loves flowers, especially my orchids.*
>
> *Anna Sanna and her family look after me, providing hot dinners that I eat in my cottage. With Christian charity they try to keep me clean even though they avoid my cabin which is crammed with books and papers from floor to ceiling. Cockroaches, silverfish and rats share my reading. All God's creatures are welcome.*
>
> *After I am gone, it may satisfy the family to feed my mouldy papers to a bonfire. I hope they at least keep my printed books.*
>
> *My nephew and nieces offer to drive me to Southport. 'KJ, it's nice waterfront there,' they coax. Anna Sanna stands looking sad near the gate. They insist I must have my outing to the Gold Coast but there is no space for her. We drive on new roads I don't know. At Brunswick Heads, I say, 'Let's swim and eat ice creams then go home.'*
>
> *'No, Uncle, there's a lovely place, right on the river. A lady wants to meet you.'*
>
> *'Ladies don't like me now I have lost my hair and teeth,' I joke. 'Perhaps she is more interested to meet Ted.' But indeed this friendly lady called 'Matron' talks with me about my books and fruit. She shows me her pawpaw tree and a spindly banana stool, her hydrangeas, cannas and gerberas. I say I prefer the exotic beauty of orchids.*

'You have green fingers,' she smiles. I offer her cuttings and information.

'Do stay with us,' she invites and I nod from politeness rather than agreement. It is unexpected that a woman expresses interest.

'Marvellous, that's settled. I'll show you a room which is empty and waiting for you.'

So, I live in that place. The people are friendly and I enjoy a pleasant holiday. The grass by the riverfront reminds me of the still waters of Finland. Will drives down from Brisbane. One time he brings his granddaughter Ruth. I watch her play on the swings and Jungle Jim.

–I remember that Granddad drove me there. I wish he took me in to meet you.

My eyes are poor. I refuse Will's religious tracts. So he reads them to me. He asks 'KJ, where will you spend eternity?'

Have I sinned? People suffered from my failings but I made restitution. How ashamed my family were that I incited priest von Essen. Of my pamphlets, wild moods and bitterness. How my workers suffered when I could not pay their wages. I remember poor Ulf Bexar, his distress that I could not pay wages so he packed his possessions and shipped back to Finland. He died in the war, left a widow and two children. Later I sent a letter to Rolf, enclosing three cheques, hardly enough, but recompense:

'I know Bexar has died but I owed him money, please take this and give it to his widow, daughter and son who are living near Terjärv.'

Rolf wrote me that he had no car but walked to Terjärv twenty miles from Jakobstad. After sleeping the night in a hostel he walked ten miles to Kolamby village to deliver the money. The widow Anna Lisa was overcome with joy that I remembered the debt. Her son Björn Bexar bought a motorbike and became a policeman.

Sofia sent newspaper cuttings about the Uleå Prophesy and how it challenged people to repent and pray, or Finland would again be invaded. Russian troops massed on the border to threaten our land. Perhaps there was something in all this praying and repenting. President Khrushchev withdrew those soldiers and left us in peace. The pressure lifted overnight. A divine power did intervene. Maybe I was counted among those who repented even then, though I kept my prayers to myself. Now I will make certain of my place in the next world, as my brother and sister urge me to do.

Yes, I have sinned, sins of omission and of commission. I have sowed much seed, and I reaped what I deserved.

I felt some peace after I read tracts Wilhelm left, and prayed. There was little else to do.

***

Nurses fuss around with pills and injections. I wave them away. I have lived enough. In my books I set out my creed as 'Give men their due'—for my family gave me little. At last I can forgive them.

Shadows crowd behind the doctors, poised to pounce on me. I hold the bed rail tight. A black crow pecks at me, cruel as a Finnish winter night. Its wings are black cassock; it has the face of Priest Gustav von Essen. My hands shake as I push it away. Birds migrate over the path of the Milky Way; it is imprinted in their genes, as in our family. The soul–bird hovers, waiting to carry me back. Where? I couldn't face return to Finland. Even more I dread the Underworld, Tuonela. I hear the swan sing as it swims around the island of the dead. The warrior Lemminkäinen tried to kill her to win Louhi's daughter, but he was beguiled by her haunting song. He drowned.

–Doctor, he's delirious. Can you give him some medicine? Help him through?

–No, I will not travel over the seas again; it is far. I feel weary. The soul–bird tells me 'You need not fear. I will carry you over the path of the *birds.' But this is my land. Bury me on a Mullumbimby green hillside. Do not take me to Tuonela. The land of the dead is dark and lifeless.*

–KJ, don't leave, I have many questions unanswered.

–*Who is that? Ruth? You go to Finland; I will not. There is nothing for me there.*

Dark Valleys and Green Hills

Death is necessary to give a final touch to our biography.

K. J. Back, *The Concentrated Wisdoms of Australia*

My grandparents lived in the 'Big House' until 1963 when Christina's health failed and she could no longer manage the upkeep of a big home. They moved into the granny flat Gloria and Victor had incorporated into their new home closer to the university in Hawken Drive.

The 'Big House' was rented to the American government and the Vice Consul lived there. Granddad's son Eric wrote:

> There was some talk of selling it to the Japanese Government and Dad turned it down—he did not want their flag on his flagpole! After Mum died and the Americans had moved out, we wanted to sell the house to wind up the estate, but Dad, a good salesman, did not have his heart in it. He had a comfortable lounge chair in the lounge, the only furniture in the house, and he would sit there and think.

Christina's dementia and cancer needed constant care. Eric continued:

> Gloria and Victor did a mighty job, as there was no let up with the workload, and they looked after Dad as well, and he had a mind of his own. They employed a night nurse. In the end I don't think Mum knew any of us, but Dad would talk to her and felt she knew him.

As Christina deteriorated, she was moved to The Chateau at New Farm. WA often visited her and talked on the present and the past.

He wrote on 30 September 1969 that as soon as he walked into her room, 'she seems to be alert and even if asleep she opens her eyes and smiles and gives me such a welcome greeting. Her eyes follow me round wherever I go and as I talk to her she's trying to say something.' But the end was inevitable. WA wrote on his card:

> CHRISTINA BACK
> Entered the Lord's presence
> August 13, 1970, aged 83 years.
> In his presence is Fullness of Joy
> At His right hand are pleasures for evermore.

The funeral was in Mullumbimby, in the little Presbyterian Church the family had attended for years. The family plot is on a small hill. Eric wrote that looking out he could say 'How Green was my Valley.'

Floods deluged Brisbane just before my wedding in 1974. Granddad's Big House, perched high above the river did not escape. His letter dated 8 February,1974 shows how WA found a bright side even in the disaster of the worst flood on record:

> We receive God's blessings daily, but very often we do not seem to realise it fully and give thanks. However when floods, fires and other disasters happen to us we can then see how well we have been cared for in the past.
>
> We are very high up, but when the river could not carry the large volume of water it spread out and sent water in all directions… A rise of another 20 foot drowned everything underneath our office—covered a car, penetrated into the strongroom where office records have been stored dating back 45 years. Many other valuables were spoilt and we had two truckloads taken to the rubbish dump to be burnt.
>
> We are very happy to be on a dry floor in the office and praise the Lord from saving us from a flood on the top floor of this building where our latest records are kept.
>
> All the family sheep stations have had over 30 inches of continuous rain, the gullies and little creeks have become inland lakes and by now nobody can ride or walk over the ground as it is waterlogged. We cannot ascertain how the sheep and cattle have fared but losses could be severe. Fences no doubt have been washed down. We cannot assess our losses until it dries up…

> We can give thanks for our Lord watches over us, and if we submit ourselves to the will of God, all will be well.
>
> All things work together for good to them that love God.

Eric told in his memoir how they took Granddad to my wedding in the hinterland, spending a few days first at their riverside house at nearby Labrador on the Gold Coast.

> Dad was very happy there. He loved the front room looking over the water, and the early morning sun. So perhaps it was one of his happy moments at that time. It was a happy wedding on top of the mountains, with views of the natural country, and with lots of music and birds.

Soon after, Granddad stayed with my parents at Hughenden. My mother Helen wrote:

> He was not, as in former times, interested in anything that was going on and what everyone was doing on the properties, but he stayed in his bedroom, just sitting in a chair with his mind far away. One day he had not been at all well and that evening he sat with breathing so fast and heavy it frightened me. I kept sponging his face as the perspiration was pouring off it and prayed, 'Lord don't let him die, don't let him die.' I knew that the way his heart was pounding it could happen.
>
> The last evening Grandad was with us, Aub said something to him about prophecy and the future for us. That seemed to unlock the key to what was on his mind and for the first time he wanted to talk. He said, 'That's what is worrying me, that some of my grandchildren might not know the Lord Jesus as their Saviour and have to go through the Tribulation and be lost for eternity.'

My father put Granddad on a plane for Brisbane. Arriving there he said: 'It is good to get back to my little bed.' And that night of 2 April, 1974, he was called home to his Heavenly Father, and was with his loved ones again. Eric wrote of his father's funeral in Mullumbimby.

> The Reverend Donald McClellan officiated. He was then Presbyterian moderator for Queensland, but more importantly he grew up knowing us all. His people lived at Wilson's Creek

near Mullumbimby and he could speak with intimate knowledge of my father and mother. There are three graves together now. To the left is my Uncle KJ Back, then my mother and father. It is a peaceful place, the green valley of Mullumbimby Creek with the hills around. I hope it remains that way.

Mr. Busing of Australian Estates Co., Brisbane told Eric 'I had to come, your father was remarkable man, and this is the passing of an era.'

Entering the Promised Land

God said to Abraham, 'Leave your country, your people, your father's house and go to a land I will show you.'

Genesis 12:1

How could the Holm children imagine that half a century later they would possess the land their grandfather Anders asked from God when he first set foot in Australia? When in 1920 they posed for that farewell photograph before emigrating, none had not heard of his prayer on arrival at Bangalow railway station on 17 January 1903. Then, he swept arms wide toward fertile hills and exclaimed, 'So this is the Promised Land. May the good Lord grant to my descendants some of this good land.'

Three of those pictured would be led to own those green acres: Martha, the eight-year old clutching her doll's pram; Ted, the elder of the two lads riding hobby horses (then aged eleven), and three-year old Anne. Flaxen haired Wally on the other horse, would live the rest of his life on his own land at Billinudgel until his peaceful death on 7 July 2015. That morning he announced, 'I am 101 years, four months and 14 days old.'

The Holm family set great store on dates and timing.

The last of the family and only sibling of that generation born in Australia, still lives alone in her eyrie, overlooking the rolling hills of Bangalow. She has spent all her years since her birth in Australia in 1923 in two sprawling white painted wood farmhouses, both perched on hills in this district. The first, which I visited as a child, was at Billinudgel. It was sold for subdivision into the residential estate called Ocean Shores.

The four unmarried siblings signed to buy the Bangalow Barby farm in 1968. They discovered this was God's provision when WA told them of Anders' prayer that God would grant this land for his descendants.

Anna Sanna and her husband knew nothing of Anders' prayer. But four of their offspring would reap the abundance of this fertile land. Three of their offspring remained single and after Martha's husband proved unfaithful she returned to the fold to help them farm and milk cows. They gave hospitality to many single men from Finland. Erik Johan interpreted and helped them find suitable land or jobs.

Eric Johan Holm died in 1955 after a hard working healthy life. Anna Sanna followed in 1964, aged 84. She told her brother Will, 'I am ready to go. I have my trust in Christ as my Saviour and Lord.'

***

Early on a Sunday morning in 2014 I drove south from Brisbane to Mullumbimby, rather too close to the speed limit. I wouldn't miss a special occasion, Wally Holm's hundredth birthday.

After the church service and the blessing from a jovial pastor, all moved to the sunny courtyard where a huge birthday cake was adorned with a doll in the Finnish costume special to Munsala. I nominated myself to sing the Swedish birthday song *Jag, må han leva* (*May he live long, to a hundred years*)—whether the company wanted to hear it or not. The MC looked baffled when I insisted, but Wally had filled his hundred years and it must be sung, even if he was too deaf to hear it. Wally left Finland at age six, and he remembered this Swedish heritage.

After cutting the huge cake, Wally sang *What a Friend we have in Jesus*, ending his speech with 'May God bless you all.' The family invited me back for lunch at the farm where Wally showed his cards and letters, from friends, the Queen, the then Governor General Quentin Bryce (who lived for decades in the Big House, remember) and the state governor. Wally's strength and good spirits owed much to his strong faith and positive nature, and also that he lived in his own home, lovingly cared for by son Lance and daughter–in–law Wendy.

With my iPad I taped more footage of Wally's memories. I edited down a ten–second snippet to include in my presentation at the Institute of Migration in Turku, Finland, three months later. And so I told Wally: 'I will take you back to Finland and people will hear your voice and message.'

Full Circle to Finland

As I looked down I saw the earth spinning around underneath us like a top...
'This,' said the Guide, 'is to be the centre and seat of all future civilisation.'

K. J. Back, *The Royal Toast*

A vortex of energy bears me northwards to Finland, land of my father's father and his forefathers. The resonance in my spirit that drew me across the Gulf of Bothnia on my first visit to Finland pales compared to this new electric sense of significance for my family, past, present and future. It's September 2008.

In the Finnair plane, I jot down my list of questions. Why did KJ never return home? What was the situation back in Finland?

Looking for clues, I open the cloth-bound copy of KJ's book, The Royal Toast, and turn up at a page titled The Settler's Dream.

> I dreamt that I was going in an aeroplane at the rate of a hundred miles an hour, straight upwards for some considerable time, until at last the earth had little or no influence over me.

KJ, even up in the ceiling of the world, you are with me! Are you following me in spirit? The family have a photograph from the time the renowned aviator, Bert Hinkler, landed on the beach at Brunswick Heads; did you write this story after seeing him?

> Then the pilot, who I afterwards learned was an angel, turned around and touched my eyes with my hand, and in so doing he said, 'Behold your little earth.' The scales fell from my eyes, and distance became a negligible quantity, enabling me to see anywhere.

My own plane noses north, weaving another circle around the world. It's so much faster than when Granddad and entourage sailed to Finland in

1924. Eric's photographs and lively commentary flash through my mind. Did he ever imagine, as a fourteen-year-old lad, how diligently a niece would one day pore over his words?

The airline captain has given updates in Finnish, Swedish and English. The last few have been limited to Finnish. Turbulence warnings, I gather. In an emergency I hope he would remember that not all on board speak fluent Finnish. Even after a semester of Finnish classes I struggle to understand. This mix of languages shows I am already in the land of my ancestors; I have a month to unearth secrets, and revelations. And I hope to improve my fluency. The tapes on my mp3 player and computer have only had a small workout; with all the extraneous noise it's hard to focus.

–*You learn the Finnish language even while driving, or flying?*

–Yes. But—maybe I have this from you, KJ—I refuse to arrive in any country and expect them to speak English.

–*Finnish pronunciation is logical. Compare the English words rough, though, thought. If you learn seven words a day, soon you will know enough to read books.*

–So you told Granddad. I would learn 17 words a day, or 70, even those peppered with umlauts. But my head aches and my brain freezes over irregular verbs and those 15 cases with inexplicable names like Inessive, Adessive, Ablative and Allative, Illative and Elative. My respect for the collective intelligence of Finnish people increases when I realise that they understand and extend words endings according to direction and location, inside or outside. And I'm baffled by long words. But the classes helped me progress beyond basic phrases.

KJ's generation didn't speak much Finnish. My earlier visits to family in Ostrobothnia were easier, coming across the Gulf of Bothnia and speaking Swedish. But Swedish is not favoured in much of Finland.

I'm look forward to arriving in Helsinki; I've never been there in earlier trips to Finland—

–*So many trips? How can you afford to travel?*

–It's important to visit your nephew Rolf again. He becomes too frail. And I'm intrigued to hear he has a folder of letters you wrote home.

–*Travel is expensive. I lived a simple life but often struggled for money—*

–Remember, Olavi Koivukangas wrote that you were a successful farmer. But I'll pass your greetings to family in Finland.

–*None are alive who knew me; who still remembers me?*

–KJ, these are family, your descendants—

–*I had no children, not that I know of anyway. You will write this in a book?*

–Your story inspires me. Please help me, KJ? I feel overwhelmed by this task!

A few hours out of Helsinki another jolt of electricity hits me. A movie brings me home before I even touch down on Finnish tarmac, and validates my trip.

I might have dismissed *Colorado Avenue* as some American film except that I note 'Swedish; subtitles.' The screen touchpad transports me to Ostrobothnia of 1905—the very place and time of my family and my research. The opening scenes—Gretchen will tell me—were filmed at Kovjoki railway station and show a steam train similar to the one KJ might have taken south. Those trees and fields might be the same ones KJ saw as he left his home in 1899. Funeral scenes are filmed in Munsala church on whose wooden pews KJ endured long sermons. The cemetery is shrouded in snow as deep and chilling as I remember from my first visit. It's a tale of emigrants to America; Erik Johan Holm spent eleven years working there before his marriage to Granddad's sister, Anna Sanna.

The movie depicts the deciding battle of the Civil War at Tampere, where Edvard fought as a volunteer of the Home Guard. Scenes of smuggling during prohibition days could translate to the ship *Equity* that trafficked arms to fight the Civil War.

The film engrosses me but, towards the end, a new tension emerges: will there be time to finish it before the plane lands? When the captain interrupts to notify the passengers of progress into Helsinki, I resent being thrust a century forward to the present. Will we arrive before the film ends? Ten minutes. Please circle some more.

The closing scene plays as the plane wheels creak down; the credits roll just as the sound system switches to bland relaxation music for landing.

Dazed, I gather my belongings, conscious that destiny has flung a laughing confirmation at me. I am in the right place and that place is my ancestral home.

Ruth Explores 2008

I will sing the people's legends, and the ballads of the nation.
To my mouth the words are flowing,
And the words are gently falling,
Quickly as my tongue can shape them.

Kalevala

Another voyage of discovery circles me around the world from Australia to a Finland speckled with flutterings of gold leaves, of russet carpets mottling the crisp green grass. As the taxi bears me to my hotel, I revel in a season that much of Australia misses. It's that glorious ruska time of birch trees turning yellow and orange and red. How I have missed birch trees.

–In spring their blossoms waft beautiful fragrance on the breezes. And the hanging birch kummer blow like fairies.

–Kummer? What is that, KJ?

–Brown seedpods that hang down and blow away like thistledown.

This is my first visit to Helsinki and I wander the streets and Senate Square, piecing together its history. Here, brutal Cossacks on horseback broke up demonstrations. In the Senate House, on 16 June 1904, Eugen Schauman, the son of a senator, shot three bullets into the hated Governor General Bobrikov, pre–empting other activists' assassination plans. Nearby I see the Governor's Residence where Bobrikov's successor, Ivan Mikhailovich Obolensky, confronted demands of a delegation backed by 20,000 demonstrators in 1905.

The dazzling white marble Cathedral's classical style contrasts with the blue and gold capped domes of the Slavic and Byzantine Uspenski Cathedral. A service is in progress as I tiptoe into this, the largest Orthodox cathedral in Western Europe, opulent in decoration and resounding music.

For lunch I feast on a range of marinated salmon, reindeer, cheese and breads, from the Old Market Hall, opened in 1889. Reinforced by a coffee sipped at the harbour front Market Square, I catch a boat to the fortress of Suomenlinna or Sveaborg. It was built in 1748 after the Russo–Swedish war, as protection against Russian expansion in the Baltic Sea. Tsar Peter the Great had made nearby St Petersburg the Russian capital and this fortress became part of its naval fortification after Russia occupied Finland in 1808. I hum the themes of clarinettist Bernhardt Crusell who was once a military musician in the grass-covered forts, and imagine him in the uniform blue jacket and yellow breeches.

Next day I board a train north to Jakobstad. Cousin Gretchen meets me at Bennäs station just outside the town and drives me to their home with a Moomin playhouse outside. After our first coffee and *bullar*, the sharing of news and gifts, she gives me four treasured manila folders of letters. There is one for each sibling of our grandparents' generation. Her grandfather Edvard noted dates when the later ones were received. His folder contains correspondence about his own attempts to emigrate, thwarted by his untimely death.

Prickles run down my spine to hold letters from KJ, dating from 1899. Some early ones are undated, pencilled scribbles on scraps of paper. Others are pages long and most are handwritten.

Where to begin? Gretchen reads the letters and my fingers fly over my laptop keyboard, to keep up with her translation. My brain races to absorb the pictures of his life, struggles and personality. Sleep is fitful—even though I'm cosy in the attic room that Gretchen's son Jörgen has given up for my visit. He ensured my computer would talk with their broadband, printer and scanner, so these letters can return to Australia with me.

–So, KJ, here I am, in Finland, with all these folders of letters to decipher. Thank heavens Gretchen and her daughter-in-law Pia can demystify the old Swedish and Munsala dialect.

–*What relatives are these you speak of?*

–I'm staying with Gretchen, Rolf's daughter. Edvard was her *farfar*.

–*He was my favourite brother, gentle and sensitive. Edvard loved books. He died young, before sailing to Australia with his wife and child, Rolf who you visit.*

–The letters tell of that. (I yawn.) We'll talk later; I'm exhausted. It's called jet lag.

Next day Gretchen drives me around villages whose names are familiar since I typed up Uncle Eric's 1924 journal from its frayed note book. I can see the places recorded in his photographs. I learn his spelling is atrocious: 'Grassern' is 'Gräsön' and 'Chitton' where they drove the cows daily to pasture is 'Tjitton'.

As with my other visits to my Swedish–Finnish family, all roads on this first day's pilgrimage lead to the village of Munsala, its church and cemetery. The autumn weather is kind. Gold leaves glow in the light and skitter along the lanes like frisky children. Yet I've been warned to wear extra thick layers of clothing, as the farmhouse has no electricity for heating. To make the most of the daylight we set out early. Gretchen has packed a thermos for tea and we buy a sticky bun loaf in Nykarleby on the way. She points to a building, the very bank where Eric photographed the family in 1924.

This reminds me of my own family's more modest three-month tour across Europe. In November 1995 we drove our three sons through the arctic winter in a campervan. On my first visit in December 1976, we did not enter the homestead as Helmi, Sofia's daughter, flinched from strangers. By our second visit in the summer 1978, she had thawed enough to hover at a distance as we stood near the family graves.

> *The first time I entered the house was in 1995 when our boys lined up on the puce-coloured divan for a photograph under the portrait of their great-great grandparents.*

I saw in the barn the very same tools crafted the boat in 1924. There, Gretchen showed me pencil marks on the wall chronicling the heights of my father and his siblings seventy years earlier. I wanted to call my boys to mark their heights alongside but they were engrossed kicking lumps of ice. Their heights might have been similar; my eldest son was fourteen just as Eric was in 1924, my middle son aged ten like my own father Aubrey; our youngest was five. We could not linger or hold up our relatives' busy lives. Rolf gave my sons fifty marks each and they whooped with delight. We hugged our farewells and drove away.

I mulled over that missed opportunity for fifty kilometres wailing: 'I want to go back and mark the heights.' But there are some things that, once the time has passed, can never be recaptured. Seize the moment. Who knows, it may create history.

I writhed for weeks.

Finding Finland

Lo! from our love, shall rise aright,
Thy sun, thy hope, thy joy, thy light,
And higher, once, more full and strong,
Shall ring Our Country's song.

   Johan Ludvig Runeberg, *The Tales of Ensign Stål*

My visit with Finnish family is packed with meetings, discoveries and talk, regaining fluency in Swedish.

How impressive that this cultured area of Finland, Ostrobothnia, produced many superb authors. KJ had fine role models and to dismiss him as an odd village scribbler devalues his talent. Ostrobothnia overall was cultured and Munsala no ordinary parish. It spawned intellectualism, Munsala Socialism and an exodus of emigrants.

The poet Johan Ludvig Runeberg was born in Jakobstad and studied first in Vaasa and Oulu, then in Turku. An excerpt from his epic poem *The Tales of Ensign Stål* has become the Finnish national anthem as *Oi Maamme* or *Vårt Land* in Swedish.

> Our land, our land, our Fatherland!
> Ring out, dear word, oh sound!

Another famous Ostrobothnian author, Zacharias Topelius, was born at Kuddnäs near Nykarleby. Eric's photograph shows their visit to his home.

I enjoy convivial family meals with Rolf and Karin at their cottage by the sea at Pörkenäs. The shore is a jumble of flat and rounded rocks.

We walk through Purmo forests bright with red, yellow and mauve moss. Gretchen's husband Anders fashions grey moss into a moustache and poses for a photo. We climb a steel ladder to the top of the 16–metre high Lostenen (lynx rock) boulder, the tallest 'erratic' bedrock in Finland, moved there by a glacier long ago. I remember Eric's photo taken at this place.

Gretchen points to a small log hut in a forest, that holds a jumble of hay and tools.

'KJ left his haversack in a similar barn to collect on his way to the train station.'

'Or to Monäs Pass?' I am reluctant to dismiss our legend.

Gretchen shakes her head.

Each night I tumble into my bed exhausted, my brain buzzing with information—and questions. Foremost is why Russians hunted KJ to Suez. Because he wrote propaganda?

The director of the Jakobstad museum—who himself played a bit part in the film *Colorado Avenue*—helps me with Internet searches for anti-Russian propaganda of the era, smuggled in from Sweden. We both realise this is futile because the writers would be anonymous. The old florid script strains my eyes, already tired from a morning of flicking through file cards of migrants. The Finnish police department must have records of criminal convictions. But should I search in Vaasa or Helsinki? What do you think, KJ?

He doesn't answer. And I can only do so much…

Around the turn of the century, half the Swedish–speaking population emigrated from Jakobstad, most to America. Finnish–speaking people now dominated the town. In the summers, occasional 'pure Finns' worked in the harbour. Crime, spies and informants to the Russians were rife. Gretchen shows me the 'gossip mirrors' angled on windows of the old houses near the port to allow clear view of activity outside.

Many recycled passports by posting theirs back after immigrating. Or people used the excuse they had lost theirs. Some bribed officials by hiding a rouble note in another person's passport.

Restless through the night, I reach for my notepad to list people to meet and places yet to visit: Jakobstad museum, Kovjoki station, Monäs from where people escaped Finland for Sweden.

KJ, where do you fit in all this?

The Archipelago

If still you hear a raucous cry
Of gulls, sea, skerried shore,
It is the resonance from a world,
A poem-world that's no more.

Arvid Mörne, *Epilogue*

In my late teens when I played music of Sibelius, my spine tingled with the sense of something beyond the dark harmonies. That clarifies when research helps me trace the events in Finland after KJ fled in 1899. The next year came the Language Manifesto, making Russian compulsory in public affairs. In April 1900, the newspaper *Nya Pressen* was suppressed. In *Grafton-affären* Jakobstad author K-G Olin wrote of this era, how out–of–work journalists published short–lived papers with bird names, which were suppressed. After the last went down, Conrad ('Konni') Zilliacus sent a cryptic telegram that 'the devil took the chaffinch!'

Concert tableaux were staged in November 1899 to raise funds for journalists' pension funds. These 'Press Celebrations' were covert protests against censorship. Sibelius composed patriotic pieces like *Atenarnes sång* ('Song of the Athenians', 1899) and *Suomi herää* ('Finland Awakens') which was revised next year into loved tone poem Finlandia.

Zilliacus went on to found the underground paper *Fria Ord* which he published from Stockholm until October 1905. Its flimsy paper was posted and smuggled into Finland and spread by a network of underground contacts; it warned of informers and spies and rallied opposition to Russian oppression.

The Conscription Edict meant that young men who didn't turn up might be deprived their right to study, access to public positions or refused a passport. Informers were rewarded. Fear spread through society. Bobrikov intimidated and divided; he enticed the Old Finns to his side.

My head buzzed with Finnish history. Gretchen offered a welcome respite, to hike twenty kilometres in the Kvarken national park of the Vaasa Archipelago. She lent me walking boots; we are a similar size.

We took a bus to Vaasa and a small motorboat across to an island called Västerö. The guide explained the wash–board moraines caused by the rapid uplift of land when glaciers melted, called post–glacial rebound. This bedrock is ancient, and a maze of low islands formed.

–So you teach me geology of my land?

–Later, I looked on Google Maps–

–What is that?

–Oh, never mind. I saw maps that showed just how close these islands are to Monäs and Udden, and wondered if our family were involved in the subterfuge that these many islands afforded.

KJ changes that topic. Is it still not safe to divulge, even now?

–Did you pick lingonberries? How I miss them.

–I swiped fistfuls as I walked, plump and dark red. Gretchen made *saft* and mousse from them.

–*Finnish winters drag on so long they shrivel our spirits.*

–When I lived in Scandinavia, I loved the crisp new world of snow freshly fallen but after three or four months I craved sun and warmth.

–*That's the problem, such extremes; all darkness and then all sun, and with little chance to shut your eyes against its glare for it burns through the eyelids just the same.*

On the walk we learned how some trees were vital for treating fevers or diarrhoea. Our boat zipped us across seas dotted with boulders, the wind frisking through our hair. A white-tailed eagle sailed through bright skies. My eyes followed the swooping paths of ducks and waders who migrated south from the tundra. Some of them travelled half way around the world. I wondered whether some of them would nest along the shores of Byron Bay. The guide pointed to birds with exotic names; whooper swan, rough-legged buzzards, red-breasted merganser and loons.

'See, those cranes take advantage of the uplifting midday winds.'

He showed us anthills where millions of ants work together and said that, if these were destroyed, so all human society would die. We cooked sausages, just like an Aussie barbeque—but the wind bit chill. We ate on the jetty because I always choose a place closest to the water.

Sofia is Strong

That villain's heart is hardened to the core,
That can a faithful maiden's pleas ignore.

K. J. Back, *The Concentrated Wisdoms of Australia*

I sit on another jetty at Udden where many activists found haven. A 1966 photograph shows Granddad's sister Sofia in this same place, aged 83 years.

She sits on a wooden seat framed by a background of reeds. Her green crocheted shawl and headscarf combat the chill; her hands knot around a walking stick. Sofia looks as if caught mid-sentence, with a half-smile, a knowing look to her eyes.

This woman was nobody's fool. Earlier, in a daguerreotype of around 1890, she was a seven-year old standing apart, chin down but looking up with a baleful stare. Ten years later we see her look direct, confident and fearless at the camera in a class photograph from the Svedberg school.

With the hindsight of a century, I know that within a few years Sofia's life will turn around. How did she cope? Was she always strong and intractable, or inspired by the activist ideas of the Svedberg school? How did she face stigma and pointed fingers, to raise a child in an era intolerant of illegitimacy?

The first time we met, Rolf and Karin commented that they saw Sofia in me. I crop and enlarge her face, see her strength tempered by a wry twinkle. That could be me in decades to come. I am intrigued by her story.

***

Much fell to Sofia's shoulders. She knew herself more able than KJ who was happiest with his head in a book. He did protest against the invaders. When Pappa was away for half a year, taking Wilhelm to Australia, Sofia ran the farm as well as he or KJ ever could.

Understand her position. Two brothers sailed away on the high seas to Australia to make their fortunes. They sent photographs of their halcyon existence in the sun; orange trees laden with fruit. KJ wrote that he only need work a day or so each week; he grew enough passionfruit, papaws and bananas to sustain him. He wrote books, read philosophy and swam in the river all year round. While her brothers feasted on bananas in paradise, Sofia existed on potato and hard rye bread. She shouldered men's work, that of several brothers—and did it well.

Edvard was a good lad, but a dreamer like KJ. And he was seven, too young to protect the horses if Cossacks chose to steal them. Much as her mother chased gypsies from the kitchen with a boiling frypan, she was wary of getting offside with the Russians. Times were tough under Governor-General Ivanovich Bobrikov. To be considered 'untrustworthy' was enough to warrant being sent off to Siberia.

Around this time the family posed for their photograph. WA bubbled with anticipation as migration plans formed. Sofia was nineteen when they sailed in November 1902, leaving her to manage the farm work and make economic decisions. Crop failure blighted the summer; villagers who flaunted the Tsar's dictates were fined or got no assistance to supplement the bad harvest.

Anna Sanna was preoccupied with her new husband and married status, building the new farmhouse at nearby Damskata. Red-eyed, Sofia's mother slumped into a *sorg* after losing another son.

With such responsibilities, is it any wonder that Sofia found respite in the attentions of a man? Sofia ignored the tell-tale signals of his disloyalty, dreaming her fiancé would set her up in a rosy life in Vaasa; marriage, a home for the family they would rear. He hailed from Korsham, on the coast where activism was rife.

In April 1903, while Anders was still overseas, Bobrikov pushed through more dictatorial powers against the activists and deported many dissidents.

Suppression pushed resistance underground. A secret society called Kagal took the name from a similar resistance movement of Jews in Russia, and the name derived from *qahal* or Kahal, meaning a church, association or a congregation. Konni Zilliacus talked of forming an Active Resistance Party. He shipped in contraband propaganda and weapons from Sweden to sheltered inlets and islands of the western coast archipelago for distribution by Kagel activists.

When he returned from Australia, Anders forbad Sofia to help distribute protest papers, *Fria Ord*, around the country.

'Use your energies in the Martha Organisation to uplift other women. Or the *Lotta Svärd*, who support our soldiers.'

Perhaps marriage would steady this headstrong daughter, so Anders quelled his concerns about the man's easy charm and smooth talk. After hours of leafing through his Bible and kneeling to pray, Anders gave his permission. The couple decorated a horse and cart for the drive to Nykarleby to buy gold rings, engraved them with their initials and the date. Sofia carded and spun the wool to make the bridal reins for the white horses that would take them to the church. They were betrothed before the priest.

Shotgun salutes fired through the village as they went to take out the banns. People offered schnapps along the way. Brännvin flowed at the bachelors' party.

Sofia glared at her wobbly fiancé. 'How many marks did you pour down your throats, that we could have put to setting up our home in Vaasa?'

If he could splash money, so would Sofia. When he visited next day, she wore a new silk gown and a frown. 'If you have no smile for me, there are others who do.'

Sofia lifted her chin and snorted. 'Who can smile when you waste money on drink? Have you no idea how much the wedding banquet will cost?'

'And how much money have you spent to prepare for the betrothal and marriage? The white drapes and wreaths, triumphal arches, flags and maypoles cost money also.' Dimples flickered into his cheeks. 'But the Backs are the cream of Munsala, they can afford it. With so many friends and relatives we will need buckets of schnapps at our wedding, to drink *skål* to the beautiful bride.'

Sofia pummelled his chest. 'If you had come to church last Sunday you would have heard Priest von Essen preach a sermon against drunkenness at weddings. You know how he promotes the Temperance Movement, always pushing booklets at us.'

As the wedding neared, Sofia was moody as a stormy sky. 'We must talk,' She twisted the engagement ring on her finger. 'I vomit, even on land. You know what that means?'

The man shrugged. He found much to keep him busy in Vaasa. How could she argue with the excuse that his work served Finland?

Whenever Sofia raised concerns, he picked up his hat and left.

'Why did you not come for Sunday dinner, yet again?' Sofia jabbed a finger. 'Let me guess. Another woman?'

'Who doesn't nag,' he muttered.

'Then you must choose between us. No, I shall choose. I will not spend my life with an unfaithful drunkard.'

'But a betrothal is legally binding; it cannot be broken.'

'It can, if the church gives consent. And you know what Priest von Essen thinks about your drinking. Of course you must return the gifts, the dowry.'

'You would raise a child alone?'

'Indeed I will.'

Sofia learned that no man, whatever his lavish endearments, could be trusted.

***

A lifetime later, the camera catches Sofia sitting at Udden, drawing strength and peace from the water. Often she found solace here when the sharp–eyed scandalmongers noted her shape. Unless she moved to Vaasa or Helsinki with a false name it was impossible to hide. How would she support a child there? Her home and life were in Munsala. Sofia stared the gossips in the eye and sniffed as they slunk away to whisper behind their hands.

Already her stomach swelled when Sofia joined the throng in the market place to celebrate exhilarating news of the assassination of reviled dictator Bobrikov on 16 June 1904. Did Sofia join the protest in Jakobstad market square on 31 October 1905 during the Great Strike? Masses of Finland–resident Swedes marched to the Lutheran church for a meeting. Priest Johannes Arvonen refused to open the door but backed down to menacing protesters.

And so did Tsar Nicholas II in the face of well–organised, disciplined and almost bloodless demonstrations by the Finns. He signed the November Manifesto that returned Finland to the situation before the 1899 February Manifesto—that is, until the second wave of oppression began in 1908. The unicameral Diet was formed and with it, women gained the right to vote and to stand for parliament.

Such events energised Sofia. Adamant that no man might rule her life or gossip dictate her future, she glared down her detractors for she wore an engagement ring when that child was conceived. Her golden rings in their snug velvet lined boxes lay safe in a drawer long after her death.

Two of her brothers were at the end of the world. Edvard married and worked his own farm. After his early death of a heart attack, just forty years old, Sofia shouldered family responsibilities alone, until her nephew grew old enough to help. She owned the Munsala farmhouse, fields and forests.

Sofia raised her daughter in her red wooden house, cluttered with the detritus of departed family.

Like Miss Havisham, she existed in a frozen time warp of deadened hopes.

But Sofia Back could stand tall.

Helmi

Thy blossom, hidden now from sight,
Shall burst its bud ere long.

Johan Ludvig Runeberg, *The Tales of Ensign Stål*

Sofia's daughter Wilhelmina—called Helmi—was born in 1904 on the day after Christmas, that highlight of the Lutheran calendar. Churchwarden Anders grumbled as if his daughter had planned that date to shame him. It made little difference that two months earlier Sofia had reached her adult majority. Age mattered naught to an unmarried mother in a small village.

It suited Anders that the shy little girl should stay close to the farmhouse. Who knew if she might be tempted to stray, as had her mother? At a precocious age she learned to read and to add columns of figures in her head.

'Helmi was very bright, but a little sick also,' Karin told me. 'She was timid, nervy and unstable. When visitors intruded, she stayed hidden, ran in and out of her room as Sofia prepared coffee and *bullar*.'

But I wonder if she was shy because she was made to be—because, being illegitimate, it was easier to keep her away from malicious whispers and crude taunts. Was she held up as an example that girls should not be enticed by smooth-talking men?

Mother and daughter looked similar in photos, but Helmi stood upright, her hands rigid. One shows the child in white ribbons and lace with a straight-lined mouth and grave, direct gaze. The name Wilhelmina means a *pearl* and paid tribute to the brother who left for Australia and to the then-princess of Holland.

Helmi would sit at the window holding the one photograph of her father, so she would recognise him if he came. Reading its inscription on the back ' To the love of my life, Sofia'. She stayed at home, waiting, and watched through white lace curtained windows as the history of modern Finland played out. Events that led to Civil War. Her sharp eyes missed little through the small frames of the windows: north, south, east and especially those facing west towards the Baltic Sea.

Finnish Jägar troops were trained in Germany since 1915. Many were Swedes resident in Finland who had taken the dangerous trek south on foot or skis, or by rail to the Lockstedt Training Corps in Schleswig-Holstein.

Amid fervent nationalism, people memorised and quoted the *Kalevala*. Vladimir Lenin was sheltered in Tampere and he supported the formation of an independent Finland in recompense.

That was granted in 1917 but it took the Civil War to make it reality. This raged between 27 January and 15 May 1918, when Helmi and her cousin Hugo were 14—he was three months older than her and made sure she knew it. The men returned from the recruitment centre to hug their mothers and girlfriends then swaggered off to the Civil War. Some returned, limping, bandages holding limbs together, shrapnel wounds splintered through their once-handsome faces.

Schoolmates enlisted in the Civil War. Of the many thousands who perished, 16 percent were between 14 and 20 years of age. She saw village boys wearing the white armband and in their hats a three-branched shoot of spruce, their blue and gold embroidered insignia marked with an S over three spruce twigs. These marked the *Skyddskår* or *Suojeluskunnat*. The rural central and northern part of Ostrobothnia was the stronghold of the freedom-fighting White Guard.

The Social Democratic Worker's Guards united on 26 January 1918 to form the Red Guard of Finland. They lit a red lantern on the tower of the Helsinki Workers' Hall as a symbol. Red Guards controlled the south, industrial towns like Helsinki and Tampere. They battled to safeguard Russian trains carrying shipments of weapons. The Whites began to disarm and arrest Russian garrisons. One was in Jakobstad.

Helmi watched their women bring in the harvest, dig out the potatoes, tend the animals, for there were few men in the village. The Russian Revolution brought food shortages. Its own citizens were starving, there was nothing to export. Cereals grown in the south of Russia were no longer available. But that was nothing to the famine that would follow the Civil War. There was little time to grieve before Anna Sanna and her husband must emigrate. First, however, they decided their eldest son Hugo, aged 16, should prepare for confirmation. He lived in Sofia's house near the church.

When Hugo planned to return decades later in 1988, Helmi was obdurate that he should not stay with them. She had felt threatened when they had waged their teenage power struggles—and Helmi was her mother's daughter.

Helmi lived life through a window. She dreamed of the day when her father would walk down the lane to the farmhouse, knock on the door and demand to meet his daughter. But he never came. Hope crumpled.

Then an idea formed; studies would open that door. She would move to Vaasa and look for him. There was an address on the back of that envelope that her mother hid in a drawer under the marriage quilt she wove. If finery and good looks meant little to him, perhaps a clever daughter would impress him. Her exceptional elementary school results qualified her for business studies in Vaasa.

At first Anders demurred. No country girls studied in Vaasa. And how would she manage alone? She hadn't been anywhere else.

KJ's ink–splattered letter of 13 December 1919 expressed qualms. Helmi wouldn't learn much that might be useful in her future. The only positive about this idea was that she could come in contact with English. That would improve the chance that Sofia and Helmi would come to Australia, where they would have better prospects.

On 9 September 1920, Edvard wrote to KJ: 'It goes well with Helmi in the school.' KJ wrote on 15 April 1922: 'I am sending you £7 and I want you to split it in the following way; £2 for yourself and your fiancée for a wedding present, £2 for Helmi to prepare for the day when she graduates, and £1 each for Mamma, Pappa and Sofia.'

By 11 July 1922, KJ hoped Helmi had graduated 'and that she can take a break from her studies. I would be glad to hear how she did.'

Helmi excelled in business school in Vaasa. Letters told she was homesick, away from the security of the farmhouse. But perhaps it was more.

Did she find her father? Did he welcome or dismiss her? Is that why she suffered what may have been a breakdown? We can only imagine.

Back to Munsala

But on cold, autumn land the ploughshare's bill and knife
Are clearing in the dead, grey clay a space for green, new life.

Arvid Mörne, *The Ploughman*

Helmi returned to Munsala, to her mother's sharp tongue and bossy ways, but they were comforting in their familiarity. She huddled in her room, rocking, rocking in the chair covered with flowered red and green brocade. She pulled a wooden stool to the window and watched the world pass by. But she only ventured outside when Sofia hounded her to work in the garden in the summer. She read the *Vasabladet* newspaper through line by line, from cover to cover and then over again. Was this a link to her father?

When Sofia berated her for sitting idle, she picked up the unfinished needlework, made a few stitches, and then threw it aside as soon as her mother turned away.

For a few years, routine prevailed. Until in 1924 WA blew a whirlwind of activity through the area when he drove up in his jaunty car, the first seen in the village. He crammed the farmhouse with people; Helmi hovered on the fringe as they welcomed his chic wife and bevy of children. With so many mouths to feed, the tiny kitchen was a frenzy of cooking and dish–washing, much of which fell to her. It was a heady summer of picnics and jaunts to islands on a launch. WA's sons built a boat, messing the barn with tar.

Then silence fell on the wooden house. The gramophone was stored in the attic along with a jumble of broken dolls in rocking cradles and blue painted coffee grinder. The wallpaper bore the sign *Gud beskydda vårt hem* (God bless our home) but it curled and stained with damp.

Unnamed photographs of long forgotten people tumbled out of drawers. Mould festered newspapers, books and devotional tracts. The translations of Australian novels by Ethel Turner. The Singer sewing machine treadle stilled.

Helmi's grandparents shuffled all the slower. Anders died. Sofia insisted

Helmi attend the funeral service, but that was the last time Helmi braved the church—until her own mother's funeral. After Sanna died in 1937, the two women rattled around together in the two-storey farmhouse.

Their female household was brightened by visits from Edvard and his son Rolf. But busy men had little time for coffee. They attacked the farm work with gusto. Rolf, with his cheery ways, was the only one able to keep Helmi in order.

The two women battled over Helmi's clothes. She refused to change, even for washing, or wear the new dresses Sofia chose for her, and shunned the frills and crisp white her mother loved. 'I do not like what you give me.' This was the only way she could stand up to her mother, by wearing the same drab brown and blue. Her stockings drifted down around her ankles.

In the early 1950s, WA visited Europe. He meant well, had sent shiploads of supplies to a depleted Finland that struggled to rebuild after continuous war since 1939. The peace terms of 1944 should have brought respite from fighting the Continuation War. But the Soviets imposed a harsh condition that the Germans must be expelled from the north within two weeks. Guns turned on former allies, who retaliated by blowing up bridges and power stations. They destroyed forests, villages and cities; burned behind them houses and barns in Lapland and lay waste to Rovaniemi.

Russians and Germans left many Finns homeless so some slept in dugouts and tents. Finland must be rebuilt. Munsala fared better than the north and east but five years of food rationing took its toll.

WA's letters, enclosing cheques, seemed to come from another world. One far from the exhaustion, the fears engendered by years of conflict, and the sacrifices that his country people made to meet Russia's impossible reparation payments by the date set, 19 September 1952.

WA engineered for Rolf to bring Sofia and Helmi to Stockholm. There he organised appointments with a psychiatrist to investigate Helmi's 'condition.'

This gave him insights to write yet more letters that advised how they should restore their lives. He tried to understand, but from the comfort of Australian isolation his solutions seemed simplistic:

> The mind has a great effect over our body and when we get downcast in mind, it effects our whole body, and after a while we begin to think we are sick and we have all sorts of ailments, whereas we have brought all that on ourselves just because we have not allowed our mind to take in new sceneries, fresh surroundings and talk to other people, and learn about their troubles and difficulties. If we can help them

out of their difficulties, which I am sure we can often do, we become a blessing to these other people.

The visit was not a success. Sofia had an accident and was miserable with a broken arm and sore face. They both longed for the red painted Munsala farmhouse.

'Once I get home I will never leave again. Travel to foreign places is too hard.'

> Your trouble, Sofia, is that you have left all these trips until you had to go away by force on account of sickness. But it's better to go somewhere when you are not sick and are feeling well.

So WA wrote on 17 May 1954 to urge them again out of their cocoon. He offered to pay for further holidays to give 'some kind of joy.'

> Having been shut up all the winter in one place, in fact a number of years without any break, it becomes like a prison house, and prisoners when they are let out of gaol they are not really responsible for what they say and do. And so it is with anyone who is shut up in the same thing day after day, year after year, and think in only one fashion. He starts to go round and round in a circle.
>
> God wants us to meet other people, to see other places and get interested in something else, instead of just being in one house, one room, one picture and the same furniture, and the same people. It gets very monotonous, and your mind does not develop. Eventually you get that way that you cannot see anything good in this world, which God has created and which God wants us to live in, and to be happy in.
>
> Just say yes, we will have some little outing, at least some *Kaffe Kalase*, also another day we can go a bit further with our experiment. So start this summer, make good use of this warm July and August, and you will come home fully refreshed.

Regardless of this advice, Sofia went alone to worship. Helmi looked out the window when the bell rang from the yellow ochre bell tower that stood adjacent to the stone church. She lived in its shadow, shunning those within it who bruised her spirit.

In 1966 Eric, Doris and his family visited from Australia. The women set a table in the orchard. Helmi joined the meal but photographs show her eyes downcast. When more Australians visited in 1974, she watched through the window. She laughed to see one fall into deep snowdrifts in the cemetery. They trudged around the farmhouse taking photographs. But on their second visit, next summer, she hovered at a distance. She understood English but would not speak with them.

Helmi refused to leave the Munsala farmhouse again, not even to shop in Nykarleby. When Sofia died suddenly at 89 years, it was Helmi who found her. And then, Helmi went to the church—alone—to hear her mother's name read out, as people who died are remembered every New Year.

After the funeral, Helmi pulled out the family records and burned many letters. Apart from her time in Vaasa and final years in a nursing home, she lived 90 years in the farmhouse.

An academic cap lies amongst the clutter in the loft but Helmi never applied her studies. Her acute mind lay waste.

Edvard and Civil War

Then from each black, accursed mouth
The cannon thundered in the South.
And with the sound
The carols drowned
Of peace on earth, good-will to men!

H. W. Longfellow, *Christmas Bells*

Through long nights Gretchen and her daughter-in-law Pia have helped me translate poignant letters from her grandfather Edvard. So my heart feels leaden as we stand by his grave near the yellow wood church in Purmo. The correspondence reveals a sad story of the one who nearly emigrated but was left behind. Fate intervened.

(Gretchen, I notice his name on the grave stone is inscribed as Edward rather than Edvard, why the English spelling? She shrugs. They were interchangeable, as were Vilhelm and Wilhelm.)

So unfolded the predicament of the son who remained in Finland. The one overlooked by visiting Aussie relatives who pay respects at Munsala cemetery. Since Edvard's marriage to Ester Ström in 1922, their farm was at Pertar near Purmo. KJ wrote after receiving a photograph: 'I am pleased to note that your intended has a good face, she also looks very intelligent and will no doubt make a good wife.'

Letters revealed Edvard's plans over many years to bring his wife and son Rolf to Australia.

(So Gretchen, you would also have grown up Australian.)

The Australian brothers urged their family to sell the land and emigrate. KJ might visit and help them move. Or might not.

> I read in your letter that you wish me to return to Finland with
> Wilhelm and his wife but I can't fulfil your wish as I have yet to do

things on my farm. But I hope to be able to travel to London next year to attend an exhibition and then I would like to continue to Finland and come and visit you. (20 January 1914)

Travel plans were stymied by Finland's disastrous Civil War. It was unsafe to write more than pleasantries in letters. No wonder the brothers had little idea of the situation.

My only information about Edvard's part in the Civil War is that he volunteered and fought in that most bitter battle at Tampere in 1918. Was he on the side of the White Army under General Mannerheim, or the Red Guards, who were communists? (Gretchen says Ostrobothnia was strongly White, the Red enclaves in cities like Helsinki and Tampere.)

A voluntary Civil Guard (Suojeluskunta, known as SK) was first raised during the Civil War and afterwards continued to train Finnish youth in athletics and military skills. It fostered physical fitness through track and field events, gymnastics, and utilised skills on cross–country skis.

I noted Tampere as my train from Helsinki passed through it. This major industrial city is situated on a wide river and lakes. My reading and the movie *Colorado Avenue* tell of three weeks' bitter civil war, of Finns fighting Finns, brother against brother, nephew against uncle.

Did Edvard fight in the Kalevankangas graveyard and house–to–house on that worst 'bloody Maundy Thursday' eve of Easter? Like most men who dragged themselves home from war wounded in mind and spirit as much as in body, he bottled tight his memories of conflict.

Finns do not talk much about war. They fight.

Peace gave little respite. People reeled with the aftermath of prison camps and executions, White and Red campaigns of terror, of starvation, malnutrition and Spanish flu. 37000 people died from these various causes. Perhaps Edvard glossed over such horrors, for KJ wrote:

> I got Edvard's letter and am happy nothing happened to you during the war in Europe. In my opinion the fall of Germany in the war was unavoidable. I was surprised to see that such a 'civilised' nation could let itself be led into such a dangerous business. (Mullumbimby, May 6, 1919)

Yet the German Jägar units were Finland's salvation! Australians took the opposite view; their country fought the Finn allies. Edvard's 'alien' brothers were suspect. What an irony that brothers should be on opposing sides, just as Reds and Whites divided families in the Civil War.

A world away in Australia, how could they understand life amongst such bloodshed?

KJ still had his viewpoint, writing on 26 July, 1919:

> According to Finns they have been oppressed under Swedish rule and it is natural that they now think themselves justified to oppress the Swedes. For six hundred years the clergy in Finland has oppressed the lay people. The day will come and not so long from now when the Finnish peasant will in his or her turn oppress the clergy.
>
> Swedish people in Finland are too few to hold freedom negotiations, but that is the Swedes' only hope, and it is possible that they could have their constitutional laws established. It is clearly impossible for Finns and Swedes to melt into one people and if it was possible it would take a lot of bloodshed. In truth the Finnish political sky looks dark indeed and the best you could do would be to move here.
>
> A lot of innocent blood will still have to flow before one's life and property are stabilised. Under such conditions all property will go down in value. On the other side in Australia everything goes up and will continue to rise due to an endless stream of immigrants that comes from Europe.
>
> I hoped that you would have had the benefit of living the

last years in free Australia where there is an eternal summer; where strawberries are ripe all year round and where one can pick fruit in the garden every day of the year. It would also be good to see Edward and Erik Johan on their own properties.

For his part, WA alienated many when he printed and distributed 500 copies of *Seven Men Went Singing to Heaven*. This well-intentioned leaflet told of an incident after the Civil War when Reds were imprisoned under the Town Hall. How a man called Koskinen was converted and started to sing what his Mother had taught him as a child and what he had heard on the street corners from the Salvation Army— '*Safe in the Arms of Jesus.*' Other prisoners were converted.

> And not only the prisoners, but it had a great effect on the other side. The Whites also saw the folly of war and hatred and they found their Lord and Saviour. I am sure you will remember the pamphlet and I thought that this would serve a great purpose. I sowed the seed in my own way and expected a harvest for our Lord and Saviour.
>
> But I found to my great disappointment that it had just the opposite effect on everyone that I spoke to, and this is the kind of reply I mostly got from most of them. 'If you are turning Red by reading these pamphlets you don't want to think that we are going to be as foolish as to turn Red because you sent us this message. I have my belief and you can have your belief, but I am not going to turn Red, no matter how many went singing to Heaven.'

WA's simplistic viewpoint grated on those who lived through the horrors of the Civil War and subsequent Red Terror and White Terror. The heart-warming story fitted WA's mindset, but Finns had little reason for singing.

The Civil War ended. Finland was free. The Promised Land beckoned Edvard.

How could WA understand the tight wedge around Edvard, responsible for his womenfolk in the midst of war? Over the next fifteen years into the 1930s, missives escalated from Australia. His brothers urged: 'Come to Australia, you will have a better life here and live longer.'

I imagine Edvard's quandary.

A World Apart

No rising hill, or mountain grand,
No sloping dale, no northern strand,
There is, more loved, to be found,
Than this—our fathers' ground!

Johan Ludvig Runeberg, *Our Land*, Tales of Ensign Stål

Edvard owned land in New South Wales since the age of eight when Pappa bought allotments for his three sons. KJ once wrote that it would save money for its upkeep if Edvard emigrated. 'If Edvard comes here I will pay him £2 from the first year to feed my hens and chickens and tend the incubator. Put his age as fifteen or else bribe officials to write a false paper.'

As thousands migrated in 1902, there was less secrecy than for KJ's escape. The family expected to join him soon. So Edvard's farewell with Wilhelm was offhand for all that they were closer in age.

KJ was Edvard's hero—even though they lived only four years together in the same house. That cold morning he left, his hug nearly choked Edvard.

'Go to school and learn. It is the path to a good future.' So Edvard attended the Svedberg school when farm work allowed. 'Send some letters to me soon and I shall write back to you with stamps of foreign lands.'

KJ promised a gold penny. Later he wrote that: 'It must have been very difficult for Edvard to wait for that gold penny that never came. I didn't send it as I meant, I have put it on hold until I can find a new one.' Disappointment did not diminish Edvard's love.

Years passed and the memory of KJ's face faded. KJ wrote often in the early years when he needed to borrow money. Or to make excuses why he could not repay the funds advanced. After Pappa died Edvard took over the care of the letters. He noted the date they arrived and filed them in manila folders, one for each of the siblings: KJ, WA and the Holm family. When KJ sent copies of his books Edvard spelled out every word, a dictionary at hand.

WA offered to sail north to help the family to voyage to Australia—he enjoyed organising people. But plans changed. Instead he bought an expensive new automobile. KJ used the excuse of business and that he was seasick most of his voyage to Australia. He gave up any pretence of visiting home.

> I should have been in Finland by now if everything had gone as we planned. But I could see that I wouldn't get you to come here and hence it wasn't necessary to travel that far. It's very sad that I can't convince you to come here as I am assured that poor Europe still has many ordeals to go through.

If only decisions were so simple! Finns must rebuild burned and shelled houses and barns, dig through mined, blackened earth. It would be a relief—but also weak—to escape this crippled country. After Edvard persuaded Ester to marry him, they dreamt of a glorious future together in this warm sunny land. There they could build a house, one with those long verandahs to catch breezes, rather than shut out drafts. They would grow bananas and oranges, cows would eat grass in the open pasture all through the year instead of shut in barns during icy months.

Edvard wrote in April 1921:

> Thank you for the letter and the book. Congratulations to the author. We waited for you to come home this summer but

> we could hardly come all of us. The old ones have no energy to do this. It's difficult to go, to leave my old parents. My farm in Australia is rented out for other people for two or three years still. Try to get someone to help milk.

How could Edvard leave them to face Red reprisals alone?

With his marriage he gained two more dependent women—for Ester's mother was also a widow. Edvard worked night and day to maintain their farm at Purmo and the family's at Munsala. He returned from the horrors of the Civil War only to find it reflected in his own home front. As Pappa's strength failed he gave little support. He sat by the big white stove, puffing clouds of smoke from his pipe. After he died, Edvard was the only man of the family. Mamma clung like an octopus.

'Come with us to Australia'. But Sofia folded her arms and refused to leave.

'Helmi is afraid of strangers, how would she cope?' she argued.

'She is shy because she is shut in the homestead all day and does not meet people. Where better to hide from gossipmongers than in Australia where no one knows her circumstances? Call yourself a widow—so many men died—and both start fresh.'

Perhaps Sofia was tempted by that logic but still she resisted. How could he stand against one who learned dominating ways from their father?

His brothers wrote 'run your own life'. But Edvard had no life away from responsibility, tensions and split allegiances. War gave battles enough for a lifetime. The easiest path was to agree.

Fortune shone on KJ and WA and led them to freedom. They were exempt from burdens of ageing, querulous parents. The duty to serve family fell square onto Edvard's shoulders. A man should leave his parents and cleave to his wife, but the phalanx of three women living alone in the farmhouse defied even the Scriptures. WA's marriage also created needs to support a wife and children but he chose that responsibility.

Edvard accepted his role to support and nurture others. It was a joy to hold and rock a baby son and to steady his first toddling steps, hear a delighted cry 'Pappa' when he rode home into the stable.

There was little chance for books and music, tending two farms divided by a seventy-kilometre horse-ride through a wasteland of snow and ice, the trees as bare and numb as his feelings. The Purmo farm was all too far and yet too close. That space of journey between farms was his only time for reflection. His horse Pelli knew the way so well she needed no direction even in black mid-winter.

Voices elbowed through his mind. 'Edvard, the potatoes must be harvested now!' What of his own harvest? Or 'Come and fix the fences, they are hard work for women alone.' He sighed for his own crumbling fences, saddling up Pelli yet again.

Teeth clenched tight, his gut churned, thoughts boiled and fermented. No one dared tell Sofia Back what many thought; that since Pappa died in 1926 she took on his mantle. His domineering ways were multiplied in her. Mamma might play peacemaker but she slumped in her own valleys of grief.

There was no escape. Women surrounded and tugged at Edvard. Rolf was too young to share such burdens, though sharp eyes noted his Pappa's sagging shoulders.

Another letter arrived bearing Australian stamps. WA's words scraped like a bayonet over bloodied open wounds. As usual he extolled the wonders of Australia. In his ignorance he belittled Finland and the effects of the Civil War, efforts to bring life back to normal. What did WA know of hunger, with his fleshy face and podgy stomach?

The Finns were confronted at each step by the homeless, the maimed, and the grief-stricken. Did WA travel to Finland and help rebuild the flattened and burned towns and bridges? Would he get his hands dirty sowing potatoes in charred fields or risk his life in that bitter warfare, fight alongside his brother? Could he imagine gagging as one fired at other humans, knowing murder to be the price of freedom? There was no room for fancy pacifism then.

Instead, WA wrote about yet more riches he amassed, more land and sheep. He lamented wool prices, droughts and blowflies. KJ wrote about birds of all colours of the rainbow, the parakeets, cockatoos and rosella.

The dark swan of *Tuonela* awaited Edvard.

While Edvard toiled to bring income to the village through the butter cooperative, WA offered advice. He left home at sixteen years of age but he pretended to understand earlier Pappa's venture, which happened long after. He claimed to be privy to the experience that 'evidently' Edvard was too young to remember anything of—his organising and building a co-operative butter factory, sawmill and flourmill combined.

> It was something that would be of great benefit to the whole community, and truly Father put his best foot forward to make it a success, but in return he only got ingratitude and abuse, and even some of his best friends became jealous of him so you do not wonder that he got tired of it and gave it up.

Pages later, WA asked about Edvard's health under all this strain. He suggested he take less interest in the business; its efficiency might drop but better than to worry about everybody's welfare. 'You would be able to give more attention to your own home, to your own relations and to yourself.'

WA sang the old refrain, unaware his letters lobbed in the household like unexploded mines awaiting an unwary foot. 'Come to the Promised Land, you will be healthier here, you will live longer and die richer.' Sell the land—their heritage, where so many memories were embedded in each stone, each sod of earth.

After each missive arrived, Mamma took to her bed, fearing Edvard would desert her. The guilt was unbearable. How could she forget the faithful years he stayed steadfastly nearby, riding to Munsala to rake her hay, shear her sheep and plant her potatoes?

Sofia worked hard on the land, but she still found time to waste money buying fancy dresses in Nykarleby. Never mind Edvard had his own farm and wife and son; if she crooked a finger he must come running. Otherwise, her eyes froze worse than midwinter in the Arctic Circle.

Two sons and a daughter had left Sanna for the ends of the earth. Her husband decamped to Heaven. This remaining son must fill all those shoes at once, even those of children dead many decades. Edvard felt like a centipede paralysed by the fear of taking a wrong step.

Big brother Patriarch tried to pull puppet strings from the end of the world. He sent carbon copies of his letters to the Consulate, to Thomas Cook and Sons, arranging passage, whether they chose to emigrate or not.

Pressure weighed on all sides: from WA, from Sofia. Ester said little when Edvard harnessed Pelli again to head for Munsala. Her slumped shoulders told all. He even felt Pappa's disapproval from the grave if a harvest yielded lower than he might have reaped. Edvard's heart compressed. He gasped to fill his constricted lungs.

So Near to the Promised Land

Be still, my soul: The hour is hast'ning on
When we shall be forever with the Lord,
When disappointment, grief, and fear are gone,
Sorrow forgot, love's purest joys restored.
Be still, my soul: When change and tears are past,
All safe and blessed we shall meet at last.

Katharina von Schlegel

WA arranged passage for the family, shutting his ears to their qualms about travel. Sofia refused to leave Finland. Ester fumed that Wilhelm made decisions where they should live and work, not knowing her or her abilities.

> I feel sure that we can give you and Ester something light on one of the stations, where you will gradually build up to normal health again. By that time you can choose for yourself what you will take up.

Thomas Cook booked two cabins, advising that 'Persons of the opposite sex above the age of twelve are not to be berthed together unless they are man and wife.'

Mamma was adamant against emigration. 'Who would lay flowers and candles on your poor Pappa's grave on All Saints' Day?' she whimpered like a wounded animal caught in a bear trap. She fretted about lying alone in a grave the length of the world away from the bones of her husband.

At WA's bidding, business people and government officials wrote a torrent of letters to offer assistance. Schwartze, Buchanan and Co. organised things as if Edvard were a child incapable of managing his own affairs.

26 July 1935

> A letter received from your brother informs me that you intend to come to London in September with your wife and son. If that is the case, would you please let me know so that someone may meet you at the railway station. We have no one in the office who speaks Swedish but several of us can speak French and German. They would be pleased to delegate someone to show something of the city.

Each visit to Mamma and Sofia, their weeping and sulking and dramas weighed like lead on Edvard's heart. Stabbing pains shot like burning comets up his arm.

Edvard folded over the back of a chair trying to ease his skittering heart. Ester cried, 'Rolf, saddle the horse to the sled. Quick, boy!'

She laid Edvard on furs and warmed his hands during the bucketing ride to Nykarleby. Doctor Hohenthal sighed. 'You need more tests. In Helsinki.'

Edvard shook his head. He must hoe Sofia's northern field and plant her potatoes before the ship sailed.

The doctor jabbed a finger. 'You must rest. Put yourself first in this equation.'

Ester cried 'Consider yourself for once—and your wife and child.'

Any travel, even within Finland, drained all his energy. Edvard had little enough.

***

> 20th September 1935
>
> Dear Sir,
>
> We have to thank you for your letter of the 15th instant, from which we note that owing to ill health you are not at present able to proceed to Australia, but it is possible you may be able to sail next spring.
>
> We are therefore advising our Brisbane office asking them to pass the information on to your brother.
>
> Yours faithfully,
> Geo. Thompson Limited, Aberdeen and Commonwealth Line

It helped to delegate the breaking of this news to a third party. Edvard need not communicate with WA. He would only pester them to undertake the journey and not inconvenience his plans.

After today's explosion, Edvard was too weak for arguments. Sofia had demanded that he assist with haymaking—as every year before. For the first time in his life, he spoke aloud words that long ran like a rat on a treadmill through his mind.

'No, I will not, Sofia—for you have drained me of my last ounce of strength!' He slammed the door with a satisfying bang and hastened to saddle Pelli.

She shrieked, 'How dare you speak to me like that?'

The reply came like a roar: 'I dare because I have nothing to lose but my life!'

Too weak to lift a pen. He lost all will to write. Or to live.

Let me rest. In peace. In my own bed. In my own land.

***

November 1935:

Ester's tears splotched the writing but the date was clear—15th October. If WA realised how serious was Edvard's condition, would he have stirred himself to write sooner? His words rubbed salt into grief.

> I have your letter of 22nd August and I am very sorry to hear that you have been so sick, but I sincerely trust and hope that you will recover your normal strength, as I feel sure that the Australian climate would be beneficial for you. And not only for you but for Ester and Rolf also.

Her eyes flicked through pages about his business dealings, concerns and expeditions across the country. He saved effort by writing one letter to all of them ('Dear Edward, Ester, Rolf, Mrs. Strom, and all Loved Ones at Purmo').

About the postponed trip WA said he 'can well picture how you would feel after making all the preparations to come but something tells me that you will be able to come out yet, so therefore work to that end, have that as your main objective.' He didn't want them to think he belittled Edvard's illness and all their concerns. As always, he simply saw their crisis through his own eyes:

> I can only say that I feel sorry, as I know what it is to be ill. I had a little taste of that, especially when nerves give way, and you feel so despondent that you cannot see any good in anything. But when a person gets in that state he is not responsible for what he says or does, and knowing all this so well, I am trying to pick the brightest and best out of a

> proposal, and that is to encourage you to cure yourself.
>
> The biggest trouble is to just get away, as it seems to be a strain to break all the ties. As you get strength you can build yourself up for the journey to Australia.

This played the well–worn record; make up your mind to venture into the unknown; the world is very small now, and once you start to travel it is only a matter of a few weeks and it is all over. Then that same chorus:

> You will be able to get into the 'Promised Land' and I hope that it will give you the benefit of all that you expect. In fact, I am sure it will. You will build up in health, you will get a new lease of life, you will start afresh in a new land, and Rolf will be able to learn the English language well and his future will be so much more assured. So just have faith and everything will come out well.
>
> Pleased to say that we are all well, and we sincerely pray to God that He will restore you to normal strength again.

Why did God not answer that prayer? Why did he allow Edvard's strength to drain? His mere forty years were too few! The choice that taxed Edvard was taken from him. Now he rested forever in his homeland.

WA penned a homily on October 17. Two days later her husband, the most caring man a woman could ever hope to live alongside, gasped his last breath. WA wrote again on October 27:

Dear Ester, Mrs Strom and Rolf,

> I don't know how to write this letter, it's so hard for me to express my thoughts. We were unpleasantly surprised here on Mullumbimby on 19 October when we got the cable 'Edward died, 4 a.m. funeral held on October 27'. I wrote him a long letter on 15th but I didn't have time to mail it. Edvard is not among us anymore and his spirit has ascended to heaven. He wrote to me on August 22nd to tell me that he never thought he would see the Promised Land.

Alone in the matrimonial bed, Ester huddled into her pillow to muffle sobs. Rolf must not be disturbed. He'd had enough sorrow.

WA's letter turned grief into bitterness.

But Ester stood up to Edvard's family. She insisted that he would not be buried alongside his father in the Munsala graveyard. He belonged in the cemetery behind Purmo's yellow wooden church, close by his wife and Rolf.

Edvard would not go again to Munsala. Ester forbade it.

Before he died, Edvard beckoned to his wife, his voice faint as a wisp of cloud. Her hair mingled with his, cheek resting against his cold, parchment skin.

'Tell me again, my love.'

He forced thin ribbons of sound through his throat. 'On gravestone–'

'No, love, the doctor has given us a stronger medicine. Stay with me and Rolf!'

He shook his head. His voice faded.

'Write my name English. Not Edvard. Edward.'

David and Goliath: Finland Vs. Russia

A powerful winter army
Of white, shimmering splinters
Is scattered, to vanish in the waves of the sea.

Z. Topelius, *Ice Breaking on the Oulu River*

Sandwiched between two invading countries, Russia and Sweden, Finns were catapulted into and out of wars they did not seek. They merely tried to protect their boundaries against a Goliath who threatened them time and time again. Finland had the longest border with Russia. Independence was hard-won and treasured.

KJ, how can I write about Finland and its turbulent battles, invasions and occupations? I can't comprehend such bruising fighting, the cities and roads bombed.

–And burned. You are blessed to have lived all your life in peace and freedom.

–Australia has never been fought over, since Captain Cook discovered it in 1770 and the British settled it from 1788 with their convicts. Indigenous people call that settlement an 'invasion'. Darwin was bombed in World War 2. Otherwise, we escaped full-scale war on our territory.

–*But Australian soldiers enlisted in world wars. Many never returned.*

–It feels presumptuous to try to write about the Finnish struggle for peace and independence. But my sons should know the strength of people from whom they came.

–*Their veins pulse with blood from survivors, people who might be knocked down but crawl back up to rebuild. Sisu.*

—And if you'd stayed home you would have built with them. Finns have struggled back with initiative, tenacity and enterprise to lead the world in education, design and technology.

Life has not come easy for the Finns, the valleys they traversed are deeper and tougher than any I have experienced. I have not lived in their skins.

However, I am tenacious in my research. I access books and attempt to read the Swedish, enlist friends to help translate the more difficult ones. With such help I face a doctoral thesis about Munsala Socialism. I download articles from the web while conscious that their veracity has limits. And for Finnish articles I must often rely on the dubious Google Translation.

After watching a film about the Civil War I squirm sleepless in bed. What can I write that will do justice to this? I make a cup of tea and Skype Gretchen's mother Karin. She thinks my Swedish is better than its reality so speaks quickly and in dialect. Sometimes I must check words to understand her meaning. I restrict my calls to Gretchen to weekends, careful of her time and work deadlines.

A family photograph shows Rolf with his parents Edvard and Ester. He looks to be about five years old. Within seven more years his father would be dead. I imagine his mother kept Edvard's memory alive with tales of his bravery.

'Rolf, your father hated fighting, but he fought in that crucial battle at Tampere, which was the turning point to victory and expelling the Russians. Otherwise, you might be speaking Russian now, forced to send your crops to Leningrad—no better than a serf.'

There was a strong pacifist movement in Munsala. Edvard rode there weekly to help his sister with farm work; he knew the radical ideas that fermented there. Was Edvard tempted to join this? Was Rolf? KJ, you could tell me?

—Neither fought in the Winter War. Edvard died six years before and Rolf was too young. But the unfair Peace Treaty created a latent time *bomb that was bound to explode soon after—*

–You mean they annexed Karelia, heartland of Finnish lore.

–So it was inevitable there would be more bloodshed—the Continuation War.

–And Rolf fought in that. He said his aunt Sofia—your sister—offered to help him escape to Sweden.

The Munsala Peace Society was the largest one in the country in the years before the Winter War and during the Continuation War. They shielded many deserters who hid in the woods, called forest guardsmen. A hub was the hamlet of Storsved and the Svedberg School which spawned progressive left ideas, and this is where Sofia studied.

I huddle under a rug through a three-hour DVD about the Winter War, so gruelling that I long for it to finish—and that was from the comfort of my lounge chair, not a dugout hole in an icy ground. I cannot comprehend living three months in temperatures around –40° winter, dodging bullets, mines and bombs.

History repeats patterns. As I type these words, television bulletins are rampant with the G20 conference hosted in my home city, Brisbane. Amid outrage that a Malaysia Airlines flight was shot down over the Ukraine and accusations of Russian involvement, many wanted to exclude President Vladimir Putin. He does appear, accompanied by attendant warships nearby at sea. Then-Australian Prime Minister Tony Abbott's vow to 'shirtfront' him brought a memorable concept to international diplomacy. 'Koala bear' diplomacy eased the tensions; Putin smiled for the cameras while cuddling a koala. He pronounced his hosts efficient and friendly but fled from the heat. And so Australia had a small taste of what Finland experienced for generations.

KJ, help me understand how the Winter War ran into the Continuation one. Or why.

–Take a step back to September 1939. The Soviet Union flexed its muscles with demands that would escalate into war. They insisted that the Baltic States and Finland allow Russia to establish military bases and station troops on their soil.

–I read that the Finnish government refused to cede their Karelian territories to Russia or to allow a Russian base near Helsinki. But on 30 November 1939 the largest army in the world attacked the Finns, who were outnumbered by the Soviet juggernaut: 450,000 men, 2000 guns and about 2000 tanks.

—But they underestimated Finnish Sisu. Just twenty years before, in 1918, they bought independence through the bloodshed of bitter Civil War.

—Knowing Russian repression, all rallied to fight against its return. If you'd stayed in Finland you might have fought also, been buried on home soil?

—Perhaps. The Soviets just followed orders from their superiors, could not think for themselves against tactical obstacles. Their only motivation was to avoid punishment, even execution, if they failed.

—The Finns were unprepared for tanks in battle but soon developed ingenious and daring tactics. Their decisive leaders encouraged resourceful men in the ranks. Long columns of Soviet tanks became bogged down along narrow single–track roads in snowbound forests. Strung out over long distances, small groups of vehicles were isolated and open to attack by Finnish troops. But KJ, what is Motti?

—You know Finns and timber. The word means 'firewood just waiting to be burned' and refers to how we measure firewood, a cubic metre of cut timber. And how resourceful Finns grasped opportunities; they surrounded and attacked the most vulnerable trapped Soviet units first 'Motti', harassed them for a day or more, so they could not eat or sleep.

—The Soviets wore thin clothes and thousands froze in the winter temperatures.

—Our men isolated the stronger pockets, sowed confusion then moved off to attack another Motti before the Soviet troops had a chance to regroup.

—Finns were well equipped and wore warm white camouflage so they could ski in to infiltrate into Soviet lines before opening fire. As Rolf did.

—They burned towns, bridges and crops, to stop the Russians from taking them. They were fit, their snipers legendary, well–trained through the youth groups and Jägar service. They inflicted heavy losses on the invading Russians. But however skilful, our men were too far outnumbered for outright victory.

I struggle through a military book, lost in maps detail which platoon or army flanks what artillery. The last chapter describes the truce on a sunny day of 13 March 1940. For the last few hours before 11 a.m. in Finland the soldiers made a last-ditch stand to kill as many as possible.

> *–Many women were widowed in that short time.* (KJ's knuckles whiten.)

> *–They were so worn from fighting, the country divided, that they welcomed any Peace Treaty to end the Winter War. But it did not last, for it sowed more latent turmoil.*

> *–Finland risked total annexation, and paid a high price to avert that; 13 percent of its economic capacity. A sore point was to lose an eleventh of its land—Karelia—to Russia. It was bad enough to lose their land, but the Russians also insisted that within ten days, 420,000 evacuees had to be repatriated in Finland.*

The cease fire brought surreal silence. And birds sang.

How do birds cope with warfare when exploding mines trash their forests? Do they huddle their heads under wings and pray that their tree will not be smashed and mashed by the tanks? perhaps they desert their nests and flee, mute with fear. Or do they sing in defiance of the mayhem, but the barrage of machinegun fire, shells and grenades, deafens all ears?

As the 'mouse tip' green shoots liven the birch trees, do they celebrate spring regardless? Do the Whooper swans beat their wings against the winds as they cry for the destruction caused by war?

> –When I played *Karelia Suite* by Sibelius I had no idea what lay beneath the notes.

> *–Australians cannot imagine the pain of losing our home.*

The Continuation War

Never can the hero falter
All his grief is put behind him.
Gentle tones from his remembrance
Bring him home and lighten sorrow.

Kalevala

There was little respite to rebuild houses and sow crops after the Winter War. A few months later, Finnish men donned uniforms for the Continuation War. Rolf Back was 17, too young for call–up when the Russian offensive began on 25 June 1941. Finnish soldiers pushed to Lake Ladoga and Viborg and retook the land of the 1939 border by 2 September 1941.

Rolf was torn between an aunt who encouraged him to escape to Sweden and a mother who said 'If you go, you are no more my son.' He risked losing a mother, as well as a father. Unknown irony lay ahead of him; thirty years later his mother, aunt and uncle would all die in the same month.

On 19 January 1942, Rolf walked to his home village of Purmo to enlist with his friends in the famed Jägar Infantry Regiment JR61. This recruited the most fit, able men and equipped them with bicycles or skis according to the season. The four elite Jägar battalions formed when Finns fought with Germany during the First World War in 1915. After the armistice, veterans returned to Finland and became the nucleus of the new Finnish army. Their reputation for toughness and peak fitness took them wherever the fighting was heaviest. They acted as storm troopers and

undertook many of the long-range reconnaissance and sabotage forays into Soviet territory behind the enemy line during the Continuation War.

Karin produces a map of 1940s Karelia and Russia and points to areas where Rolf fought. She points 'that name is familiar, he talked of that.' I highlight Teeri Syväri. But I become lost in variable Swedish, Finnish and Russian place names. This map is in Swedish and my atlas shows Russian names. I know Viborg is Viipuri, but what is Petroskoi now? St Petersburg?

Australia and Germany were foes through two world wars. But Finland's relationship with Germany veered back and forth, more often allies except for the Lapp War of 1945. During the Civil War, Finns were wary of Germany as an ally of the Soviet Union. Then Adolf Hitler planned an assault on the Soviets. He invited Finnish officers to coordinate Operation Barbarossa. Germany took responsibility for the 500-kilometre Finnish Lapland front and in secret sold arms to Finland.

−KJ, you corresponded with many Finns and those piles of newspapers in your shack kept you up to date of the encroaching war. You know the impossible demands made by the Soviet foreign minister Vyacheslav Molotov. That the Finns resisted granting a mining license at the Petsamo nickel mines but could not resist the use of Finnish railways to transport Soviet troops to their base at Hanko?

−*Like pawns on a chessboard, Finns were pushed further to the edge until cornered. Soviets made them destroy their own Finnish fortifications built in the Åland islands.*

In Helsinki, I visit an exhibition of the bombing of Helsinki between 1939–1944. An ingenious air raid defense minimised damage. The Finns built a fake Helsinki next to the real one and built bonfires to fool the Russian bombers! Fighting began in June 1941 and by the end of September the Finns regained the land from a line just past the former border.

Rolf was one of the Jägars who held these lines. He took patrols over the border to blow up tanks, fuel and wage guerrilla warfare. After his bullet wound healed he returned to the front and helped stop the Russian offensive at Tienhaara in Spring of 1944.

Sofia urged Rolf to escape to Sweden over the Monäs Pass. He wrestled with his moral dilemma then said 'I'll go back to the war.' The wording 'back to the front' indicates that this was after he was in hospital with scarlet fever, or else the second time when the bullet was removed from his knee. When he already knew first-hand the horror of life in the '*Korsu*' bunkers and trenches, dug into the ice.

The bunker was a hive of young men on the brink of their lives, existing on charged adrenaline where fight was the only option, for flight brought death. Deserters were shot by firing squad. But they had seen enough slaughter already—on all sides.

On 9 June 1944 the Soviets fought back with a major offensive in the Karelian Isthmus and around Lake Ladoga. Fierce battles broke through the Finnish lines. With reinforcements from Germany, the Finnish army halted the Soviet in early July but lost the hundred kilometres gained to bring them back to the borders of the end of the Winter War.

Rolf was amongst those who stopped the Soviets at the Battle of Tali–Ihantala even though outnumbered in manpower, tanks and weapons. Exhausted, the nation craved peace, and to rebuild and to replant crops.

After a poor harvest in 1942, many died of starvation. An armistice was brokered in 1944. KJ, Tell me more, please.

> *–Commander–in–chief, Carl Gustav Mannerheim was made president with the brief to secure the best possible peace terms. The cease–fire ended military action on 4 September 1944, and a day later the Soviets stopped fighting. The armistice was signed on 19 September. But this peace was troubled.*

> –Russia demanded impossible concessions of Finland.

> *–The Finnish army must expel all German troops within two weeks then be demobilised.*

> –Imagine the feeling of impotence, to disband one's army when living next door to Russia! Even if those remaining men were exhausted and wounded.

> *–As the Finns could not meet the deadline, they were forced to fight the Germans, their former allies, in the Lapland War.*

> –Another war, KJ! With no respite of peace between.

> *–The Finns had always insisted they fought as co–belligerent with Germany to protect themselves and regain their territory. They stated they would only fight the Soviets as far as was necessary to regain the territory ceded by the 1940 treaty.*

But in spite of being the aggressors who started the war, the Soviets demanded enormous reparations, and though negotiations reduced these by half, they insisted payments should be at the 1938 rate. This constituted half of Finland's annual gross domestic product in 1938.

After the peace came the mammoth task to rebuild. The Finns were impoverished, but rich in *sisu*.

Hero Rolf

How pitiably small seem human griefs,
The sea and sky sublimely spacious.
A solitary boat. At the tiller, a solitary man.
With nothing more to win or lose.

Arvid Mörne, *A Boat in the Bay*

When I went to Finland I hesitated to ask Rolf intrusive questions but he opened up to tell stories that may have been bottled up for half a century. He shared war memories and sang Russian songs for my camera.

Of all the Australian visitors, I heard what many others did not. Rolf and Karin decided to give me the parish records and help me decipher them into a family tree. They entrusted to me the folders of letters and helped me translate the Munsala dialect and old Swedish. Perhaps this was because I visited with ever increasing knowledge of their language, instead of expecting to speak English, or because of my passion to understand our culture and heritage.

When I lived in Sweden I faced the ski tracks—and faced my fears of falling and letting go. As a child I would hold on when going down a slippery slide, and avoided water slides. But who could live in the north of Sweden, woven by ski tracks, without donning skis? Two-year old children zoomed past on tiny skis as I picked myself up again and again. I came to enjoy it, and managed modest cross-country slopes but blanched at the prospect of slalom.

Antoni and I celebrated our wedding anniversary picnic on a rug near a floodlit track. We ate marinated herring on hard bread and toasted each other with champagne as passers-by threw startled glances behind. Decades later, when we visited Australia's Snowy Mountains, I had lost my skill; forgotten to bend my knees, backside out. I spent most of the time working out how to drag my splayed limbs upright.

So I am in awe that Rolf fought in this crack unit, the Jägars—on skis!

He went on thirty patrols over the Soviet lines into Russian territory, wearing a white camouflage cape.

It was an adventure, that first spring of 1942. They flirted with the Lotta Svärd women of the voluntary auxiliary, looking as dashing as drab grey uniforms allowed; people respected their Jägar collar patches, green with a gold frame. A chinstrap held their peaked visor cap. They jaunted off to war on bicycles through forests, determined to retake the Karelian Isthmus that the Russians annexed after the Winter War.

During winter, 'Ski guerrillas' operated as small squads or platoons and included top class skiers and peak fitness athletes. They were trained for clandestine operations and took 50 patrols in 1943. The following year they undertook nearly a hundred missions. Some went to sabotage the Murmansk railway.

Soldiers drew cards to decide who would go on each sortie into enemy territory. 'The first time I drew a card,' Rolf said, 'but not again. I went free will. I don't let a card tell me when I should be killed. I choose it myself.'

Amongst the books, letters and memorabilia of the war, is a pack of cards.

Concoctions of chicory, dandelion root and weeds made poor substitutes for coffee. Rations were sparse, so they ate what they could. After the war, a relative who took Rolf to a Stockholm restaurant consulted on what he would order from the menu.

'I have eaten boot leather,' Rolf shrugged. 'So I eat anything.'

Karin shows me the alarm clock that Corporal Rolf carried all through the war, tied to his knapsack, or beside his bunk in the dugout Korsu. It now sits on the mantelpiece of their seaside cottage at Pörkenäs.

Any soldier who battled on the Karelian border with Russia must retain dark memories. Finns fight to the last man, will shed every last drop of blood for they know too well their enemy—Russia. In their underground bunkers at night, their commander Harry Järv studied and encouraged others to do so, poring over books sent by his schoolmaster from Vaasa—to take their minds off the horrors of the day.

A documentary describes the bitter battles on the isthmus of Karelia that formed a thin bridge to Russia. If this 'lock' gave way, Helsinki and all of Finland fell. If the River Svea was lost, so was their country. Rolf spent much of his time behind enemy lines.

'I had a machine gun.'

Although Germany helped with armaments, those were often insufficient against the Soviet might of tanks and aircraft. Many Finns supplied their own weapons or were assisted by their community. What they lacked in weapons and anti-tank weapons they made up for with ingenuity. They improvised

TNT charges packed inside a sheet metal box, with a wooden handle and a fuse system. They made 'Molotov' Cocktails from glass bottles filled with flammable liquids and a simple hand–lit fuse. This lethal weapon became a symbol of the Finns' courage in their fight for survival. The name was a joke against Stalin's foreign minister.

In June–September 1944, the Red Army struggled through obstacles of rivers, lakes and thick wooded forest of the Karelian Isthmus. They lost almost 600 tanks on the Finnish front in ingenious tank traps.

Rolf tells humorous stories of patrols with boys from Purmo and of a man from Munsala, who stepped on a mine. His foot was blown off, hands fractured. This man visited him in the last weeks of the war.

'Back' he asked, 'do you believe you will go again over to Karelia?'

'Yes, I shall.'

'Bring my best greetings to the rest of my leg. I remember my foot often.'

'All right, I'll do it.'

Years later I will sit in a Noosa coffee shop with a Swedish friend as she helps me translate more of this story. I discover that Rolf downplayed his own bravery. A book [5] tells of a nine–man patrol into No Man's Land on a cold clear winter day in 1943. They knew the terrain from summer exploits. Two stayed watch and seven moved closer. Their Swedish leader, Malte Erikson chose to go alone to blow up the Russian camp. As he returned to the waiting comrades a mine exploded. Malte's comrades bound his leg so he would not bleed to death. Rolf tied two pairs of skis together and hauled Malte back through deep snowdrifts to the medical station.

'The real hero was Harry Järv,' Rolf says. 'He went on 189 patrols.' And the Soviets offered a reward of three million Finnish marks for another famous raider Lauri Törni.

Rolf was wounded in the knee, not by enemy fire but an accident with a pistol in the trench in July 1943. A colleague sat on the table edge, playing with a Parabellum pistol. A shot rang out and wounded another comrade in the arm and leg, then the bullet settled in Rolf's knee—three wounds from one bullet. The 'wounded train' took him to Jakobstad military hospital where the bullet was removed. He struggled to get through the door when he arrived. Because of the anaesthetic he could not feel that his leg was still outside the door.

While there, he first saw Karin Cederberg, then a schoolgirl running messages. She became his wife and the love of his life.

Rolf's damaged kneecap and leg never recovered but he returned to the

---

5   *Livets Färdväg* by Robert T. Tallgren

front and fought for two years. All Finnish men must rally against the Russians.

War did not come easy to sensitive men like the Edvards, the Rolfs. They faced pressure on all sides to fight and save their country from Russian occupation.

I imagine them tossing in their bunks, wide eyed through long winter nights or restless summer evenings. In fitful sleep, their minds relive the horrors. They thrash through nightmares, call out in hoarse voices, sleepwalk out of the safety of the Korsu, to be retrieved by a colleague—and pushed out to fight next day. Even if their hands shake like autumn leaves and they cannot fire straight; even if they can barely walk on arthritic or wounded legs. Mortality is all around, it surrounds them and stalks, it may strike at any moment, they smell it, grimed into their bloodied hands after dragging a wounded colleague from behind enemy lines to the medic station, they taste it on their own tongues from shrapnel wounds.

At the end of each bullet they fire, each grenade lobbed, are husbands, fathers, brothers, sons. Bells toll through generations; their rigid metronome echoes out of belfries across the land. But Finland is free. And its men and women would rally again if the bugle called.

Rolf's Birthday—and Death

Noble son of Finland's blue lakes
Free I was born, and free I want to die.

Z. Topelius, *Ice Breaking on the Oulu River*

My 2008 visit to Finland drew to an end. We drove to the Pörkenäs cottage to celebrate Rolf's 85th birthday with *kaffe* and the cake Gretchen has baked.

As weight-effective gifts, I had brought various Australiana 'souvineers' (Eric's adolescent spelling is contagious), and chosen for Rolf a toy kookaburra. For Rolf, humour has been his defence and salvation against the horrors of war. Karin told of his nickname 'Silly Back' and his greeting 'Happy Ascension Day' regardless of the date.

As a more personal gift I decided to paint a portrait with my travel set of watercolours. Intermittent autumn sunshine lured me onto the balcony although my fingertips became chilled. With extra pullovers I sat in the crisp air, watching squirrels frisk in the birches.

Looking through my laptop photographs I was tempted to copy the Rolf of our visit in summer, 1977. A photo showed him at my farfarsfar's stuga when he took Antoni and me to spend a night in the family cabin on Anders Back's land. But I opted instead for Rolf with a roguish half-smile at the window of his home at Pörkenäs. In this he stood with arms loose on his hips, framed by a vista of flat grey sea and flanked by fir trees and a jumble of rocks typical of Finland.

In the cropped photo blown-up on my computer screen, I saw the real

Rolf. My pencil outlined the shape of his head in lines of features that could make any one of my family. A darker 4B lead sent hair flopping over his eyes, just like many of my brothers; I noticed the chin so like my father's. As his crinkles of smile appeared I realised similar indentations form my own smile. I saw a man whose joking sustained him through minus 40–degree frostbitten toes in the war. Although reared at the other end of the world, I share the laughter lines and offbeat humour with my father's cousin, and perhaps with his uncle KJ, whose wit livened the letters that lie near me on the table.

Even with language constraints, we can share jokes.

Rolf was genial, easy–going. Yet I wondered, after all he has suffered, if he hid a dark side, suffered from a depressive streak that lurks in so many Scandinavians, or the Seasonal Affective Disorder activated by the long dark winters. My father was prone to tortuous moods, even in Australia's lavish sunshine; is there a gloomy gene in our metabolism at either end of the world? And Dad never fought the Russians.

If so, this was an aspect I never saw in Rolf. Instead, with each meeting this outgoing, generous man became more the father I wished I had.

Rolf was a baby when WA made his triumphal return in 1924 but his youth was coloured by letters bearing bright Australian stamps from unknown uncles. His father's plans to emigrate were dashed. Edvard died two weeks after Rolf's twelfth birthday. He grew up under a cloud of grief.

The burden that contributed to forty–year–old Edvard's death fell on Rolf's shoulders. He was the man in a family of strong women; his grandmothers Sanna Back and Lovisa Strom, a skilful herbalist; aunt Sofia; her daughter Helmi, and his forthright mother Ester.

That night of Rolf's 85th birthday, I sang him the Swedish birthday song, *Ja må han leva* flavoured in my Aussie *Svenska*. Rolf also gave gifts: 'I remember in 1995, three young boys came to Finland. They have little money and when I gave them some they whooped with joy. And for that I like to give another money. I hope you can go in a shop in Helsinki or where you like and buy something for these young men today, just to remember Finland.' (I chose pens crafted from birch wood as a reminder of Finland's forests.)

Then Rolf produced two small boxes. 'These rings belonged to Sofia. One is her engagement ring and the other for her wedding. You choose which one you will keep.'

My eyes brimmed with tears. I chose the engagement band as it contained the hopes and dreams of my great aunt. Which were dashed just a week before the wedding. Many women donated their rings to the state to buy guns, or later to put towards the war reparations. They were given replacements made from iron or tin. Sofia treasured hers, even though she discarded the man who left her with an illegitimate child.

From my childhood I remember just two gifts that my own father gave me. Both fostered my budding love of music; a toy xylophone, the other a music box. But Dad, who grew up in the Depression, negotiated a cheaper price to remove the pretty case. It rusted.

A ring is the symbol of eternity, of love. This I found with my Finnish family.

I know that, like gold, our relationship is eternal, even across the wide seas, even past the door of death. For the hole in the centre of a ring represents a gateway or door which leads to events both known and unknown.

There were more tears as we parted, for this was my last night with Rolf and Karin before flying home. We all knew the chances of meeting again were slim.

'Next time, we meet in heaven.'

***

Two years later:

Why am I sleepless tonight? I have soaked in a bubble bath, read a book, with no particular worries on my mind. Yet after tossing for several hours, I struggle out to the computer; the time zones are right to talk with Gretchen on Skype. There is no answer; perhaps she is at the hospital. Rolf was operated on for a malignant skin growth, which has spread to secondary throat cancer.

I decide to edit the video files from that last night at Pörkenäs into segments small enough to email to Finland. There's Rolf, opening his gifts, singing his Russian songs, some of which have a bawdy tone. Telling of exploits over the enemy border, the lighter version. I feel he is with me. Over thirty years, my four or five visits with him forged a love deeper and more real than that for my own father. Rolf has been generous, as Dad could not be, stretched by his eight children. (How to remember names? Any one will do...)

My father did not support my education, for 'Christ will return any day'. When Gretchen went to study at university, Rolf encouraged.

'As a rule knowledge is no weight to carry in our luggage.'

Intuition prepared me to hear that Rolf passed away that night. Amidst the loss and grief, I thank God that I was given these opportunities to know and love Rolf and that he filled the father–shaped hole in my life.

Rolf, you were the father I wished for over all those decades. My life has been richer for knowing you.

To Russia With Caution

28 December 1941 - Zhenya died. 25 January 1942 - Granny died. 17 March - Lyoka died. 13 April - Uncle Vasya died. 10 May - Uncle Lyosha died. 13 May at 7.30am - Mama died. The Savichevs are dead, everyone is dead. Only Tanya is left.

Pocket book of Tanya Savicheva, age 12.

Finns know Russians too well. For centuries they have squirmed under their thumb, at times defending themselves against onslaughts, and living with the uneasiness of such rumbling neighbours.

After hearing Rolf's stories I determined to pay tribute to him by visiting Karelia where he fought in the Continuation War. We had hoped to drive our campervan to St Petersburg in 1995. Time ran out then, as did our funds, so the expensive visa costs turned into a waste.

–A good thing, too. How could you be so naïve to consider going to Russia?

–Times change, KJ. I suggested to Gretchen that together we might travel from Helsinki to St Petersburg by train, passing through areas over the border where Rolf went on patrols.

–You thought to put Rolf's daughter into danger? Foolhardy woman!

–But we would see little during the four–hour journey, hardly worth getting visas. A feasible option was the visa–free cruise with overnight ferry each way and two nights in St Petersburg. We discussed back and forth on Skype. Then Vladimir Putin's army invaded the Ukraine. Russians acted true to form.

–You see? Russians never change.

–It was the other side of Europe but talk was rife that President Putin wanted to restore the borders of Catherine the Great. That included Finland. Gretchen watched the situation for weeks before she agreed to join us on the cruise.

Antoni and I sailed by overnight ferry from Stockholm to Helsinki a day before. Shrouds of mist hid the view of the archipelago I'd been anticipating. Chill winds and speckles of snow—in May—cut a fitting reminder that I had arrived in the land of my ancestors. We waited on the platform at the Helsinki railway station to greet Gretchen and Anders, then repaired for a coffee to catch-up and regroup.

'There's time to see the stunning Rock Church before sailing,' I suggested. 'Tram number two then a short walk.' The others eyed our collective luggage and vetoed that for a taxi directly to the wharf.

We opted for the cheaper inside cabins, putting our budget to the Palace Bridge Hotel. There we would make good use of its spa and saunas. From our dining table in the bow we feasted on a smorgasbord dinner with complimentary vodka and returned for breakfast—without vodka.

As we had pre-booked a day tour of St Petersburg, the customs officials waved us through.

–*They didn't check the name to find that Rolf fought their forebears?*

–Or they wanted our money to be spent on babushkas, garnet jewellery and fine chocolate. Soon we walked onto Russian tarmac. Bright sunny skies shone on us—an auspicious blessing as this city averaged just fifty fine-weather days per year.

Our tour stopped first at St Nicholas Cathedral, bright blue and white against a matching sky, and topped with sparkling gold domes. Ten minutes to absorb the scene, then back in the bus. At the Peterhof Orthodox Cathedral of Peter and Paul green and gold domes top baroque red brick. This church houses the Romanov graves dating back to Peter the Great, along with the remains of Nicholas II and his family, executed at Yekaterinburg at dawn of 17 July 1918.

Never mind the gold dome of St Isaacs Cathedral. Gretchen and I froze in horror. Drums thundered. The military were out! (Calm down, KJ!)

–*Madness! Had Putin's forces moved north from Ukraine?*

–Soldiers were everywhere. They marched wearing fatigues, khaki, others in brown with red caps. Female corps stepped out, jaunty in blue uniforms with orange caps. (Rolf, you could tell what corps they were.) Bands rumbled, canons blared.

Our tour guide Olga reassured us; this was just a rehearsal for Victory Day celebrations two days later. To mark the date that Hitler's Operation Barbarossa, the German invasion of the Soviet Union, was repulsed on 8 May 1944.

The bus turned a corner and there it stood—the Bronze Horseman. Empress Catherine the Great commissioned this statue as a tribute to Tsar Peter the Great—and also to shore up her own credibility. I had read a series of novels starting with *The Bronze Horseman*, fascinated by Paullina Simons' stories of the Nazi siege of Leningrad that lasted 872 days from 8 September 1941. It described the other side of the story—the Russian experience—the contrast to Rolf's fighting in the border area. Thirty kilometres from Leningrad, the Finns halted their offensive at the pre–World War II border between Soviet Union and Finland. Perhaps Rolf also fought so close?

The novels are grim reading, interspersed with an intense love story to keep the reader engaged. A million died, half of them from starvation as the Nazis bombed the storage where food was kept. People ate anything they could scrounge; cats, dogs, sawdust, wallpaper paste, leather. It was dangerous to leave children alone. Several hundred people were tried and imprisoned for cannibalism.

Leningrad would not fall, so the legend went, as long as the Bronze Horseman statue stood in its centre. Sandbags and a wooden shelter protected the statue until the siege was lifted on 27 January 1944.

The Bronze Horseman statue rides over its cliff of red granite hauled from Lahta in the Gulf of Finland. This 'Thunder Stone' pedestal—reputed to be the largest stone ever moved by man—took 400 men nine months to haul up the Neva River.

Olga shepherded us at a fast trot through the kilometres of galleries in the Hermitage. On our walk back to the hotel we sustained ourselves with detours into chocolate shops and souvenir outlets. They offered a free nip of vodka to help open wallets.

We soaked in the spa and broiled in all the saunas, Russian and Finnish; hot, steam, and dry. Then padded into the elevators in slippers, glowing pink above our hotel dressing gowns. Sleep was bliss after a sauna. As Finns well know.

A highlight was the blaze of colourful intricate mosaics in the Church of the Resurrected Saviour, known as the Church on the Spilled Blood. This was built on the spot where Tsar Alexander II was mortally wounded on 1 March 1881. The bomb thrown by a revolutionary set Russia on a bloody path for the next century. Yet it could be said that Alexander II was a good guy. He emancipated serfs and ratified the law regarding compulsory military service, limited corporal punishment and made the judicial system answer to the law.

We toured the St Peter and St Paul fortress, the cells where revolutionaries from the 1905 revolution were held. Many did not emerge. Plaques on the walls noted prisoners. One struck me; look at this! It could have been KJ.

Maria Vetrova, 1870–1897

> Participant of the Narodnik (Populist) Revolutionary Movement, worked in illegal revolutionary printing house. Imprisoned from 23rd January until 12th February 1897. Cells 3, 7, 8, 6. In prison went ill, had mental problems and hallucinations. Burned herself with a kerosene lamp in the cell 7. Died in four days in cell 6.

> –KJ, come down, you are safe now. (I strain to hear his voice, thin as a thread.)

> –*Go away, you may draw attention to me. How did you find me up here?*

> –An old-timer told me that you built a tree house on your land, in which you could hide if threatened. You are safe now. But how sobering to think if you hadn't escaped conscription to the Russian army, you might have been jailed here, even buried in their soil.

Outside in the square, another rehearsal was in progress for more celebratory concerts. We tramped along Nevsky Prospekt then huddled against a torrent of rain in a canal boat, warmed by coffee and vodka.

We walked all day and into the night. As respite for my aching knee, we braved the daunting subway. Antoni negotiated the token machine and led the way through turnstiles. Gretchen and Anders looked doubtful. They preferred riding bicycles in their flat hometown, Jakobstad. It took two minutes to descend an escalator into the world's deepest metro, 105 metres below ground. Opened in 1955 as the city recovered from ruins and the horror of the siege, people craved beauty. They decorated each station with elegant chandeliers, statues, mosaics and golden carvings.

So, even the hated Russians had redeeming factors. They surmounted grim experiences with art and music. Shostakovich dedicated his massive *Seventh Symphony to Leningrad* as a symbol of resistance to Nazi totalitarianism—or any militarism. 'Neither savage raids, German planes, nor the grim atmosphere of the beleaguered city could hinder the flow,' he recalled. 'I worked with an inhuman intensity I have never before reached.' In *Testimony*, he wrote that he composed the first movement 'invasion theme' before the siege and he had 'other enemies of humanity' in mind. The Leningrad he described was one 'that Stalin destroyed and Hitler merely finished off.' But after the war began he referred to it as the 'German' or anti-Hitler' theme. Whatever its genesis, there must be hope for any country that can marshal exhausted, malnourished musicians to rehearse and record a mammoth symphony lasting an hour and a quarter to boost morale. I feel for the wind and brass players, so depleted that lung capacity could barely cope with the challenges.

Next morning canon fire woke us. The Victory Parade. Soldiers and officials strutted their rows of medals. People sported St George orange and black ribbons. I hesitated before accepting one. Gretchen refused. I hesitated before accepting one. I brace for KJ's reaction.

—*You wore that ribbon? I'm ashamed of you!*

—No, I just kept it for the memory.

Jubilant young folk enjoyed the excuse for celebration. Elderly drawn faces and teary eyes intrigued me. Were they children who survived but lost their family?

A visit to the Bolshoi theatre is a bucket list item, and my former teacher Valentin Sakharov played in its orchestra until he defected during the Cold War. 'You must suffer for your art' he would intone, describing his teenage studies at the military musical academy. How guards patrolled the corridors and banged on studio doors when practice paused. The father he never met was a Russian war hero. My tone and technique had bloomed under his regime of long hours' daily etudes and scales, playing the hardest possible reeds with a bulldog firm mouth position.

But we were cash–strapped and exhausted from walking all day. The spa suited our bodies, pockets and moods. But a free concert in St Isaac's square featured soloists from the Bolshoi singing songs of the war era. Gretchen and I both wiped away tears to hear a song that we knew from Rolf's party pieces. (We treasure the footage I filmed of him.)

Strolling back to our hotel, we browsed through stalls of painting and bronze works, babushkas and knickknacks. Nesting dolls attracted me as I had come to feel like one, nestled into the snug arms of generations of my ancestors.

The heavens erupted with vicious thunder to drench rain. We scuttled back to warm hotel rooms. How did citizens or soldiers cope—of either side—shivering through such deluges and snowstorms with no shelter or prospect of a hot dinner? During the siege, temperatures dropped to −40 degrees in a city void of heating.

—Northerners picture a Hell of freezing and frostbite, rather than broiling heat.

It was a relief to return from St Petersburg without mishap.

Finland shares a long border with Russia. That would be vulnerable if Russians tried to act on nostalgic memories and re–acquire the realm of their once glorious Empire.

Now, Finnish family eye current world events, report surveillance flights inside Finnish airspace. Karin refuses a medical appointment with a Russian locum when her usual doctor is absent.

I hope and pray that this country of my heritage remains free.

In 1988, Anna Sanna's sons Hugo and Wally Holm refused flights to Finland via Moscow for 'Russians have long memories'. The tickets were changed to a longer route via London. And you, KJ, never returned to Finland.

Back to Helsinki and Jakobstad

As grim as the gale on the tundra the winds of autumn run free.
They drag the squalls from the east and snow from the lowering north.
The lonely tree whimpers, it quakes on the wind-possessed earth.

Arvid Mörne, *The Lonely Tree*

Our ship docks in Helsinki and we head for the railway station to board the train north to Ostrobothnia. Now I view the large cobbled square with different eyes.

Here, as the crippling St Petersburg General Strike spread to Finland, the Finns rallied against their Russian oppressors. In this same square, the young poet Arvid Mörne gave a passionate speech on 30 October 1905 to rally 20,000 protesters. His words fired a spontaneous demonstration of marchers past the Senate Marketplace to the governor's residence, singing the Runeberg words to *Björneborgarnas marsch*.

> Not yet is Finland's manhood dead;
> With foemen's blood a field may still be tinted red!

Their boots tramped through the Senate Square, where Cossacks stood at the ready.

Mörne headed a delegation that pushed up the stairs to demand Governor General Obolensky, who had replaced the assassinated Bobrikov, should resign.

Just as the senators came to accept this, events turned around. Senator Sohlman moved to announce this decision from a balcony. Someone in the crowd cried, 'The Cossacks are coming!' The horde ran. Twenty people were hurt, many badly. This false alarm triggered memories of the Cossack riots of the past years when Bobrikov sent Cossacks on horseback with whips to disperse them. In an instant, the aggressive demonstrators turned into a herd who fled for their lives.

Historical stories flashed through my mind as our train neared Jakobstad. At our destination, the railway station called Pännäinen/Bennäs, A. V. Huldén laid bombs under a wagon in 1905. A Russian colonel survived a double explosion. The activist was not convicted as many railway staff were involved in or supported the resistance.

Gretchen ensconced us in her attic room. I opened a book, *Moomin in November* by Tove Jansson. My eyes widened. *There are some that go and some that stay.* How true this is of my family!

During the next days I revisited my band of researchers, historians and relatives. In mid–May temperatures hovered close to zero at nights. Antoni created a new family legend; he cycled to Pörkenäs for dinner wearing his shorts, leather jacket and an Aussie flag as bandana on his head. My other visits had been too hectic to enjoy the sea. This time I curled up on a wooden bench and absorbed the gentle lapping of waves on rocks. The Finnish flag swirled overhead. If only I could stay here all week, all year! Absorb the changing seasons that northern Australia lacks.

To get the family's feedback I rehearsed for them the paper I would read at the Institute of Migration conference in Turku next week. Woven into it was the letters they gave and helped me translate. What a responsibility—to bring the story full-circle home, condensed and with an Australian accent.

'Hanko is not far from Turku,' I said, 'so I hope to go there and stand on its wharf, put myself in the shoes of those who sailed from there.'

My relatives shook collective heads. It would be impossible to go onto the wharf, busy with trucks and containers, and locked. Use your time in Helsinki or Turku. 'At least I could stand on the rocks and see that last glimpse of Finland, look to their horizon ahead.' They resisted saying that horizons at sea are similar.

Karin showed me photographs of Rolf in his uniform and in his prized Ford car '*Karolina*' that his uncle Wilhelm helped him buy. Books about the Continuation War were marked with lines referring to Rolf's part in it. With my iPad, I photographed these for later translation by kind friends.

Gretchen prepared a dinner of my favourite fish, *sik*, with salad, potatoes and dill. Then we devoured her *bullar*, apple and blueberry cake.

Once again she drove me to the Munsala house and orchard whose apple and cherry trees KJ planted. 'Remember, Gretchen, how often he wrote in letters his letter to send cherry stones?'

—You saw the spruce trees in the cemetery. Did they tell you that I planted them?

–KJ, you're back! Yes, I visited there—as a horde of Aussie relatives have before me. Your cherry trees thrive. I ate their fruit with my muesli this morning.

–Even with all my fruit trees in Australia, I missed wine currant berry and gooseberries. In 1910 when I was a successful farmer, I had a thousand orange and mandarin trees, a hundred persimmon trees, twenty fig trees and many acres of bananas…

***

His voice fades, lost in his reveries. So I wander outside and reflect, propped by a gnarled cherry tree. WA had visited his parents, knowing it was their last meeting. But KJ fled with hasty farewells. He carried his father's disapproval like a cross to his back, never made the journey of resolution. Harsh words spoken long ago festered. Even his successes were dogged by impossible standards.

'See, Pappa, how I have built farms, I employ many workers; my timber is the showpiece of Wilhelm's house at *Cedarholm*. But at the other end of the world he will not see or believe that the no–hoper son had made good.'

How sad to die unreconciled.

Leaving Home

Many precious crafts have been wrecked upon the submerged rocks, by which the sea of life is infested.

K. J. Back, *The Royal Toast*

Back track to my 2008 visit which drew to a close, and the to–do list lengthened. People to visit, packing, scanning photographs and documents. I must buy gifts for family and friends back home, and as a thank-you for this family's hospitality.

Gretchen and I embarked on a flurry of shopping and last-ditch visits on her free day. We started at the markets, site of the Great Strike demonstrations in 1905, and now a cheery mix of stalls. I bought a bunch of dried flowers for Karin and chose an orchid for Gretchen. She steered me to Marimekko for bright scarves and purses for my sisters and son's partners. A bottle for Anders, Gretchen's husband, required a special trip to the state (and only) alcohol supplier, ALKO.

Gretchen directed me away from tourist traps to small shops where I could buy handcrafts direct from the artisans—birch carved butter knives and straw Christmas decorations. Bookmarks woven with Jakobstad's symbols of an anchor, cross and heart. Wooden candlesticks and vases painted in folk art of flowers, leaves and dots challenged my credit card. A carved violin in which a thermometer serves as a bridge as a gift for Antoni.

We repaired for lunch to regroup and boost our energy. My 'to visit' list had two places left: Monäs, from where people escaped to Sweden, and Kovjoki Station, which Gretchen steered me towards as KJ's final departure point. Time was short so she vetoed Monäs. As we drove to Kovjoki, I looked out the window at forests, typical of any in Finland, except that KJ walked amongst those trees. Were these rocks and hayfields his last glimpse of his homelands?

The station is no longer used but well preserved. Deep red trim and a brick roof enhance the cream paint. Seats look out to the parallel lines across which thousands left their home. The opening scenes of *Colorado Avenue* were filmed here. Perhaps this burgundy painted carriage was the one seen in the film. I climbed up three steep steps to peer in the window at the hard benches on which KJ may have jolted his way south to Hanko.

> –KJ, I admit I'm stubborn, and you did advise WA to travel south by train. That story of you crossing the ice came from somewhere. But now we've translated your letter—
>
> –*I wrote it should be destroyed. They knew this would put me in danger!*
>
> –You weren't captured after all. The family tried to keep the Russians off your scent, still covering for you. But your letter instructed them how to travel:

> In Hanko you buy your tickets. It is a city with Swedish-speaking inhabitants, much like Nykarleby, but a little larger than Kyrkbacken in Munsala. When you have your tickets you only have to show them to the agent and proceed to go on board, and you will be taken to Hull without much ado. A Swede or Norwegian will take you to the train and send you to London.

Late into the night we wrestled, bleary eyed, to finish translating the letters in the folders. We unfolded a page that solved the riddle of whether KJ's escape route was across the gulf or south from Kovjoki station to Hanko.

KJ, you've been playing me for a fool with your smokescreens. Your letter showed—a pity it is undated—that you did travel from Hanko. Here it is, clear as the sea at Udden, and a thermometer was the clue!

> The heat is not so painful here on the nights and in the afternoons, that's the best you can ever wish. And if it's too warm at midday, it will be freshened by the sea breezes and the sea is so nearby that you can see it. Midday is about 37 degrees. This night the temperature is not going below more than 24.
>
> And if somebody should believe that I have been mistaken I can mention to you that I bought this thermometer in Hanko and there is written Celsius on the backside of the thermometer.

> –Because you had Mat's passport you could travel legally, right?

My train will travel through Kovjoki on its way south tomorrow. Correct me if I'm wrong, please?

—You won't push me back on the carriage, or make me go back in time?

—No, KJ, I don't have the heart. You've been through enough. Rest in peace.

Finding Sibelius

Millions of years ago, in my previous incarnations, I must have been related to swans...because I can feel that affinity.

Jean Sibelius

It is now mid–May 2014, a similar time to when KJ left his home—as I am about to head south also, first to Hanko and Turku then on to Australia. Walking between Munsala church, cemetery and farmhouse, I absorb colours, landscape and vegetation similar to his last view.

KJ, I have just farewelled our family, boarded the train south, on the same route that you took. Here comes a quick glimpse of Kovjoki where—yes—you boarded your train for Hanko. The deserted railway station passes in a flash.

***

Back in Helsinki Station. As Antoni and I walk through the cobbled streets I muse over what might have been. KJ might have trodden his paths with more confidence if he had a life partner as a sounding board for his ideas, to stabilise, encourage and lift him from his depressions. To throw his often–brilliant ideas back and forth, like rune singers, elaborating and developing.

This visit celebrates our forty–year wedding anniversary. Antoni will return to Australia a week before me, as I will head west to Turku and the Institute of Migration Conference. We enjoy *Rosenkavalier* at the Opera House, followed by a supper at a restaurant overlooking a floodlit Senate Square—the best view in Helsinki.

Next day, we wander up Esplanadi Park, bright with daffodils, a brass band playing in the clam–shaped bandstand. In the park are statues of the famous poets Runeberg (sculpted by his son Walter), Topelius and Eino Leino. Viktor Jansson's fountain statues depict a boy riding a fish and the Mermaid (modelled on his daughter Tove). Also known as 'Play' its water nymphs frolic with a fish on waves. It stands outside Kappeli Restaurant, a hub for authors, artists and musicians since it was built in 1867. This ornate building proves just the place for our romantic final luncheon.

Kappeli was Helsinki's nerve centre, a meeting-place for poets and musicians. Including Sibelius, who often met with his cohort of Finnish artists –Aino Järnefelt, Leino, and Gallen-Kallela. He gathered as usual at Kappeli before leaving for Stockholm for a couple of days to complete a musical composition. Sibelius returned to find the same group sitting at Kappeli. One said: 'Listen here, Jean – either you stay outside or stay inside, but stop coming in and out all the time!'

It was there that Sibelius and his friends celebrated the assassination of Bobrikov, becoming so merry that he was arrested for 'unwarranted happiness.' Six months later, on New Year's Day, the composer told Kagal women's leader Dr. Tekla Hultin of his intention to compose a Requiem for the assassin. *In Memorium* was completed in 1909. In 1917 he set the *Jäger March* to lyrics by Heikki Nurmi, smuggled in from Prussia and given to him by his ear doctor Dr Wilhelm Zilliacus.

Like my own forebears, Sibelius was Finland Swedish, but his personal life typified the struggle between the Swedish and Finnish language groups. He married into a Fennoman family, his mother–in–law was Russian. To compose his choral symphony with Finnish text was seen by the Swedes as selling out. But Sibelius also said 'For me, music begins where words end.'

Would our celebration have been enhanced to know all this? Sufficient to enjoy the atmosphere and each other's company before Antoni caught the airport bus for his flight home. I would follow after visiting two cities high on my list: Hanko and Turku.

Hanko Port

Out of the purest notes I build a bridge
To the world, to sorrow, and to anguish.

Karl August Tavaststjerna, *När jag drömmer*

The day beams bright and sunny as I set out to visit Hanko on May 18—a week before KJ's departure date over a century before. For the first time I have ventured out on a day trip without my coat, though extra layers weigh down my shoulder bag. The journey from Turku to Hanko is 50 kilometres, two connections each way. After travelling across the world, how could I baulk at two hours to Hanko?

I perch on a concrete stairwell at Karjaa station, opposite a retired steam train, to wait for my bus connection. Unlike the north, gardens bloom with spring blossom and flowers: daffodils, lilac and tulips. Birch trees sport delicate green leaves. Wind and sun weave gentle shimmers through them. Animals, released from their barns, cavort in fields and nibble bright grass.

A billboard advertises '*Sisu*' described as digging through a cement wall with a spoon, but you keep going. I have inherited my portion. Despite the odds that there may be little to see, I am heading to Hanko. I was stubborn, coming late to accept that KJ sailed from Hanko. Now I must see that place, to imagine myself in his shoes as he—and later his siblings—waved goodbye to his homeland.

My bus into Hanko runs parallel to railway tracks that bore my relatives. Did they buy their ship tickets on the trains from agents? I imagine Anders Back was too organised to leave it to chance, had bought them in Vaasa. And a copy of *Emigrant's Interpreter*.

Ships sailed on Saturdays. I calculate; according to the family Bible, KJ left on 26 May, a Friday. The train from Ostrobothnia took two days at that time. Did he travel direct to the port or was there time to meet with activist Matti Kurikka, to plan meeting in Australia? Was he tempted to join the Utopian community?

I alight at Hanko railway station; it's standard modern style for the original was damaged in the 1940s. A red brick water tower stands tall above the low wooden houses painted cream, blue or sand yellow—unlike that ubiquitous red of the north to contrast against snow. Hanko was chosen for its winter harbour.

True, the wharf is locked behind tall fences to protect the containers and trucks that await ships. Around 1900 butter was a major export from Finland and containers were loaded from Hanko. I wonder at a possible irony, if butter from Byron Bay's Norco factory reached as far north as Scandinavia?

In a café on the waterfront I enjoy a smorgasbord lunch, with its dozen types of herring—how I will miss them! Then I head for the museum in a low stone barn flanked by a canon. There I buy a book[6] and compare its photographs to locate the Emigrants' Hotel: 'Boulevard 15, near the pizza place.'[7]

Chimneys top tall red brick walls of the ground floor and wooden upper level, white wood trim to the windows, door and balcony. Adjacent hugs a low cream coloured wooden house, with carved cornices and red roof. There were two separate entrances, one for men and the other for women, with a large hall and kitchen in the middle. It was built in 1902 between the emigration office and the bank.

It's deserted now. Over the years, excited emigrants tossed restless in the three-tiered bunks inside. Granddad was one of 23 000 who left Finland in 1902 alone—about half from Ostrobothnia. I imagine these quiet streets flocked with a thousand emigrants buying loaves of bread at the market, eyes popping at first sights of tomatoes and oranges. So the family must have been agog at Granddad's photograph marked '3 year old orange tree' to impress the folks at home.

Did shipping company agents meet them at the railway station and help them through the paperwork? The fierce competition for business sometimes led to fist-fights.

My next vantage point is the Emigrants Cliffs. I walk round the bay, through sandy moraine and pine trees, past the faded spa resort favoured by Russian nobility in the times of Finland's Grand Duchy. My camera at the ready, I stand on the chunks of flat granite rocks where emigrants danced through their last night in Finland around a flagpole. Wheezes of an accordion encouraged them into polkas and ring dances. I look back over the town and forward to the horizon—the horizon that expanded before them as their ships sailed.

Next morning revellers would have reeled from unaccustomed spirits.

---

6   Marketta Wall, *To America America; Hanko as Port of Departure for Emigrants*.
7   The following pages owe much to this book and to the Institute of Migration exhibition.

Reeking of the cure–all Hoffmann's Drops (a quarter ether and three quarters spirit) they straggled down to the harbour to watch cargo loading, flinching as the winch squealed, porters clanged trunks and saws grated. If their eyes watered, they blamed the steam that billowed from smoke stacks.

'With all the money I earn, I'll return and buy a bigger farm,' they reassured red–eyed mothers. But all knew that they might never again be circled by these arms. Hugs tightened as the ship hooted its final whistles. The travellers swaggered up the gangplank and found a space on the deck to wave handkerchiefs and hats as sailors untied the ropes. The engine coughed to life and rumbled as the ship moved forward to brave the waves.

Steerage space was stuffy and damp with the engine's oily breath. They crowded onto benches aboard; sixty people attempted to sleep on wooden three–storey bunk beds with mattresses two centimetres thick. Cabin space was little better, delineated by a chalk mark. There were no pillows or mattresses.

A photograph taken a year before Granddad emigrated shows a lad eager to take on the world. But when KJ left that port, in May 1899, he might have hidden in his bunk until the ship was safely away. Did he then slink onto the deck to warm his spirit with a final glimpse of this security beacon?

Work would begin on Byron Bay lighthouse a year after KJ arrived at the most easterly point of Australia. That would eventually comfort his lonely nights and remind him of Finland.

Past the archipelago, the ship bucked through grim waves like a rocking horse.

But the Turku Memorial Statue shows birds in flight. Three cranes head out to sea to the expanding horizon. For me they represent the Back siblings: Karl Johan, Wilhelm Anders and Anna Sanna.

Bringing Them Home

No rising hill, or mountain grand,
No sloping dale, no northern strand,
There is, more loved, to be found,
Than this—our fathers' ground!

Johan Ludvig Runeberg, *The Tales of Ensign Stål*

I feel honoured to bring the Back stories home to Finland through my conference presentation at the Institute of Migration in Turku. In the red stone building I check the data projector talks with my slides and the link to the recording of my grandfather WA from the 1963 interview:

> Go forward. It's the thing what we have in front of us, not what we have been in the past and what have been doing wrong because it's from mistakes and everything that has been in the wrong direction when you're trying to learn from that and rectify that.

—Granddad, did you never stop to draw breath in your whirlwind life? I haven't added punctuation to your long sentences.

I decide to begin my presentation with a multilingual 'Good morning, *god morgon,* Hyvää huomenta.' The polite Finns keep straight faces when my basic linguistic skills render a dubious meaning by failing to pronounce the 'y' with a 'u' inflection.

It is a pleasure to bring these stories back to Finland. I show a film of the *bon vivant* Wally Holm at his hundredth birthday celebration. A year later he will be buried with a rock from Munsala on his coffin, after which a huge blue–iced cake he would have loved will be shared by the many who pack the church to farewell him.

On my last day in Turku I manage a quick viewing of the Institute exhibition. I bless my iPad because I can photograph the exhibits and absorb them later, enlarging details with a swipe of my fingers. Solid wooden trunks and leather suitcases contained the emigrants' possessions for their journeys. Woollen long john leggings and singlets. Photographs of family and sweethearts. Of crowds milling at the dock, the lighthouse that beamed reassurance on them. Ships and maps. There are many books and journals that I have too little time to browse. *Next visit.*

There are many displays about American emigrants. Some show Finns in Australia, their old Queenslander–style wooden houses, bungalows surrounded by fruit trees. Children in traditional folk costumes who maintain the memories of a homeland they have not seen. Queen Elizabeth II heads a certificate of naturalisation. Shells, a dry starfish, ships in bottles and an aboriginal boomerang.

But I must return home that night.

First I enjoy lunch with Olavi Koivukangas on a riverboat. He sent me his book years ago, roused my appetite for Finnish heritage, mentored me over these years of my research. Students row races, encouraged by the crowd. Olavi and his wife help me with my luggage and deposit me at the railway station, *en route* to Helsinki then Australia.

After six Finnish rail journeys in the past weeks I'm adept with the process: check the number on the ticket and the sign that shows where to stand on the platform. The sleek trains, decorated with whooper swans, are efficient and punctual. Free Wi-Fi. Thoughtful design provides passengers with luggage lockers and an upstairs childproofed area. In the small cabins it's possible to ring on mobile phones and not disturb other travellers.

As I settle into my seat, the past weeks unfold in my mind. My exciting days in south–west Finland. But there was no time to visit the Sibelius Museum. *Next time.*

My train weaves between fields and lakes; Christmas trees with candle tips. Again, my instinct is to reach for my camera again but I have enough footage. Camera, iPhone and iPad burst to their data limit. I'm loaded with DVDs of war films for my research.

After three weeks in Finland I extended my vocabulary but determined to learn more Finnish before further visits. During these weeks I have deepened family ties, made friends and renewed relations with people. Many are on hugging terms and I look forward to meeting again.

Before catching the bus to the airport, I have one hour free to scuttle through an exhibition of Tove Jansson's paintings and drawings. What an artist she was, far beyond her Moomin characters. I cherish a photograph of her, swimming in a lake, a wreath in her hair. Perched on the rocks—so typical of Finland—is her summer stuga. I wish I could have met you, Tove. Thank you for the quote that solved my manuscript's structural issues.

How my knowledge of heritage has deepened and expanded in the past decade, this past hectic month! A few years ago I knew little about my heritage. Now my mind teems with letters, stories and anecdotes; KJ's vernacular seeps into my own.

The question has been put to me in varying tones, ranging from the tactful to the blunt: why am I drawn to the black sheep brother rather than Granddad, whose story was so vibrant? KJ, after all, became a recluse. But I'd always wondered: why?

Russians would not have pursued him at Suez unless he buried secrets from his past in Finland. He escaped, but did he spend the rest of his life coiled, ready for fight or flight? Long after he found safety on vantage points overlooking Byron Bay, KJ lived with one eye ever open for the Russians.

Those who remember him from his declining years paint an unattractive picture, though most are too well-bred to malign the dead. Nick, my old-timer fountain of information, called him an eccentric. In his voice I heard the restraint, the euphemism. KJ was remembered as a bachelor, short of graces, even a tramp. He was not always so. Photographs around 1915 show a sensitive man and aesthete, a lover of books and of beauty. His portrait made a statement: a book in hand and an orchid in his buttonhole. Another photograph showed him relaxed and smiling amongst his farm workers from Finland. He sat at ease in this landscape, grounded on his own earth. In his younger decades, KJ ran successful farms and a sawmill.

In Granddad's letters we often read exasperation; 'I had to rescue him from bankruptcy and he didn't thank me for it.' My own father 'took after' KJ with unfortunate habits like leaving pawpaw to ripen on the windowsill, or bananas to brown and collect swarms of fruit fly. Both deserved more credit for their inventive minds that verged on genius, though some ventures dissipated into the mess of their muddled instability.

I have discovered why that refugee KJ lived as a reclusive hermit in the bush, why he failed to reach his potential. And why he wrote home to '*Burn my letters!*'

If only we could fulfil your last wish, to publish your account of the family history. My version may have errors, fallacies and confusions. But I did my best. I knew all along there was more to you, KJ. You had redeeming features to balance your foibles. My goal was to find them and to redeem you in the eyes of your family.

Forgive me for putting words in your mouth. Now I will leave you in peace, Karl Johan. Thank you for sharing your life with me.

KJ does not answer, but I sense that he rests at last.

Homing Bird

I see the giant orbs spring forth, and blazing
With silver sparks as they commence a racing
Through bottomless and endless seas of space.

K. J. Back, *The Royal Toast*

Helsinki cries with rain as I leave. The trees glisten. It was frosted with snow when I arrived three weeks ago; now at 15°C, I shiver—and it nears midsummer!

My plane circles for a last view of splashes of colour on patchwork fields, the island dots of the archipelago. Like a *haminja*, the trail of wake follows a ship. I imagine KJ on it, a hundred years before; I feel the turmoil that churned his gut; his mix of exhilaration yet desolation; his fear of freedom.

I pull out KJ's book and return to his description of an imaginary flight.

> As I looked down I saw the earth spinning around underneath us like a top, but she was going so fast that all the towns and cities on the earth looked to me like fence-posts viewed from an express train travelling at the rate of sixty miles per hour. Now we descended to a lower altitude, and in so doing we began to travel with the earth.

You wrote that in 1918, aviation's childhood. You visionary!

***

My ears pop as the plane ascends. This country of lakes fades into that surreal no–man's land of blue; water and sky dotted with clouds. For twenty hours my mind will process the pictures, memories and sensations, the tastes and aromas of Scandinavia. Ice–age rocks take on troll–shapes in my fitful dozing.

The cabin lights dim and I curl up as the temperature drops. I think how we might have stayed in Scandinavia except for the long winters. But, spoiled by Australia's lavish sun, the cold chilled us to the very marrow of our bones.

As the angle of the world tilts it shows different perspectives of the brothers who were opposite personalities, two sides of a coin. KJ, poet and philosopher, was the first Australian Finn to publish. He retains more respect amongst the Finnish family than the southern one. The Australian branch sees WA as white sheep to KJ's black one; the Finns notice his dust-stained wool. Displays of the wealth of 'Australia's richest Finn' may have been tactless to those struggling to rebuild a homeland bruised by war and famine. WA's success was all too visible to the modest Swedes.

What have I learned from the brothers? How do their strengths and weaknesses emerge in my life? We are all mixtures of personality traits.

Granddad has passed on his ingenuity, vision and breadth of experience. Often I quote his motto of 'Just do it.' He had faith and an ability to turn difficult situations to positives, to innovate and find opportunities at every turn.

I feel an affinity with KJ because he was an author, and a self-published one.

Granddad took seriously his role as patriarch and had a genuine care for his flock of descendants, relatives and emigrant Finns. He was concerned to establish his sons and grandsons. WA inspired us all with his generosity and enterprise.

I have looked under the surface of dates, events and actions to find the persons and motivations beneath. To understand what drove the brothers and a sister to leave their native land and settle at the far end of the earth. They welcomed the opportunities of wider horizons.

My great-grandmother Sanna Back farewelled sons and a daughter, knowing she might never see them again. I shiver to put myself into her worn boots and thick wool stockings.

Then comfort encircles me as it has done so many of my forebears, in the words that have become an unofficial Finnish anthem:

> Be still, my soul: Thy God doth undertake
> To guide the future as He has the past.
> Thy hope, thy confidence let nothing shake:
> All now mysterious shall be bright at last.
> Be still, my soul: The waves and winds still know
> His voice who ruled them while he dwelt below.

Snuggled under my Marimekko rug, I hum myself to sleep, as did so many who faced far worse challenges. As my planes follow the night, I peer out my window searching for the Southern Cross.

Hours later we fly over red plains and hills. Somewhere there, my maternal grandparents settled on land such as this below me, empty, parched expanses. There Grandpa managed the largest stations in Queensland. Grandma was the only white woman for hundreds of square kilometres. Pioneer women bore children and raised those who survived infancy into resilient people. Such is the strength of the forebears who formed me, from both arms of my family tree. My grandmothers were strong uncomplaining women who supported husbands through fire, drought and floods. With a strength of spirit, they created what they lacked.

Living in an immense land gave me a sense that distance is for conquering. This created a gypsy in me who traversed Australia and lived for seven heady years in Europe.

My birthplace, somewhere amongst those flat expanses below me, shaped me even as I resisted it. Since then, I adopted with enthusiasm the land of the Midnight Sun, exhilarated by Northern Lights. My soul lifts at Scandinavia's snow and the lilt of its speech.

My heart lifts as we circle lower over sapphire seas dotted with islands and golden beaches. A fragmented person left for Europe in her twenties. She returns whole.

I discovered my family in Finland and Sweden—but now I am going home.

Timeline

1809	Finland became Grand Duchy of Russia with own laws, language, religion.
1871	Anders Back married Sanna Ohls 21 February.
1876	Munsala family home built.
1881	Tsar Alexander II assassinated; Tsar Alexander III increased repression.
1894	Nicholas II became Tsar.
1898	Nikolai Bobrikov appointed Governor General of Finland.
1899–1905	First Era of Oppression.
1900	Finn army strike. Erik Johan Nyholm exempt from conscription; married Anna Sanna.
1903	Anders and WA arrived in Sydney 17 January.
1904	General Strike Finland, 12–19.11. Helmi born 26 December.
1905	'Bloody Sunday' led to Russian Revolution 12–19 November.
1905	Konni Zilliacus shipped weapons to Jakobstad 8 September. Unrest until November Manifesto.
1906	Michelin founded Senate with equal voting and human rights; Finnish women lead European peers to vote.
1907	Russification resumed.
1908	WA naturalised, February 18; married Christina Hart November 4.
1909–1917	Second Era of Oppression
1910	Finnish autonomy curtailed.
1913	WA sold Mooball farm, moved to Mullumbimby. Press published plans for complete Russification.

1914	WA opened Mullumbimby office.
1917	February Russian Revolution. Tsar abdicated 15 March, assassinated 16.7.1918. SS Equity shipped arms to Vaasa 1 October. Finn Independence declared 6 December.
1918	Finnish alliance treaty with Germany. Civil War 27 January—15 May.
1919	Second Conscription Referendum rejected 20 December.
1919-20	Hollingworth estate purchased Goonengerry timber rights. Cedarholm built.
1920	Holm family arrived Byron Bay 3 January 1921.
1922	WA bought 124 acres at St Lucia on terms. Edvard married Ester Ström 6 November.
1923	Cedarholm sold to Dr. Gibson. Rolf born 7 October.
1924	WA and family sailed to Europe for yearlong tour.
1927	St Lucia land resumed for University of Queensland.
1928	KJ bankruptcy proceedings; concluded 8 September 1931.
1935	Edvard booked passage to Australia, cancelled due to ill health. Died 17 October.
1937	University of Queensland foundation stone laid 6 March.
1939	Winter War from November 30 until 12 March 1940. Russians bombed Helsinki, occupied Finland. Treaty of Moscow annexed Karelia.
1941	Finland invaded Karelia, declared war on Soviet Union. Siege of Leningrad 8 September—January 1944.
1942	Rolf enlisted 19 January; wounded 27 July 1943.
1944	Spring offensive Karelian Isthmus. Ceasefire 4 September, armistice 19 September. Lapland War September–April 1945 against Germans.

1946	Voluntary liquidation of Coronation Park Company.
1948	WA Civic Farewell from Mullumbimby and move to Brisbane.
1950s	Hawken Drive Big House built.
1974	Ruth marriage. WA, Sofia, Ester Ström and Hulda Nyholm died.

Books quoted or consulted

AUSTRALIA

Australianus (pseud of K. J. Back), *Concentrated Wisdoms of Australia*, Sydney, 1918.

Australianus (pseud of K. J. Back), *The Royal Toast*, Sydney, The Kingston Press, 1920.

Back, Eric, *William Andrew Back, Esq. and Mrs Back, from his arrival in Australia From Finland in 1902 until his death in 1974.* Brisbane, 1991, unpublished memoir.

Blainey, Geoffrey and Hutton, Geoffrey, *Gold and Paper 1858–1982: A History of the National Bank of Australasia Ltd.* Macmillan, 1958 and 1983 pp. 121–125.

Bunbury, Bill, *Timber for Gold: Life on the Goldfields Woodlines*, Freemale Arts Centre Press, 1997.

Daley, Louise Tiffany, *Men and a River: Richmond River District, 1828-1895*, Melbourne University Press, 1966.

Evans, Raymond, *The Red Flag Riots: A study of intolerance*, University of Queensland Press, 1988.

Flett, Yvonne and Alick, *John James and Harriet Hart: A partial history of one family in England and Australia, 1856-1937*, Lismore 1988, unpublished memoir.

Hollingworth, Nicholas, *The Mullumbimby Sawmill*, Brunswick Valley Historical Society, Mullumbimby, 2012.

MacKinnon, Neta, *What They Did: Families of the Brunswick 1890-1950*, Brunswick Valley Historical Society, Mullumbimby, 1998.

Siemon, Rosamund, *The Mayne Inheritance*, University of Queensland Press, 1999.

Tsicalas, Peter, *Mullumbimby: Boom and Bust 1908-1928*, Brunswick Valley Historical Society, Mullumbimby, 2012.

Tsicalas, Peter, *Mullumbimby: Foundation Events 1848-1908*, Brunswick Valley Historical Society, Mullumbimby, 2011.

Tsicalas, Susan, *A Century of Schooling in the Wilson's Creek, Huonbrook and Wanganui Valleys, 1908-2008*, Wilsons Creek–Huonbrook Centenary Committee, 2008.

Vader, John, *Red Gold: The tree that built a nation*, New Holland Press, 2002.

Walker, Shirley, *Roundabout at Bangalow*, University of Queensland Press, 2001.

FINLAND AND RUSSIA

Anderson, T., *Symphony for the City of the Dead: Dmitri Shostakovich and the Siege of Leningrad*, Candlewick Press, 2015.

Åkerlund, Bror, *Munsala Socken Historia*, Munsala kommuns förlag, 1972.

Clements, Jonathan, *Mannerheim: President, Soldier, Spy*, Haus Publishing, 2010.

Edwards, Robert, *White Death: Russia's War With Finland 1939-1940*, Phoenix, 2006.

Goss, Glenda Dawn, *Sibelius: A Composer's Life and the Awakening of Finland*, University of Chicago Press, 2009.

Irincheev, Bair, *The Mannerheim Line 1920-39: Finnish Fortifications of the Winter War*, Osprey Publishing, 2009.

Irincheev, Bair, *War of the White Death: Finland against the Soviet Union, 1939-40*, Stackpole Books, 2012.

Jansson, Tove, *Moominvalley in November*, Penguin, 1968.

Jacobsen, Roy, *The Burnt-Out Town of Miracles*, John Murray, 2007.

Jowett, Philip and Snodgrass, Brent, *Finland at War 1939-45*, Osprey Books, 2006.

Katchadourian, Stina, *The Lapp King's Daughter: A Family's Journey Through Finland's Wars*, California, Fithian Press, 2010.

Koivukangas, Olavi, *Sea, Gold and Sugarcane: Finns in Australia 1951-1947*, Turku, Institute of Migration, 1986.

Linna, Väinö, *The Unknown Soldier*, Collins, Putnam's New York, 1957.

Linna, Väinö, *Under the Northern Star*, transl. Impola, Richard, Aspasia Books,

Beaverton, Ontario, 2001.

Lönnrot, Elias, *Kalavala*, transl. W. F. Kirby, J M Dent, London, 1907.

Marani, Diego, *New Finnish Grammar*, transl. Judith Landry, Dedalus, 2011.

Moberg, Vilhelm, Series: *The Emigrants; Unto a Good Land; The Settlers; Last Letter Home*, Minnesota Historical Society Press, 1995.

Moynahan, Brian, *Leningrad: Siege and Symphony*, Atlantic Monthly Press, 2013.

Nyholm, Runar, *Udden in Munsala*, Nykarleby-Oravais hembygdsförening, Vaasa 1982.

Olin, K-G, *Grafton-affären*, Olimex, Jakobstad 1999.

Polvinen

Quigley, Sarah, *The Conductor*, Random House, New Zealand, 2011.

Rayner, Richard, *The Cloud Sketcher*, HarperCollins, 2001.

Runeberg, Johan Ludvig, *The Tales of Ensign Stål*, Princeton University Press, 1938.

Rundt, Dennis, *Munsalaradikalismen: En studie i politisk mobilisering och etablering*, Turku, Åbo Akademis förlag, 1992. Simons, Paullina, series especially *The Bronze Horseman*, HarperCollins, 2001.

Skrivargruppen, *Mellan Lojlax och Åkvarn, Berättelser ock hågkomster från gången tf samlade av Munsala byaforskare*, Munsala, 1997.

Tallgren, Robert T., *Livets Färdväg; Krokiga Stigar Glädje & Smärta* (Life Route; Crooked Trails Joy & Pain), Maxmo, Sven-Erik Syréns förlag, 2011.

Wall, Marketta, *To America: Hanko as Port of Departure for Emigrants*, 2013.

ARTICLES, CONTRIBUTIONS

Bonetti, Ruth. 'Munsala: St Lucia.' Wilson, Kim. *Brisbane Art Deco: Stories of our Built Heritage*, Jubliee Studio, 2015.

Bonetti, Ruth. (2015): 'Two Finnish Migrants Down Under: An Australian bibliographical perspective', *Participation, Integration, and Recognition: Changing Pathways to Immigrant Incorporation*, Migration Studies C24, Turku, Institute of Migration, pp.167–176.

Bonetti, Ruth. (2015): 'Finland Through Australian Eyes', *Siirtolaisuus-Migration Quarterly*, Vol 1/2015, Turku, Institute of Migration, pp. 36–42.

Acknowledgements

Many have supported and assisted the journey to bring these two books to print. I am very grateful to all.

Special mentions go to:

Professor Olavi Koivukangas mentored, encouraged and commented on the manuscript.

Gretchen, Rolf and Karin Back generously shared information; much is recorded as audio and video. Birgit Dahlbacka in Munsala gave insights into Munsala village history and genealogical charts; to the director of Jakobstad Museum, Guy Bjorkland and to historian authors Bengt Kummel and K.G. Olin.

Carl G. Friedner and Marie Campbell assisted with further translations of letters, books and theses. Nigel Holmes and Dr. Peter Fenoglio restored photographs from less legible versions. Thank you Peter, for capturing the cover concepts.

Thank you for encouragement from writing buddy Debbie Terranova, insights and editing from Anne Hamilton, further edits by Laura Back, Bob Johnson and Jeanette O'Hagen, and support from Omega Writers Inc.

Paul–Antoni Bonetti advised and edited footage for my crowdfunding campaign to assist publication costs; thank you to those who supported this.

Of the cousins and siblings who shared material, special thanks to John Back and Jenny Starky.

Antoni, thank you for sharing the journey, for carrying my bags and baggage along the way.

About the Author

Ruth Bonetti grew up in the arid Queensland outback, intrigued by the strange-accented relatives she met on holidays near Byron Bay. She preferred Mozart to hillbilly music, books to horses. Ruth's gift for classical music became a passport to the world.

Destiny led her to live in Sweden, directly across the Gulf of Bothnia from her grandfather's birthplace in Finland, where she researched this story. Ruth is author/editor of a dozen publications about music, education and performance, five through Words and Music and two with Oxford University Press.

Ruth Bonetti is a Fellow of the Migration Institute of Finland where she presented a conference paper in 2014, published in *Participation, Integration, and Recognition: Changing Pathways to Immigrant Incorporation*. She has published in the Institute quarterly journal, *Siirtolaisuus-Migration Quarterly*.

Book 1 of the *Midnight Sun to Southern Cross* Saga

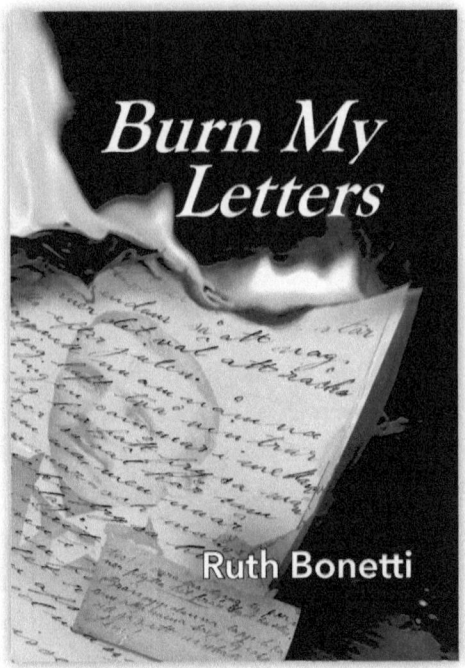

Burn My Letters: Tyranny to Refuge

ISBN: 978-0-9875442-2-3

At the end of the 19th century Finland is a dark and repressive place. Pacifist and political dissenter Karl Johan Back is conscripted to fight for the Russian despots that occupy his country. In 1899 he flees to an untamed land on the far side of the world. Finding refuge on ridges overlooking the Byron Bay lighthouse in northern New South Wales, he plants orchids and grows lush tropical fruit.

Intrigued by her 'black sheep' great-uncle, Ruth Bonetti pieces together the motives that propelled his flight. Along the way she discovers much about her own voyage of self-discovery.

Finnish relatives share a treasure-trove of letters that provide answers to the many questions raised by Karl Johan's quest for freedom. Why did Russian military police pursue him as far as Suez? Why did he publish under a pen-name? And, most intriguing of all, why did he implore his family to burn his letters?

Available at www.ruthbonetti.com

There is nothing dull about this historical search, from the start I was drawn into the story, entertained, amused, challenged and moved.

–Jeanette O'Hagan

Ruth's writing is cohesive and easy to read. It capably supports the delightful ebb-and-flow of interesting situations, dramatic overtones, curious characters, evocative imagery and collective wisdom.

– Mazzy Adams

An excellent, challenging book. For anyone not only interested in European history but Australian stories of refugees who arrived here years ago, this is a must read.

– Mary Hawkins

I absolutely loved Burn My Letters. I appreciated it was based on a true story. It took hold of my imagination. Some moments I wept a little, then later giggled, then held my breath in anticipation of the outcome of another adventure.

– Jenny Bardy-Back

www.ingramcontent.com/pod-product-compliance
Lightning Source LLC
Chambersburg PA
CBHW020645300426
44112CB00007B/252